Sibshops

Sibshops
Workshops for Siblings of Children with Special Needs

by

Donald J. Meyer, M.Ed.
Director
Sibling Support Project
Children's Hospital & Medical Center
Seattle, Washington

and

Patricia F. Vadasy, M.P.H.
Research Associate
Washington Research Institute
Seattle, Washington

Illustrations by Cary Pillo Lassen

·P·A·U·L·H·
BROOKES
PUBLISHING C°

Baltimore • London • Toronto • Sydney

Paul H. Brookes Publishing Co.
P.O. Box 10624
Baltimore, Maryland 21285-0624
www.brookespublishing.com

Typeset by Brushwood Graphics, Inc., Baltimore, Maryland.
Manufactured in the United States of America by
Sheridan Books, Inc., Fredericksburg, VA.

The illustrations appearing on the cover and in this book are the original
work of Cary Pillo Lassen.

Preparation of this book was supported, in part, by
Project #MCJ-535077-01-0 from the Maternal and Child Health Program
(Title V, Social Security Act), Health Resources and Services Administration,
U.S. Department of Health and Human Services.

First printing, August 1994.
Second printing, March 1996.
Third printing, February 2000.
Fourth printing, November 2000.

Library of Congress Cataloging-in-Publication Data
Meyer, Donald J.
  Sibshops : workshops for siblings of children with special needs / Donald J.
Meyer, Patricia F. Vadasy : illustrations by Cary Pillo Lassen.
    p.   cm.
  Includes bibliographical references (p.   ) and index.
  ISBN 1-55766-169-3
  1. Handicapped children—Family relationships. 2. Handicapped
children—Home care. 3. Brothers and sisters. I. Vadasy, Patricia F. II. Title.
HV888.M495   1994
362.4′043′083—dc20   94-8827
                                                                           CIP

British Library Cataloguing-in-Publication data are available from the
British Library.

Contents

Foreword

Hanging out with a group of 5th-grade girls is good for the soul, if not for getting a balance on the important things in life. These last few Saturday mornings I've been engaged with a group of girls, all sisters of older siblings with disabilities, and we go bowling. I personally don't like to bowl, but these girls do and so I do. I'm really there to listen, learn, and laugh a bit. These girls came together at a Sibshop, where brothers and sisters of children with special needs are provided an opportunity to meet other siblings in a relaxed, recreational setting. A helpful mom got the girls together, provided transportation and some minor organization, and bingo! They discovered that they liked each other and bowling. They formed a friendship around their common interest in bowling and their siblings. I listen and hear talk of school, clothes, music, a bit about boys, and some about disability and their families. They talk of their Aunt Blabby and we laugh some more. Not heavy meetings, just a fun time together, realizing that they share so much including the sibling experience. They wear their Sibshops shirts when they bowl and teach this college professor about important things like families, disability, and bowling!

A few years ago, Don Meyer and Pat Vadasy sent me their information about Sibshops and explained how they were implementing these workshops in Washington. It wasn't long before I began hearing about the excitement that Sibshops were causing among young people who had brothers and sisters with disabilities. Finally, someone was attending to these special needs by detailing a set of fun activities that get to the heart of the sibling experience. I've been so fortunate to use *Sibshops: Workshops for Siblings of Children with Special Needs* with many groups, and the reaction is always the same—this curriculum guide gets to the point and we have fun at the same time.

Don and Pat have blazed a trail in helping siblings explore their feelings in creative, light, and fun ways. They have skillfully organized a learning program primarily for siblings, although parents, too, are a vital part of the Sibshop experience. Don and Pat have developed a set of activities that bring difficult issues to the forefront and let young people talk about what is usually not talked about. Their work is simply remarkable because brothers and sisters are empowered to help each other and, in so doing, help themselves.

Parents and professionals know that siblings who have sisters or brothers with disabilities have special concerns. Growing up with a disability in the family is often stressful and unfair; but it can also be a source of power and inspiration. Siblings I've met often talk to me about their need to be recognized and respected as individuals. They need us to acknowledge their special feelings and concerns and help them deal with a whirlwind of feelings and emotions. Of course, as all of us who have sisters or brothers know, many of these feelings are just a part of the sibling experience. It's natural to have a love–hate relationship, and love usually triumphs. Building on the robust nature of sibling relationships, Don and Pat help siblings to confront their natural feelings in proactive, positive, and fun ways.

I once heard a professional suggest that all siblings who have brothers or sisters with disabilities need counseling. This is not my experience at all. Some siblings do need counseling, but not the majority. However, I believe that all siblings need opportunities to express their feelings and concerns. They need opportunities to learn from others and to realize that their experience is not so unusual, that they are not alone, that they share a number of bonds with other brothers and sisters who feel the way that they do. This is the power of *Sibshops*!

This book is about learning. Thanks to *Sibshops*, brothers and sisters are helped to learn about the full range and depth of their feelings. They learn to handle situations in positive ways. They learn to talk and share, to help each other. They learn about their parents. They learn that they are not alone, and they learn about their love.

I think what I like most about *Sibshops* is the humor. Sometimes when I reread it, I feel that it would play well on the "Late Show with David Letterman." (I think David would like Aunt Blabby.) The humor provides a powerful tool in helping siblings, parents, and teachers focus on the important issues, while not getting overwhelmed. We learn more when we laugh.

So what will you do with this book? If you're like me, you'll use it to help get some groups going, you'll use the many suggestions to improve your parenting or clinical skills, and you'll pass the resource along to others. Kids need us to use Sibshops to help them. Maybe if you're lucky, some 5th graders will invite you to go bowling after a Sibshop.

Thanks, Don and Pat, for writing this powerful book. So many of us are in your debt!

Thomas H. Powell, Ed.D.
Dean
School of Education
Winthrop University
Rock Hill, South Carolina

Preface

The fact that you are holding this book suggests that you already have an interest in the well-being of brothers and sisters of children with special health and developmental needs. Perhaps you are a parent of a child with special needs who wants to create peer support and educational programs for brothers and sisters in your community. Or, maybe you are an adult sib who wishes that there had been programs like Sibshops when you were younger and would like to share your experiences either as a Sibshop facilitator or as a member of a program for adult siblings. Or, perhaps you are a human services professional who realizes that there is much more to serving "families of children with special needs" than just meeting with children's parents. Regardless, this book is for you.

It is our hope that this book will be somewhat different from other books you have read. Here are our goals for *Sibshops*:

1. *To increase the number of programs, services, and considerations for brothers and sisters of individuals with special health and developmental needs.* With this book, we hope to give you the rationale, tools, inspiration, permission, and encouragement to make community-based programs for siblings as available as Parent-to-Parent programs are for parents of children with special needs. As important as these programs are, however, they are not enough. We hope to provide you with information that will allow you to challenge current practices to assure that siblings' issues are addressed. We seek fundamental change in the way schools, clinics, agencies, and organizations "do business" with respect to brothers and sisters. As a friend puts it, we hope to subvert the dominant paradigm!
2. *To increase the reader's understanding of specific issues experienced by brothers and sisters of individuals with special health and developmental needs.* A working knowledge is essential to creating programs and services for brothers and sisters. The first part of the book will provide an overview of the unusual concerns and unusual opportunities experienced by siblings as reported in the clinical and research literature and by siblings themselves.
3. *To provide specific information for local agencies and parent groups to create programs for siblings of individuals with special health and developmental needs.* The second part of this book will be devoted to the Sibshop model, a lively peer support, educational, and recreational program for school-age brothers and sisters. In this section, we present activities that can be adapted for different disabilities and illnesses as well as ages. We also discuss programs for adult brothers and sisters, as they are among the most underserved of family members.

We first presented some of the information in this book in a manual published by the University of Washington Press. Preparing this new volume was a welcome opportunity to update what we have learned about brothers and sisters of people with special needs and expand upon the original text. To make this book as comprehensive and useful as possible, this edition contains six times the content of the previous edition.

Throughout, we have tried to write this book in a style that is accessible and even enjoyable to read. We know that most people who wish to create services and programs for brothers and sisters are not academicians. We also know that most readers, even academicians, seem to enjoy and learn more from books that don't appear to be designed to induce sleep. We know that there is much good news to share about siblings of people with special needs. We hope to present the information that follows with the grace, vitality, and insight we frequently see in brothers and sisters of people with special needs.

We hope you will let us know if we have accomplished our goals.

Acknowledgments

We are fortunate to have many friends who share our commitment to providing services for brothers and sisters of people with special needs. Many of the people listed below have pioneered programs for siblings in their communities; others have provided us with support, advice, and encouragement over the years and in the preparation of this volume. While their contributions are varied, each shares our belief that brothers and sisters deserve our time, effort, and consideration. We are grateful to them all: Allene Anderson, Jennifer Annable, Tizzy Bennett, Martha Blue-Banning, Monica Burnham, Sally Burton, Shirley Butwin, Sarah Cheney, Kelly Coulter, Terri Dawson, Juli Del Monego, Jan Doody, Jan Erion, Teresa Farmer, Rebecca Fewell, Tom Fish, Jan Fleming, Cheryl Fraser, Patty Gerdel, Lisa Glidden, Tracey Gooding, Hod Gray, Karen Grossman, Anne Guthrie, Peggy Hart, Susan Janko, Norma Johnson, Christine Jones, Gail Karp, Maxine Hayes, Margaret Lewis, Debra Lobato, Emma Longan, Patty Lott, Susan Macek, Mary Marin, Karen Mataya, Mike Matteson, Nancy Meltzer, Fay Morgan, Mary Nessle, Maren Noyes, Patti Par, Geri Pettit, Tom Powell, Florene Poyadue, Nancy Ratokalau, Paula Recchia, Margaret Roberts, Brian Ross, Betsy Santelli, Joanne Scaturro, Elaine Schab-Bragg, Greg Schell, Lisa Sessions, Kathleen Shivell, Jenny Stamm, Ellen Thaler, Josie Torres, Marianne Tucker, Ann Turnbull, Jenny Waldon-Weaver, Pearl Wollin, Theresa Wong, Debbie Yanak, Pam Younghans, and Geri Zatlow.

We would also like to thank the U.S. Department of Health and Human Services for funding the Sibling Support Project as a Special Project of Regional and National Significance, thus making this book possible.

Finally, a special acknowledgment is reserved for Erica Lewis Erickson, who reviewed drafts of this manuscript and field tested many of the activities contained herein. As a staff member of the Sibling Support Project, Erica is an important part of any success the project enjoys. Anyone looking for an example of a "sibling's successful adaptation to life with a brother or sister with special needs" need look no further!

For Terese Marie, Gina, and Angela

1
What Are Sibshops?

For the adults who plan them and the agencies that sponsor them, Sibshops are best described as opportunities for brothers and sisters of children with special health and developmental needs to obtain peer support and education within a recreational context. They often reflect an agency's commitment to the well-being of the family member most likely to have the longest-lasting relationship with the person with special needs.

However, for the young people who attend them and the energetic people who run them, Sibshops are best described as *events*. Sibshops are lively, pedal-to-the-metal celebrations of the many contributions made by brothers and sisters of kids with special needs. Sibshops acknowledge that being the brother or sister of a person with special needs is for some a good thing, for others a not-so-good thing, and for many somewhere in between. They reflect a belief that brothers and sisters have much to offer one another—if they are given a chance. The Sibshop model intersperses information and discussion activities with new games (designed to be unique, offbeat, and appealing to a wide ability range), cooking activities, and special guests who may teach participants mime, how to juggle or, in the case of one guest artist who has cerebral palsy, how to paint by holding a toothbrush in your mouth. Sibshops are as fun and rewarding for the people who host them as they are for the participants.

Sibshops seek to provide siblings with opportunities for peer support. Because Sibshops are designed for school-age children, peer support is provided within a lively, recreational context that emphasizes a kids'-eye view.

Sibshops are *not* therapy, group or otherwise, although their effect may be therapeutic for some children. Sibshops acknowledge that most brothers and sisters of people with special needs, like their parents, are doing well, despite the challenges of an illness or disability. Consequently, while Sibshop facilitators always keep an eye open for participants who may need additional services, the Sibshop model takes a wellness approach.

The goals of the model that guide Sibshop activities are discussed below.

WHO ATTENDS SIBSHOPS?

Originally developed for 8- to 13-year-old siblings of children with developmental disabilities, the Sibshop model is easily adapted for slightly younger and older children. It has been adapted for brothers and sisters of children with other special needs, including cancer, hearing impairments, epilepsy, emotional disturbances, and HIV-positive status. Sibshops have also been adapted for use with children who have experienced the death of a family member. Children who attend Sibshops come from diverse backgrounds including suburban communities (e.g., Bellevue, Washington; Springfield, Massachusetts; Tallahassee, Florida), urban communities (e.g., Detroit; Washington, D.C.), rural communities (e.g., Wyoming, Iowa), and communities with unique cultural heritages (e.g., Alaska, New Mexico, Hawaii).

WHO SPONSORS SIBSHOPS?

Any agency serving families of children with special needs can sponsor a Sibshop, provided it can offer financial support, properly staff the program, and attract sufficient numbers of participants. However, we strongly recommend that agencies work together to cosponsor a local Sibshop. (This important topic is further discussed in Chapter 5.) We have found that Sibshops are well within the reach and abilities of most communities. They are not expensive to run, and logistically are no more difficult to coordinate than other community-based programs for children, such as Scouts or Camp Fire.

WHO RUNS SIBSHOPS?

We believe Sibshops are best facilitated by a team of service providers (such as social workers, special education teachers and professors, psychologists, and nurses) *and* adult siblings of people with special needs. At the very least, the team of facilitators will need to: be knowledgeable of the disability or illness represented, possess a sense of humor and play, enjoy the company of children, and respect the young participants' expertise on the topic of life with a brother or sister with special needs. Qualifications for Sibshop facilitators are further discussed in Chapter 5.

WHAT IS THE OPTIMAL NUMBER OF PARTICIPANTS FOR A SIBSHOP?

Sibshops have been held for as few as 5 children and as many as 45. Around a dozen children, with at least two facilitators, is a comfortable number.

WHEN ARE SIBSHOPS OFFERED?

Usually Sibshops are offered on Saturdays, often from 10 A.M. until 2 P.M. This allows ample time for games, discussion and information activities, and making and eating lunch. Of course, Saturdays from 10:00 to 2:00 will not be ideal for all families or communities. Each community will need to determine the best day and length for its Sibshop, as further discussed in Chapter 5.

HOW OFTEN ARE SIBSHOPS HELD?

Depending on the needs and resources of the community, Sibshops may be offered as frequently as weekly (as with a 1½-hour after-school program) or as infrequently as yearly (as with an all-day Sibshop that is a part of an annual conference for families from around the state or nation). Generally, Sibshops are presented monthly or bimonthly.

Sibshops may be offered in a series (e.g., five Sibshops, meeting once a month, with one registration). Offering Sibshops in series can provide a stable group that can form an identity during the months they are together. However, it can be difficult for some participants and families to commit to a series of dates due to interference with other activities. Sibshops may also be offered as stand-alone events (e.g., bimonthly meetings with separate registrations). The stand-alone events offer families flexibility, but participants will vary somewhat from Sibshop to Sibshop.

WHAT ARE THE GOALS OF THE SIBSHOP MODEL?

> Goal 1: Sibshops will provide brothers and sisters of children with special needs an opportunity to meet other siblings in a relaxed, recreational setting.

The chance to meet other brothers and sisters in a casual atmosphere and join them in recreational activities has several benefits for participants. First, it can help reduce a sibling's sense of isolation. Participants quickly learn that there are others who experience the special joys and challenges that they do. Second, the casual atmosphere and recreational activities promote informal sharing and friendships among participants. Friendships begun during Sibshops and continued outside the program offer siblings ongoing sources of support. Third, the recreational aspect of the Sibshops makes them enjoyable to attend. If children perceive the Sibshop as yet another thing that they have to do because of their sibling, they may find it hard to be receptive to the information and discussion presented in the workshop. Furthermore, when a sibling workshop does not offer anything that is personally satisfying for the participant, he or she is unlikely to attend in the future.

Recreational activities and the importance of play during Sibshops are discussed further in Chapter 9.

> Goal 2: Sibshops will provide brothers and sisters with opportunities to discuss common joys and concerns with other siblings of children with special needs.

At Sibshops, participants share stories, experiences, and knowing laughs with peers who truly understand the ups and downs of life with a sibling who has special needs. This opportunity allows participants to learn that they are not alone with their experiences and their often-ambivalent feelings.

> Goal 3: Sibshops will provide brothers and sisters with an opportunity to learn how others handle situations commonly experienced by siblings of children with special needs.

Brothers and sisters of children with special health and developmental needs routinely face situations that are not experienced by other children. Defending a brother or sister from name-calling, responding to questions from friends or strangers, and resenting the time and attention required by the sibling with special needs are only a few of the problems siblings may experience. At a Sibshop, participants learn how others handle difficult situations. This experience can offer a sibling a broad array of solutions from which to choose.

Activities that promote discussion among sibling participants are presented in Chapter 8.

Goal 4: Sibshops will provide siblings with an opportunity to learn more about the implications of their brothers' and sisters' special needs.

As noted above, brothers and sisters have a need for information to answer their own questions about their siblings' special needs as well as the questions posed by friends, classmates, and strangers. Sibshops offer participants opportunities to learn about the effect that a sibling's illness or disability will have on the special child's life, schooling, and future.

Informational Sibshop activities are discussed in Chapter 10.

Goal 5: Sibshops will provide parents and other professionals with opportunities to learn more about the concerns and opportunities frequently experienced by brothers and sisters of people with special needs.

Because they may be unaware of the wide range of sibling concerns, some Sibshop activities attempt to help parents and service providers better understand "life as a sib." One activity allows parents and professionals to meet with a panel of young adult and adult siblings to learn about the special joys and challenges of growing up with a special brother or sister. Parents learn about what the panelists appreciated in their parents' treatment of the children in their family, and also what they wish their parents had done differently. This and other programs for parents are discussed further in Chapter 11.

To advocate effectively for increased services for brothers and sisters, it is critical to learn more about issues affecting their lives. The chapters that follow provide an overview of the unusual concerns and opportunities experienced by brothers and sisters of people with special health and developmental needs.

2

Unusual Concerns

Is there any relationship more ambivalent than that between brothers and sisters? In families with only typically developing siblings, brothers and sisters fight and argue and laugh and hug, often within the same hour. A 3-year-old's name for her 8-year-old sister may be "dummyhead" one minute, and "sweetie-face" the next.

Siblings, because of their shared experiences, know each other in ways no one else will ever know them. Being a sibling, someone once told us, is like living in the nude, psychologically. Sisters and brothers know the chinks in the armor all too well. Like younger siblings, older siblings can be brutal and loving as well. As another sister told us, "I can always count on my sister to give me an unvarnished view of how I am leading my life. Yet she will be the first to defend me if she feels I am being attacked by someone else."

> I was green with envy at first. My sister was just lying in bed and receiving all this merchandise: nightgowns, sheets, stuffed animals and books. Will it ever end? Then I thought: What am I jealous of? Here I am being healthy and standing upright; my sister was lying in bed with her life being threatened. These presents were not going to help her sickness any. Then I started to feel sorry for her! I was so confused! (Amy, age 14, in Murray & Jampolsky, 1982, p. 45)

> We are not heroes any more than we are victims or sufferers. I am just a person, with a brother whose condition makes an added complication in my life. And that, like everything else in life, has both its pluses and minuses. (Pat, in Remsberg, 1989, p. 3)

> Siblings of children with chronic health problems are simultaneously vulnerable for psychological problems and precocious development. In fact, both outcomes may be true for an individual over time. What can be interpreted as inconclusive literature may be an accurate reflection of sibling status. (Leonard, 1992, p. 501)

Given that most brothers and sisters harbor a wide range of feelings toward their siblings, it is not at all unusual to learn that siblings of people with special needs also experience ambivalent feelings

7

about their brothers and sisters. After all, a relationship in which one sibling has a disability or illness is still a sibling relationship. Adding a special need to the equation appears to enhance the inherent ambivalence.

However similar they may be, there can be some important differences when one of the siblings has been diagnosed with a special health or developmental need. In this chapter we review the unusual concerns that siblings of people with special needs may experience. This overview is based on the clinical and research literature and what we have learned working with siblings and parents for over 10 years. Whenever possible, we let siblings speak for themselves. One unusual concern *not* covered in this chapter is siblings' lifelong and ever-changing need for information. An extensive discussion of siblings' informational needs may be found in Chapter 3. Chapter 4 reviews the equally important but less reported unusual opportunities recounted by brothers and sisters of people with special needs.

It is difficult to make generalizations about siblings who have brothers and sisters with special needs, because this is only one aspect of their lives. Disabilities and illnesses affect people from all walks of life, and siblings will experience these conditions in innumerable ways. However, in listening to brothers and sisters, we hear recurring themes, despite the diverse backgrounds of these siblings. Here, then, is a discussion of these themes. To be sure, no one brother or sister will experience all of the concerns discussed below, but all will share some of them.

OVERIDENTIFICATION

> Yes, I worry a lot. I worry that my leg will get cut off also. I think about it and then I wake up and I go into the kitchen. All the time I worry about it. (10-year-old boy, in Sourkes, 1990, p. 6).

A 4-year-old boy worries that he might catch his sister's cerebral palsy and lose his ability to walk.

Because her older brother and sister have seizures, a 10-year-old girl wonders when hers will begin.

Unable to see the blackboard clearly, an 8-year-old boy wonders whether he will lose his vision the way his brother did.

After doing poorly on a spelling test, a 9-year-old girl thinks that perhaps her brother isn't the only one in the family with a learning disability.

On the eve of his 16th birthday, a boy worries deeply that he, too, will start showing signs of schizophrenia, just as his sister did soon after her 16th birthday.

Overidentification occurs when a sibling wonders whether he or she shares—or will share—a sibling's problem. Frequently (but not always) irrational, these fears can be very real, especially to young children, who often indulge in "magical thinking" and who have an immature concept of contagion. "Well, we all got chickenpox," a sibling may wonder. "Why shouldn't we all catch cancer?" Although younger children are more open about fears of catching a disease or acquiring a disability, Sourkes (1990) doubted that there are many siblings who *haven't* worried about acquiring their sibling's special needs.

Severity appears to influence overidentification. Grossman's 1972 study of college-age siblings of people with disabilities suggested that overidentification is more likely to occur when the disability is mild, and especially if it is "invisible." The logic is apparent: Jennifer's sister has been diagnosed as having epilepsy, an invisible disability. Michelle's sister was diagnosed as having a genetic disorder that causes her to look and act differently from other family members. Because Jennifer's sister is like her in so many ways, Jennifer may be more likely to worry that she, too, has epilepsy.

Age also appears to influence overidentification. Miller (1974) suggested that overidentification is less likely to occur if the child with the special needs is younger than the typically developing child. A 10-year-old child whose older siblings all have learning disabilities may be more likely to fear that he or she also has a learning disability than a 10-year-old child whose younger brother just began experiencing seizures.

The risk of overidentification is one of the many reasons that brothers and sisters need accurate information about their siblings' disabilities and illnesses. Information that may be obvious to adults may be not be to children. For instance, younger children need to know that they cannot "catch" their siblings' disability. One third of the siblings interviewed by Koocher and O'Malley (1981) said they worried about getting cancer themselves.

Siblings who *are* at higher risk for acquiring a disability or illness need to know what their chances are. Usually their risk is much lower than they might imagine. For instance, siblings who have seen their previously healthy siblings develop serious mental illnesses frequently worry that they also will succumb to the illness, although their chances are only 1 in 10 (compared to 1 in 100 in the general population), and negligible after age 30 (Dickens, 1991). Most siblings appreciate straight talk about their siblings' special needs.

EMBARRASSMENT

> Sometimes, he's embarrassing, though. He likes to brag about things that aren't true to gain acceptance. I can see kids laughing at him because of his bragging. I'm not sure if I'm embarrassed because of his physical handicap or because he acts the way he does. (Beth, age 16, in Binkard, Goldberg, & Goldberg, 1987, pp. 5–6)

A sibling with a disability or illness can be a source of embarrassment for typically developing brothers and sisters. They may get embarrassed by the unwanted attention the child, and consequently the family, receives when the child with special needs has behavior problems:

> At church we had the collection. Then the pastor started to say a prayer. In the middle of the prayer David started to play his favorite tune—"Happy Birthday"—on the kazoo! (He must have sneaked it

in with him!) Everybody laughed! I felt so embarrassed. I was glad when it was time for Sunday school and David went off for a walk with one of his helpers. (Angela, age 10, about her brother who has autism, in Burslem, 1991, p. 13)

Differences in appearances can also make siblings feel overly conspicuous:

As Red got older, people would stare at him and speak under their breath, as if my brother was some kind of side show. To this day, people still do that. (A. Jones, personal communication, 1991)

In some instances, siblings may be acutely sensitive about the appearance and behavior of their siblings, lest others—peers especially —conclude that they share their brothers' and sisters' special needs.

I was certain that everyone was looking at my brother with his obvious handicap and wondering what was wrong with the rest of us. (Marge, in Helsel et al., 1978, p. 110)

In these instances, embarrassment will be more common when the problems are mild or invisible. Visible disabilities, siblings tell us, at least provide a reason for unusual behavior. A brother with a mild learning disability who is given to asking strangers rude questions can be more embarrassing than a sister who uses a wheelchair and makes occasional noises.

Siblings may experience embarrassment and unwanted attention when they are asked questions about their brothers' and sisters' special needs. These questions can come from friends, classmates, and even strangers:

When I finally found out what happened, it was so hard to talk about it, especially when someone says, "Hey what's wrong with your sister? Why is she in a wheelchair?" People can be such jerks sometimes! They just don't understand!! (Joanne, age 16, in Murray & Jampolsky, 1982, p. 36)

Developing strategies to spare a typically developing child embarrassment first requires analyzing the cause of the embarrassment. Is it something that can be changed, such as an age-inappropriate bib on a sibling who drools, or a behavior, such as singing during the sermon at church, that could be changed through a carefully considered behavior program? If changeable, then the family can work toward decreasing the sibling's embarrassment and improving the life of the person with special needs at the same time.

However, it is equally likely that the source of embarrassment is something about which little can be done. In these instances, there are two strategies parents may wish to consider. First, they should remember that most children go through stages when they are easily embarrassed, and these experiences may be unavoidable. Early adolescents have a particularly strong need to conform. It can make a teenager miserable to be seen with her parents, much less with a sister who looks and acts differently.

> Being an older sister to David was difficult. When I became a teenager, I tried to pretend he didn't exist. Adolescence is an emotional roller coaster, and I spent most of those years on unsteady ground. It was too uncool to admit to having a retarded brother. And there were times when I wanted to drop through the earth rather than acknowledge our relationship. (Herndon, 1992, p. 2)

During this time of raging conformity, the best strategy may be to give the typically developing child "space," psychological and otherwise. Given permission to walk on the other side of the shopping mall or attend a different church service, most siblings will eventually reintegrate their brother or sister, according to their own agendas:

> As time moved on, I pretended I wasn't embarrassed by Jennifer. But I really was when friends were around. By the time I was 14 or 15 though I realized my good friends loved her too. I hadn't realized that before. I hadn't given her a chance. (Cassie, age 19, in Binkard et al., 1987, p. 16)

Featherstone (1980) wrote that parents can help their children by allowing them some control over situations. A second strategy is to acknowledge the embarrassment. One mother told us, "When my son comes up to me and says, 'Mom I get so embarrassed when she does that!' I tell him, 'Yeah, I really get embarrassed when she does that too!' "

Denying siblings "permission" to be embarrassed by their sibling (as in "He's your brother; you shouldn't be embarrassed by him!") is more likely to invoke guilty feelings than to reduce embarrassment. It also will send a message that children cannot bring their concerns to their parents. Acknowledging that a sibling with special needs is sometimes difficult to live with not only reflects reality (after all, what sibling—special needs or not—is always easy to live with?), but it also sends a message that brothers and sisters can feel free to talk about their feelings with their parents. Good communication among siblings and parents is, along with information, the primary means of minimizing siblings' concerns.

> My parents always wanted us to express our feelings. They'd say "If you're uncomfortable when Jennifer is around your friends, don't feel guilty. Those feelings are very normal." (Andrea, age 19, in Binkard et al., 1987, p.18)

Luckily, for most siblings, embarrassment is transitory. As described in the section on unusual opportunities, most brothers and sisters have a remarkable ability to reframe difficult situations in a more positive light:

> I don't feel embarrassed about him. With his kind of handicap, well, he does strange stuff. But it's like the stuff everybody's little brother does. It's sort of what you'd expect from little brothers. (Mary, age 17, in Binkard et al., 1987, p. 11)

GUILT

Relationships between brothers and sisters and their siblings who have special health or developmental needs resemble those of typically developing siblings in most ways. However, siblings of individuals with special needs are far more likely to experience guilt than siblings of individuals without special needs. And guilt, although it represents the darker end of the emotional palette, nevertheless comes in many hues. Brothers and sisters may feel they caused their siblings' disability; they may experience survivor's guilt; they may feel guilty about their own abilities or harboring less-than-charitable feelings about their siblings.

Feeling Responsible for the Disability or Illness

Siblings who feel somehow responsible for their brothers' or sisters' disability or illness may experience irrational, but nonetheless real, guilt. They may feel that they are somehow being punished for something they said, did, or thought near the time of the diagnosis. Koch-Hattem (1986) reported on interviews with 33 siblings of pediatric cancer patients. Of the 33 siblings, 9 reported that when the individual patients were diagnosed, they considered the possibility that the illnesses would not have occurred if they had treated their brothers or sisters differently.

> I blamed myself [for my sister's illness]. I constantly felt guilty around her. I wanted to punish myself somehow. . . . I knew inside it wasn't my fault but I was so hurt, lost, and mixed up that I blamed myself. (Joanne, age 16, in Murray & Jampolsky, 1982, p. 37)

The implication of this type of guilt is obvious: brothers and sisters, especially younger siblings, will need to be reassured that the disabilities or illnesses did not result from anything they did.

Survivor's Guilt

Brothers and sisters may experience a form of survivor's guilt. A sister's secret prayer might be:

> "Dear God, why did this have to happen to Colleen? She's so little and so sweet and now she's in the hospital with all these tubes com-

ing out of her. She has all these seizures and seems in such pain. She doesn't deserve this. Why couldn't it happen to me?"

Three of the siblings interviewed by Koch-Hattem (1986) expressed a desire to trade places with their siblings. One 15-year-old sister of a 9-year-old boy with acute lymphoblastic leukemia said:

"Sometimes when I'm in there with him taking shots, I'll just say, 'Why couldn't it be me instead of him?' He's so little and so young that I probably could take shots better than he could." (p. 114)

Guilt over Abilities or Health

Since we were twins, my brother and I were always together. And so from the earliest time I can remember, I had the responsibility of watching after him. A lot of times I felt guilty because I was invited to go to parties, and I went to school. They enrolled him in first grade, but he was only there a very short time. I of course was allowed to go and I felt very guilty about that. (Fish, 1993)

Brothers and sisters of people with special needs often learn to value and appreciate their health, their family, and other aspects of their lives that their peers may take for granted. While they appreciate the ability to do things that others—such as their siblings—cannot do and the advantages they have, they sometimes feel guilty for their good fortune.

I guess it was in junior high that I started to be aware of some of Tom's disorders and be sad for him. He was falling behind me. When I got to junior high and was having such a good time myself, I realized that the whole experience wasn't going to be the same for Tom as it was for me. I was sad but I didn't know what I could do. (Mark, age 24, in Binkard et al., 1987, p.27)

I feel bad when John sees me going off with my friends and wonders why he doesn't have many. He'll be at home when I'm out having fun, and it makes my mom feel bad. I feel guilty and don't know how to handle it. (Sue, age 17, in Binkard et al., 1987, p.13)

Guilt over Typical Sibling Conflicts

One 9-year-old girl described often being angry at her 4-year-old sick brother who "was a pest, interfering with my homework and possessions." She related how in a moment of acute fury she chased her little brother around the apartment. Her mother picked up the child and shouted: "Don't you hit my child!" The sibling described feeling during this episode, as well as during many others in her life: "My parents act as if I wasn't also their child." (Bendor, 1990, p. 23)

Although difficult for parents to watch, teasing, name-calling, arguing, and other forms of conflict are common among most brothers and sisters. While parents may be appalled at siblings' harshness toward one another, much of this conflict can be a beneficial part of normal social development. Bank and Kahn (1982, p. 199) noted that a "constructive function of sibling aggression is that it forces the participants into a social 'laboratory' where they learn how to manage and resolve conflicts." They further noted that:

> The ability to deflect aggression, to use it wisely and at the right moment, to use humor, to surrender without debasing oneself and to defeat someone without humiliating that person are all skills that children and adolescents can eventually use in relationships with peers, spouses, and ultimately with their own children. (p.199)

Bank and Kahn also reported that children they have interviewed have told them that a moderate amount of aggressive interaction (that is not interfered with by parents) is a necessary and positive part of the sibling relationship.

Presumably, lessons taught and relationships built through sibling conflict will also apply to the sibling who has a disability or illness. A brother who has Down syndrome might be better equipped to face life in the community if he has learned to defend himself within the essentially loving confines of a family. A sibling who has shared a rich, if sometimes rocky, relationship with a sister who is disabled may be more likely to continue that relationship as an adult.

Regardless of how adaptive or developmentally appropriate it might be, however, typical sibling conflict is more likely to result in feelings of guilt when one sibling has a special health or developmental need. When conflict arises, the message sent to many brothers and sisters is, "Leave your sibling alone. You are bigger, you are stronger, you should know better. It is your job to compromise." Because of their "advantages," brothers and sisters may feel they are not permitted to get angry or tease or argue with their siblings.

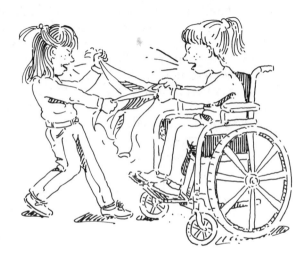

> You know, I would complain about something my brother did and everyone would say "Now you know he doesn't really know what he is doing. You're the one who is okay and you need to understand." And I used to get so frustrated and really copped a lot of resentments about that it was not okay for me to get angry with him, but it was okay for him to do whatever he wanted. (Fish, 1993)

While no parent should ever tolerate physical abuse among siblings, brothers and sisters—even those with special needs—should be allowed to work out their conflicts as best they can. Because sibling squabbles can be so painful for parents to watch, it is often helpful to remove oneself from the situation. It has been our experience that sibling squabbles resolve in 30 minutes when parents intervene and 30 minutes when they do not. Parents who deny their children the right to have conflicts, said Bank and Kahn (1982), run the risk that "the children may express their anger in secret and forbidden ways" (p. 203).

Guilt Regarding Caregiving

> I had to go to my parents and make them talk about it. It was always this given that I was going to take the responsibility over and what ended up happening is that I got really miserable. I love my brother dearly, but I don't want to be a parent. I had to set a very strict boundary: No, he cannot live with me, and I still stand by that. They felt I had really let the family down. They said: "You're going to let him live on the street!" No, that's not what I'm saying. What I am saying is that we have to look into other options. Living with me is not one of them. (Fish, 1993)

> I am Douglas' sibling. I wanted to be a sister and very much wanted a baby brother. But I never planned on being his everything. For years I was just that. (Zatlow, 1992, p. 15)

Some family theorists such as Duvall (1962) have observed that families, like individuals, proceed through a life cycle consisting of overlapping stages. Just as an individual grows, develops, matures, and ages, families also are "born," grow, change, and age. Events such as divorce, desertion, or death will profoundly affect the family life cycle. As noted elsewhere (Meyer, 1986), few changes will have a greater effect on the life cycle than the presence of a child with special health or developmental needs.

One poignant example is Duvall's (1962) seventh stage, "families as launching centers," which begins when a family's first child leaves home and ends when the last child leaves the nest. For a family with a child with special needs this "launching" stage may take place much earlier (for families who institutionalize their child) or may extend for the life of the child if the child lives with the parents as an adult. Regardless, entering adulthood will be an especially troubling milestone for families of people who have disabilities. For the families Wikler (1981) studied, the 21st birthday for a young adult with a disability was the second most stressful crisis for parents, following the initial diagnosis. The 21st birthday can be a double crisis: While it normally symbolizes independence, parents may be reminded of their child's many needs before he or she can achieve independence. Furthermore, the 21st birthday will signal a transitional crisis: Schools cease to provide services after this age, and adult services are often inadequate.

Crises such as these will affect other family members as well. Brothers and sisters, who would otherwise be planning to "launch" from their families, may feel guilty about moving away from home and leaving their parents to care for their siblings' special needs (Grossman, 1972). One sister commented that going away to college was initially a relief: She did not have to care for her brother who has Down syndrome; she could sleep in. By mid-college, she felt guilty about not helping, and felt the need to provide her parents with respite (Nester, 1989, p.1). Other siblings have expressed similar feelings:

> As Paul finishes his college years, he's thinking more and more about leaving their family home, but finds it difficult to imagine his mother coping with their home and sister by herself. His father died a couple of years ago, and the loss of a good and kind man . . . is still keenly felt. (Binkard et al., 1987, p. 24)

> When I moved out of my mother's house, I was distraught and overwhelmed by responsibilities. Even the process of moving had to be negotiated on a compromise; I agreed to be near enough to my mother and brother so that I could get to them quickly in the event of problems. This proved to be prophetic, for there were countless days and nights when I was called upon by my mother to help her in a crisis and handle my brother on difficult days. (Zatlow, 1992, p. 13)

Even when siblings do stay to offer assistance to their siblings, conflicting loyalties and needs can produce guilty feelings:

> It was grueling; I had no relief, no support, no options. My life was revolving around Kevin and his care. If I wanted to go away for a few days, I couldn't. The guilt was overwhelming. What do you tell your friends? No, I can't go out; I have to feed my brother? (Pat, in Remsberg, 1989, p. 10)

Shame

Shame, where guilt intersects with embarrassment, is a powerful and painful experience for some brothers and sisters. Because of the stigma of a disability or illness, siblings can feel that their family is now "marked," and wish that their family would just fade into the woodwork (Sourkes, 1980).

> Julie went through a long stage of being embarrassed about her sister. This continued into her teenage years. "There's a constant conflict in you," she remembers. "You don't want to say anything because you don't want your parents to feel that you are ashamed." (Remsberg, 1989, p. 15)

Shame can have long-lasting consequences. One prominent professional in the field of developmental disabilities told us that much of her success is "shame-driven." She grew up with a brother who had Down syndrome, although she did not learn the name of her brother's disability until after his death when they were both in their early teens. Life with a brother who was different was a constant source of embarrassment for this individual. When her mother would pick her up from school, she would dive into the back seat of the car, afraid that classmates might see her with her brother. After his death, guilty feelings about her embarrassment gave way to shame. Now in counseling, she tells us that her pursuit of academic degrees and work in human services is a means of compensating for her perceived transgressions against her brother. Her shame, she feels, keeps her from enjoying her successes.

Although little has been written about this topic, siblings we know who have shared similar stories seem to share characteristics. First, most were born before the 1960s, an era when John F. Kennedy, Hubert Humphrey, and others sought to reduce the stigma of disabilities and illnesses by discussing them publicly. Today, with legislation assuring access to public education and increased visibility of people with special needs in popular media, the stigma of having a brother or sister with health or developmental needs is not what it once was (although one can easily imagine the stigma felt by a sibling whose brother or sister is HIV-positive or has a resistant strain of tuberculosis).

Second, they came from families where the disability was rarely, if ever, discussed, and the disability was clearly traumatic for the parents.

> In our family, there exists a way of being, a denial of the truth. . . . there was a strong message that you don't go outside of the family for anything. You stay inside, you keep family secrets, you don't seek outside help from anyone. I'm the first one in this family to seek therapy and I've had to go through a lot of shame and guilt about doing that. (David, age 29, in Leder, 1991, p. 26)

Finally, these instances usually seem to occur in families where there are only two children, one who is affected and one who is not. Additional children in the family, as Dyson (1989) and Kazak and Clarke (1986) have found, appear to dilute the consequences of growing up with a sibling who has a disability or an illness. Other siblings can provide a typically developing child other children with whom he or she can identify and a built-in informal means of support.

For the simple reason that they are healthy and their sibling is not, sisters and brothers of people with special needs are at risk for a variety of guilty feelings. Although open communication is desirable for any parent–child relationship, it is especially important when that child has a sibling with special needs.

ISOLATION, LONELINESS, AND LOSS

In *A Difference in the Family*, Helen Featherstone (1980) wrote: "In dealing with the wider world of friends, classmates and teacher, able-bodied children at times feel painfully different" (p. 144). A sibling's disability or illness can cause brothers and sisters to experience various feelings of loss and isolation.

Especially if there are only two children in the family, typically developing siblings may miss having a brother or sister with whom they can seek advice, or share their thoughts, hopes, and dreams. They may also long for the rough-but-loving relationship many siblings share:

> It was hard. They were telling me stuff that I really didn't understand. At that time he and I were really close. He was getting sick and we couldn't do much. I was wondering why he couldn't do things anymore. And if I got into an argument and hit him I was always afraid my hit would cause him to die. I felt lonely not having a brother to play with or beat up. (Don, age 18, in Murray & Jampolsky, 1982, p.40)

Isolation from Parents' Attention

When parents are consumed with a child's disability or illness, typically developing brothers and sisters can feel neglected and isolated from their parents. These feelings are especially keen during times of stress for the family, such as diagnoses or hospitalizations. Of course, this comes at times when siblings need more, not less, emotional support.

> Even if you feel bad for your sick brother or sister, you still want your parents too. (12-year-old girl, in Bendor, 1990, p. 24)

> I spent a lot of time with baby-sitters and television, and less with my parents and the relatives who visited only to see Lisa. It seemed as though she were the only one anybody cared about. In this, I was the typical sibling of a victim of childhood cancer. (Ellis, 1991, p. 2)

Cairns, Clark, Smith, and Lansky (1979), in a study of school-age children with cancer and their healthy siblings, found that siblings showed greater distress than did patients in the areas of perceived social isolation, perception of their parents as overindulgent and overprotective of the sick child, fear of expressing negative feelings, and (for older siblings only) concern with school failure.

Parents, overwhelmed by a child's many needs, may be too exhausted or simply unable to recognize a brother's or sister's calls for attention (Schorr-Ribera, 1992). Several brothers and sisters of children who have epilepsy reflected on how their sibling's disability caused them to feel isolated from their parents:

> I probably will never forget the loneliness during that period of time. The feeling that I had was that I wasn't worth as much as Jessica. (Collins, 1991)

> The only way I could get them to pay attention to me was to get mad. That would get their attention. (Collins, 1991)

> I wouldn't talk to my parents about being lonely because I wasn't sure that they'd understand me—the way I felt. (Collins, 1991)

> I didn't do my schoolwork. I guess I wanted to see how my parents would react. I wanted to see if they would pay attention or yell at me or ground me or something. (Collins, 1991)

Other siblings, seeing the pain caused by a sibling's special needs, may elect not to come to their parents with their troubles. These siblings, wrote Featherstone (1980),

> may, then, endure many of [their] feelings alone and without support, even when parents are tactful and eager to help. Conscientious, sensitive parents often have conscientious sensitive children; seeing how pushed and saddened their parents already are, such children hesitate to burden them further. (p. 61)

One adult sibling we met told us that it took her 5 years to tell her parents she had been raped. She thought they had "enough to worry about" with her brother, who has autism. Another sister wrote:

> I felt I had to hold my feelings in when I was around my parents. I let my feelings out only when I was with my close friends. (Honey, age 16, in Murray & Jampolsky, 1982, p. 54)

Of course, when a child is facing a health or developmental crisis, it may be impossible for parents to meet all their children's needs for emotional support. During trying times, many families enlist the support of a favorite relative or adult friend who provides the healthy child with time, attention, and an "open ear."

Isolation from Information, the Process

> My parents, my two older sisters and my grandparents would all leave to go to the hospital while I sat at home with a baby-sitter. All I wanted to know was what was happening and why everybody al-

ways left me. No one took the time to explain to me that my sister was basically dying. (Doherty, 1992, p. 4)

Several [sibling group] members described the pain of having to give up a beloved bird or dog after the sick child began treatment. Pets carry germs and pose a serious threat to the infection-prone child whose immunity is suppressed when he receives chemotherapy. Two parents did not give an explanation to the healthy siblings for putting a pet to sleep or giving him away. The siblings felt devastated and angry. (Bendor, 1990, p. 24)

Adult brothers and sisters occasionally report growing up in families where their siblings' disability or illness was rarely discussed. They report the irony of this situation: In many ways, they knew their siblings better than anyone, yet they knew little about the illness or disability or its implications.

There are several reasons for this situation. Some siblings tell us that their parents wished to protect them from the stress and sadness they experienced, and "spared" them information about their siblings' special needs. Other siblings grew up with a sibling whose disability (e.g., epilepsy) or illness (e.g., schizophrenia) was so stigmatizing that their parents sought to keep the problem a family secret. Topics that were taboo outside the home were also frequently taboo inside the home, leaving siblings to feel alone with their questions and concerns.

Other siblings report feeling "left in the dark" for legal reasons. Foster brothers and sisters of children who have complex psychosocial needs have told us of their frustrations: They must live with a foster sibling's often-difficult behavior, yet they are not permitted (intrepreted to mean *trusted*) to know details of the foster sibling's background.

Regardless of the reason, when there is insufficient communication about the brother's or sister's problems, a typically developing sibling can experience a unique loneliness. One brother shared what it was like to be spared information about his sister's cancer. He felt his parents sheltered him, assuring him "not to worry." He now feels that remaining uninvolved and uninformed has a cost:

> I didn't understand the full extent of my sister's disease—I just thought that the doctors would take care of everything and I didn't think about how tough it was for my sister in other ways. (Peter, in Ellis, 1992, p. 5)

Not understanding the implications of his sister's illness and being reassured that he need not worry caused him to feel isolated and confused, especially when his parents left and went to the hospital:

> I became a latchkey child in a lot of ways—always left by myself, so I feel that essentially I became a peripheral member of my family during that time. I wasn't included at all. (Peter, in Ellis, 1992, p. 5)

Isolation from Peers

> Until this group, I had never met another sibling. It wasn't until the tender age of 39 that I met another person like myself. (Marilyn, in Fink, 1984, p. 6)

> Right now, I think it would be helpful if I could understand more about what he goes through and why my folks have such different expectations for him. If there were groups for siblings, I'd like to talk to them about parents and their different expectations. (Mary, 17, in Binkard et al., 1987, p. 11)

Since the 1980s, we have learned one simple yet far-reaching lesson from the hundreds of parents and siblings we have met, and it is this: Siblings' experiences parallel parents' experiences. Brothers and sisters will encounter joys, concerns, and issues regarding the person with special needs that closely correspond to those of their parents. And, although brothers and sisters have the longest-lasting relationship in the family, siblings (as we see again and again) have, compared to their parents, far fewer opportunities to gain access to programs, services, and professional support.

Nowhere is this more evident than in the area of peer support. Many parents count on sharing the good times, the not-so-good times, and helpful information with a peer who is also the parent of a child with special needs. Some parents connect with other parents through common-sense efforts in programs such as Parent-to-Parent, or fathers' programs, or mothers' groups (Meyer, Vadasy, Fewell, & Schell, 1985). Many parents maintain informal contact with other parents of children who have similar special needs. For most parents, the thought of "going it alone," without the benefit of knowing another parent in a similar situation, is unthinkable. Yet this happens routinely to brothers and sisters. The siblings Bendor (1990) interviewed made periodic but vain attempts to share feelings of frustration and loneliness with friends. The siblings reported that friends were either uninterested or unable to respond helpfully (p. 25).

> I'd like to join a group for siblings if there were one. I guess I'd even be willing to try to start one if I knew other brothers and sisters who would like to join. Sometimes you feel like you're the only one who's gone through this. I haven't ever been able to share most of my feelings. (Beth, age 16, in Binkard et al., 1987, p. 6)

Despite the tremendous success of peer-support programs for parents, there remains a dearth of such programs for brothers and sisters of children with special needs. The need for such opportunities is clear: McKeever's (1983) study of children with cancer revealed that siblings were more in need of support than were other family members. Numerous authors (Lobato, 1990; Murphy, 1981; Powell & Gallagher, 1993; Seligman, 1991) have suggested that support groups can provide young siblings with opportunities for "catharsis, support, and insight concerning relationships with family members and others and techniques for managing various situations" (Murphy, 1979, p. 359).

Like their parents, brothers and sisters appear to benefit from groups in which they can voice their fears, hopes, and doubts. Groups specifically for brothers and sisters demonstrate that somebody cares about the issues facing them and values the important role they play in the family.

As revealed in subsequent chapters, brothers and sisters, while they have unique concerns, are not the at-risk population once described in the research literature. Like their parents, the vast majority of brothers and sisters of people with special needs do well despite challenges brought about by the siblings' disability or illness. Consequently, programs for brothers and sisters should reflect siblings' and families' strengths while acknowledging their concerns. (To be sure, there will be some family members—parents or siblings—who will have needs that go beyond what a peer support group can provide. In Chapter 5 we discuss how to recognize siblings in need of therapeutic programs, and where to refer them.)

RESENTMENT

> "How is Andrea, your sister, doing today? Is she home from the hospital yet? Will she get better soon? Send her my love." When your brother or sister is sick, this is what you might hear. This is all I heard

> for about a year after Andrea was sick. I was so sick of hearing about all this stuff about Andrea I could scream. Why doesn't anyone ever ask me how I am doing!!! (Amy, age 14, in Murray & Jampolsky, 1982, p. 51)

Resentment, a strong sentiment frequently expressed by brothers and sisters of people with special needs, is unlikely to go unnoticed by parents. A group of parents of children with muscular dystrophy with whom we met said that among the most pressing concerns their typically developing children experienced was resentment. Their observations serve as an overview of the types of resentment mentioned by siblings of children with diverse special needs. The parents volunteered that their children resented the attention the siblings with muscular dystrophy received, the amount of care and time the siblings required, the perceived unequal treatment for children in the family, being expected to do more around the house and help their siblings with toileting and other needs that the siblings cannot do for themselves, and the limitations on their and the families' lifestyle imposed by the disability.

Loss of Parental Attention

> I remember the toys, gifts, and candy that were given in surplus to Lisa in a futile attempt to ease her pain. I felt jealous, neglected, and isolated because of Lisa's illness and the subsequent attention that was given her and taken from me. (Ellis, 1992, p. 2)

One form of resentment occurs when siblings perceive that the child with special needs is receiving more than his or her share of the family's emotional or even financial resources. From the sibling's perspective, the child with special needs becomes the sun in the family's solar system. The siblings of children with cancer interviewed by Koch-Hattem (1986) said their siblings were receiving more attention, caring, and material possessions since having been diagnosed with cancer. Although many were realistic about the need for these changes, all displayed some degree of envy.

Young siblings may lack the cognitive and affective capabilities to appreciate that their parents' behavior is a response to the genuine needs of the child with a disability, rather than a lack of love or appreciation for their typically developing children. Bendor (1990) noted that some of the children interviewed were frightened by their feelings of anger, and, developmentally, the options available to them for expressing or mastering their negative feelings were limited.

However, even when they do comprehend their siblings' needs and their parents' stresses, brothers and sisters may be faced with another dilemma. One sibling to whom Bendor (1990) spoke summed it

up this way: "The worst thing about all the anger you feel inside is that there is no one to blame" (p. 24). Without the target that blame provides, siblings may turn inward, feeling guilty about their anger.

Unequal Treatment and Excessive Demands

"You should be ashamed of yourself," her mother told her. "You should be able to control your temper. She can't help it. You can." (Julie, in Remsberg, 1989, p. 15)

I guess I have more resentment now about the attention my brother gets than when we were younger. When we were younger, he seemed like a little kid and it was OK for him to get a lot of help. Now it seems like my mom will sit for hours with him while I'm just expected to do my own homework for myself. . . . Nonhandicapped kids can get pushed aside when their brothers or sisters have handicaps. Andrew seems to get help naturally—it's like attention to his needs is "built in to the system." (Mary, age 17, in Binkard et al., 1987, p. 10)

I mostly missed my mom a lot. She was always away at the hospital with my sister. My brother and I had to stay with Mom's friends or our neighbors all day. When my sister came home and she was mean or bad, she got away with it. If I hit her I got spanked. Why was she so special? (Forrest, age 10, in Murray & Jampolsky, 1982, p. 48)

Brothers and sisters report resentment when children with disabilities or illness are indulged or overprotected, or permitted to engage in behaviors unacceptable by other family members. Miller's

(1974) study revealed that parents were much less tolerant of siblings' negative behaviors toward their siblings with mental retardation than they were of similar sibling behaviors toward other, typically developing siblings. Further, Miller found that siblings without disabilities were more likely to be punished if they did not engage in a prescribed activity with a sibling with a disability than if they avoided a similar responsibility for a typically developing sibling. Podeanu-Czehotsky's (1975) study of the families of children with cerebral palsy found that in some families life was normal, whereas in other families the child with the disability was indulged and became "a tyrant causing hidden or open conflicts among siblings" (p. 309).

Growing up, siblings may find them themselves facing a difficult dilemma: they may appreciate that their siblings have bona fide needs, yet, because of their still-egocentric view of the world, they resent them for having these needs. One 16-year-old responded this way when asked what was the most difficult aspect of having a sick sibling: "Having to care so much and being burdened by the responsibility of caring" (Bendor, 1990, p. 28). The girl then described staying home night after night to help her mother when her sick sister had high fevers and was vomiting. She wondered if she was selfish for resenting this role.

When we listen to brothers and sisters at Sibshops or during sibling panels, they frequently complain that their siblings "get away with murder." Family rules about behavior, chores, bedtime routines, and so forth often do not apply to the child with special needs. Brothers and sisters frequently insist that their sibling *could* comply with many of the family's rules and requirements "if only my parents would make him [or her] do it."

Siblings' views deserve to be heard, even if, as children, they lack a parent's understanding of the "bigger picture." Their alternative perspective—which almost always focuses on what they believe their sibling can do—can provide parents and service providers with fresh insights regarding a child's actual abilities. "My brother never has to unload the dishwasher because he has Down syndrome," one brother told us. "But he can do it. I know he can, because when my parents aren't home, I make him unload the dishwasher."

Parfit (1975) has recommended that parents avoid overprotecting children with disabilities by discussing with their typically developing children the behaviors that are unavoidable due to the siblings' disabilities, and discipline that can help modify the problem behaviors. Brothers and sisters, then, can advise parents of behaviors for which their siblings should be held responsible: "Children are often more sensible and sensitive about such matters than adults" (Parfit, 1975, p. 20).

Resentment Regarding Failure to Plan for the Future

> Julie feels that her mother overprotects Kathy and babies her more than necessary. But, "It's too sensitive an area between us to talk about. If I ask 'What's she going to do if you're gone?' the subject is changed." (Remsberg, 1989, p. 16)

In families where there is a child with developmental disabilities, frequently there is an assumption—often unspoken—that brothers and sisters will someday become guardians of their sibling as adults. An especially poignant concern for many adult brothers and sisters regards their siblings' future and the role they will play in that future. Psychiatrist E. Fuller Torrey (1992), a brother of a woman who has schizophrenia, has noted: "Demographically, we will outlive our parents; demographically, we will get involved with our siblings."

When parents fail to involve siblings in planning for the future for the person with the disability, resentment is likely to occur. "My parents won't consider letting Bobby try a group home," one sister told us. "That's all well and good now, but what happens when they die? Will he have to come live with me?"

We will never forget the testimony of a young woman who participated in a sibling panel we hosted. This woman, a mother with two young children, clearly loved her parents and her sister, who has cerebral palsy and emotional problems. However, her resentment toward her parents was unmistakable. With tears welling in her eyes, she told how her parents, who had grown too frail to take care of her sister's many special needs, "dropped the sister on her doorstep." Her sister's presence and many demands, she said, had been extremely difficult for all members of her young family.

Failure to plan adequately for the future can cause resentment among surviving siblings as well. Adult siblings—generally sisters—have told us how they have somehow inherited all of the responsibilities associated with caring for the sibling who is disabled. "[My siblings] are all patting me on the back, telling me what a good job I'm doing and all that, but they don't help at all" (Fish, 1993).

Even when parents plan for the future, their expectations can cause guilt and resentment. "My parents never wanted my brother to live outside the family home," one sister told us, "and when we talked about what we would do when they were gone, it was apparent that they wanted Jim to come live with me. I love my brother. I will always be involved with my brother. But I don't want him to live with me." Other adult siblings have told of promises extracted by dying parents that they will take in their siblings with disabilities.

Advanced medical technologies allow people with disabilities to live longer than in previous generations. Social policy and diminishing economic resources dictate that people with disabilities will live in the community and closer to their families than in previous generations, when the state assumed an *in loco parentis* role for adults with disabilities. Therefore, it is reasonable to expect that adult siblings of the baby-boom and post–baby-boom generation will be more involved in the lives of the brothers and sisters with disabilities than any previous generation. Unless parents and service providers involve siblings in the planning for their children's future, many adults with disabilities will soon have sibling guardians who are both ill-prepared for the job and resentful of the responsibilities placed on their shoulders.

INCREASED RESPONSIBILITIES

> When my parents went out for the evening, they would hire a baby-sitter, but baby-sitters didn't know how to handle a little girl who screamed all night and bit herself and did things like that, so they would get me up to take care of her. So from the time I was five years old, I was being responsible and helping and doing things. My two brothers have had a much harder time with it, especially the brother who is less than a year older than my sister. He won't even talk about her, and this has been 30 some years and he will not talk about her. (Fish, 1993)

About caregiving responsibilities, Milton Seligman (1979) wrote:

> The extent to which a sibling may be held responsible for a handicapped brother or sister bears a strong relationship to the perception and feelings children, adolescents, and adults have about their handicapped sibling and their parents. Available research supports the notion that a child's (especially a female child's) excessive re-

sponsibility for a handicapped sib is related to the development of anger, resentment and guilt, and quite possibly subsequent psychological disturbance. (p. 530)

Early research on siblings of children with developmental disabilities frequently focused on the caregiving demands assumed by siblings, especially sisters. Authors such as Farber (1960) and Fowle (1973) observed that sisters, especially oldest sisters, were more adversely affected than brothers by the presence of a child with a disability. Other researchers from this era, including Cleveland and Miller (1977) and Gath (1974), felt that oldest daughters were often pushed into a surrogate parent role with the child with special needs, especially in large and low-income families. This heavy caregiving responsibility, they felt, often isolated them from their age mates. If they have too many responsibilities, older sisters may be at risk for educational failure and increased disturbances (Gath, 1974), and stress (Farber, 1960).

Cleveland and Miller's (1977) research suggests that oldest female siblings may experience a sibling's disability as a double-edged sword. Their research revealed that oldest sisters were most likely to enter helping professions and to remain involved with the sibling with a disability as an adult; it also showed that this group was most likely to seek professional help for personal problems.

How much of this research—some of it 30 years old—remains valid? What effect, if any, have programs (e.g., respite care, special sitters, "Special Saturday," day care for children with disabilities) and movement toward community-based schooling and life had on the caregiving demands placed on brothers and sisters?

In a more recent study of preschool siblings of children with disabilities conducted by Lobato, Barbour, Hall, and Miller (1987), sisters were found to have the greatest degree of responsibility for child care and household tasks, although the difference was not statistically significant when compared with brothers of children with disabilities and with siblings of typically developing children. However, the sisters of children with disabilities received significantly fewer privileges and experienced more restrictions on social routines compared with matched controls. Brothers of children with disabilities experienced the opposite—more privileges and fewer restrictions on social activities. According to Lobato and her colleagues, the sex of the typically developing siblings appeared to shape the daily living routines among families with children who have disabilities but not among control families.

Stoneman, Brody, and their colleagues have conducted extensive research on caregiving responsibilities of siblings of children with developmental disabilities. In one study of younger siblings of children with and without disabilities (Stoneman, Brody, Davis, Crapps, & Malone, 1991), younger siblings of children with disabilities baby-sat, monitored, and helped care for their older siblings while the comparison group performed significantly less total child care and never baby-sat their older siblings.

During observational studies conducted by Stoneman, Brody, Davis, and Crapps (1987, 1988, 1989), children with disabilities (ages 4–8 years) were videotaped with their older siblings (ages 6–12 years). According to the authors, siblings of children with disabilities—especially older sisters—more readily assumed the role of manager or caregiver for their brothers or sisters.

That older sisters assume greater caregiving responsibilities in families where there is a child with a disability is hardly surprising. After all, many oldest daughters find themselves assuming the role of surrogate mother, regardless of the presence of a child with a disability in the family. However, when Stoneman et al. (1988) compared older sisters in families where there is a disability to a comparison group, they found that the older sisters of children with disabilities baby-sat and had more child-care responsibilities than any other groups of children. Also, the more family responsibilities these sisters assumed, the less they participated in their own activities outside of the homes and the more conflict was found with the children who have the disability.

In their 1988 study of older siblings, Stoneman et al. found that for brothers and sisters of children with disabilities an increase in observed sibling conflict and a decrease in positive sibling interaction was associated with child-care responsibilities, which was not found with the comparison group. This finding apparently does not apply to other domestic chores. In fact, the authors noted, increased older sibling responsibility for other household chores corresponded to less, rather than more, observed sibling conflict.

As expected, the authors (Stoneman et al., 1988, 1991) found that responsibilities assumed by the siblings of children with disabilities (e.g., helping with dressing, feeding) tended to be greater when the child with the disability had fewer adaptive skills. Less adaptively competent children, suggested Stoneman and Brody (1993), seem to place greater demands for caregiving on siblings, regardless of the birth order.

It would be far too easy and unrealistic to recommend that brothers and especially sisters of children with special health and developmental needs be spared domestic duties. After all, "special needs" invariably translate into increased caregiving needs and household chores. Besides, the responsible attitudes that so many siblings seem to have are, in part, a result of successfully handling duties performed in service to their siblings and families.

I didn't resent [her] dependency, though. It's been my whole life. I always had to bring Sandy to the bathroom and help her get ready before I could go to school. (Rachel, age 21, in Binkard et al., 1987, p. 20)

As a child, I know I was a very important part of Martha's life. I was the only one she would go potty for. I was the only one who could braid her hair, take her into a store, and stop her tantrums. (Westra, 1992, p.4)

The research of Stoneman et al. (1988) suggests some general guidelines for assigning domestic chores to siblings of children with special needs. First, the type of chores assigned should be considered. Are child-care demands resulting in the conflict described by Stoneman et al. (1988)? If so, parents may wish to consider offering siblings a choice in the household responsibilities they assume. Parents can offer siblings an opportunity to contribute to the family in other ways—shopping, meal preparation, or cleaning.

Second, the amount of demands placed on the typically developing child should also be considered. Parents should be advised to compare their children's level of child-care and household duties with those of their peers in order to determine if their chores are excessive or preventing them from participating in at least some activities outside of the home. Responsibility is great, but so is soccer, being in the school play, or learning to play the saxophone.

Third, who is assuming the caregiving demands should be considered. It is not surprising that it is sisters who bear the brunt of the caregiving responsibilities. Brothers, according to Grossman (1972), are often exempted from demanding caregiving duties. Parents should be encouraged to make sure the chores are spread equitably among brothers and sisters.

PRESSURE TO ACHIEVE

Ever since I was a child, I have been put into that role—rescuer, perfect child, the one who would make everything right. And all the time while this craziness was going on in my family, I was trying to maintain my grade point average to go on to college and become a doctor. (David, in Leder, 1991, p. 22)

I couldn't express anger. There was lots of denial and I had to remain well-behaved all the time. (Selma, family therapist, in Fink, 1984, p. 6)

Over the years we have had the good fortune to talk to many parents about their children. Some of these parents have told us of a situation they believe to be unusual: One child attends a special education program, while another child is enrolled in a program for gifted children.

The perceived pressure on siblings of people with special needs to excel in academics, sports, music, or even behavior has long been

noticed by clinicians. Earlier writings suggested that parents placed the pressure on their typically developing children, as if to compensate for the "failure" of the other child's disability. Whether consciously or unconsciously, parents can pressure their children to compensate for the limitations of the child with a disability, creating resentment and anxiety for typically developing siblings (Murphy, 1979; Schild, 1976).

Grossman (1972) found that this pressure to achieve was especially true when the child with the disability was a son. Older, only daughters are particularly prone to dual stresses, suggested Cleveland and Miller (1977). These daughters feel pressured to make up for the parents' unfulfilled hopes for the sibling with the disability; they also experience the increased parent-surrogate responsibilities that are most often delegated to daughters rather than sons.

While parents may be the source for some of the pressure siblings experience (as one brother told us: "My parents expect me to take up all the slack!"), it may be that siblings place much of the pressure on themselves. Coleman (1990) studied siblings of children with developmental disabilities, ages 12–14 years, and compared them with siblings of children who had (only) physical disabilities and siblings of typically developing children. Specifically, Coleman investigated the siblings' self-concept, their need to compensate for the child's deficit, their actual achievement, and parental demandingness. Coleman found no significant differences among the groups with regard to the subjects' self-concept. However, there were significant group differences with regard to need for achievement, with siblings of children with developmental disabilities scoring higher than siblings of children with physical disabilities only, or no disabilities.

For the siblings of children who have developmental disabilities, Coleman (1990) found that as their academic achievement increased, their self-concept decreased. There was no such relationship found between self-concept and achievement for the other two groups. Finally, Coleman found no significant differences among the three groups regarding siblings' perceptions of parental demandingness.

I put pressure on myself; whether my parents encouraged that stance I don't know. (Cynthia, in Leder, 1991, p. 210)

Suggesting that parents attempt to compensate for the loss associated with having a child who has special needs by placing pressure on their typically developing children may be too simplistic and unidirectional. Siblings may place pressure on themselves for a variety of reasons. Coleman (1990) speculated that her finding of an inverse relationship between achievement and self-concept may be a result of internal conflict and could stem from survivor guilt or setting unattainable achievement goals. This hypothesis would certainly apply to the sister mentioned earlier in this chapter who felt that her success in human services was "shame-driven" and could not enjoy her many accomplishments.

But there can be other reasons as well. The motivation may be attention: As one sister told us, "Growing up I did well in school because that was my way of getting attention from my parents." Another brother said he did well in school to counteract the profound loss that his parents experienced about his sister's disability. Another sister volunteered that success in academics was her way of demonstrating to the world that it was her sister, not she, who had a disability.

High achievement in academics, sports, or behavior may seem like a dubious "unusual concern." After all, Grossman's (1972) study revealed that not only were there no significant differences between college-age siblings of people with and without mental retardation in academic achievement, overall academic functioning (including social adaptation), intelligence, and anxiety levels, but also the siblings of people with mental retardation scored higher on measures of overall college functioning.

Indeed, the conscientious attitude some siblings have for their schoolwork would suggest that their need to achieve is, in fact, an "unusual opportunity." And it may well be. However, parents and service providers should be alert for siblings whose efforts are compulsive or neurotic (e.g., the sibling who cannot be satisfied with a B+ average), or for siblings who are unhappy, despite many successes.

3

Information Needs of Siblings

Throughout their lives, brothers and sisters will have a need for information about their siblings' condition. Their need will closely parallel their parents' informational needs, yet parents have distinct advantages: Being adults, parents' understanding of the world and the way it works is more mature and benefits from a longer lifetime of experiences. Also, parents have far greater access to information—written and otherwise—about the condition and its implications than their children do.

Siblings have a compelling need for information about the condition of their brother or sister with a disability and its implications. They need information for reassurance, to answer their own questions and questions posed by others, and to plan for their future. And, unless their brother or sister has a terminal condition, the need will be lifelong, and the topics ever-changing. Throughout their lives, the types of information siblings need—as well as how it is optimally presented—will vary with the siblings' age.

INFORMATION NEEDS VARY WITH THE CHILD'S AGE

Preschoolers

Debra Lobato (1990) has written that children's understanding of their siblings' special needs "will represent a unique blend of what they have been told, overheard, observed, and conjured up on their very own" (p. 21). When siblings lack adequate, age-appropriate information and a mature understanding of the world, misunderstandings will be neither unusual nor surprising.

> I remember walking into my sister's room one morning [and] seeing large clumps of blond hair on her pillow. "Mommy, why is Lisa's hair falling out?" I asked. "She's sick," was the only reply possible from my mother; she had no time for lengthy explanations to a three-year-old. So I was left to solve the mystery by myself. (Ellis, 1992, p. 1)

Typically, young children interpret their world in terms of their own immediate observations. Because they have a limited range of experiences from which to draw, they frequently engage in magical thinking.

> "My kitty is sick!" (said a six-year-old girl who came to me, crying). Her cat had been coughing up hairballs and this little girl was afraid that it caught cancer from her brother, who had been throwing up from his chemotherapy treatments. She looked at me, sighed deeply, and said, "This chemo has been hard on all of us." (Schorr-Ribera, 1992, p. 2)

To prevent such misconceptions, preschoolers need to know that they cannot catch their siblings' disability, nor did they cause the condition. These concepts—while obvious to adults—may not be clear to a young child who has caught her sister's cold and has a preschooler's sense of causality.

Children ages 2–6 are very concrete thinkers. Explanations of disabilities or illnesses to children at this age should be as clear as possible. Debra Lobato (1990) noted that children as young as 3 can recognize some of their brothers' and sisters' problems, especially when they have had contact with other children and their siblings are older than they are.

> John plays cars with me and he loves to break dance. Sometimes he pulls off a shoe and I have to put it back on, but he's just slower than us, that's all. (a 4-year-old brother, in Fink, 1984, p. 6)

Lobato counsels that 3 years is not too early to share comments about a child's disability or illness. One means of explaining a disability is to describe it in terms of differences in behavior or routine. Thus, a 4-year-old who accompanies his 2-year-old sister to an early intervention program may understand his sister's disability this way: "Down syndrome means that you have to go to school to learn how to talk." Cerebral palsy, to another preschooler, might mean "you have a hard time walking, and a lady comes to your house to help you learn how to eat." While clearly incomplete, these definitions can be the foundation for more involved explanations at later ages.

School-Age Children

During their grade-school years, siblings need information to answer their own questions about the disability or illness as well as questions posed by classmates, friends, or even strangers. Older children may harbor private theories to explain their siblings' problems—even when accurate information has been provided. Sourkes (1990) recounted the observation of a 10-year-old boy whose teenage sister had a leg amputated due to osteogenic sarcoma:

My sister hurt her leg on the chain of her bike. She didn't even notice it until I pointed it out to her. I don't ride my bike anymore. I'm afraid to. One night I went out and I broke the chain on my bike so that I couldn't ride it. I told my mother that the bike broke by itself, but I really broke the chain. (p. 3)

Other siblings, according to Koch-Hattem (1986), may hold beliefs about the cause of the condition that place the blame on the child with special needs. "She probably got it because she never drank water or something" (Koch-Hattem, 1986, p. 113), said one 13-year-old sister of a 7-year-old Wilms' tumor patient. Blaming the patient, Koch-Hattem wrote, "may be a reflection of the sibling's own anger, a part of the belief system of the sibling or family, or a projection of guilt onto the patient" (p. 113).

My sister's diagnosis is very strongly connected in my mind to nail polish. She was getting into that kind of stuff and I wasn't and so I thought it was kind of gross. I thought she got a rash because of the nail polish, which then caused the cancer. (Naomi, age 22, in Sourkes, 1990, p. 12)

More so than preschoolers, school-age children may have more specific questions. They may ask: "Why does she have to go to the hospital?" "Why can some people with cerebral palsy walk and some can't?" "What does amniocentesis mean?" "What's physical therapy? Does it hurt?" "Why is Stephanie getting so fat?" "What does retarded mean?" Yet obtaining this information can be a problem for siblings of this age.

Teenagers

Even adolescents may have misconceptions about their siblings' problems. Some may assign a psychological or metaphysical reason for the diagnosis. One teen commented:

Well I think maybe it was God's way of telling our family to pull together. There had been a lot of arguing and a lot of dissension in my family and maybe this was his [sic] way to bring us together. (Sourkes, 1990, p. 4)

Like preschoolers and school-age children, teenagers often have specific questions about their brothers' or sisters' special needs.

Why was his hair falling out? Why was he going to the hospital all the time? Why was he getting bone marrows all the time? It never occurred to me that he might die. What was happening? I didn't get to go to the hospital to see him. What was leukemia? Why was he getting so many presents? (Chet, age 14, in Murray & Jampolsky, 1982, p. 35)

AVOIDING MISCONCEPTIONS ABOUT THE CONDITION

> My mother didn't tell me what was going on because she wanted to protect my feelings. I was so angry because Jeana and I were so close. I was so terribly afraid. I didn't know what was happening; I was afraid of the unknown. If you know what the problem is, you can face up to it and work it out; but if you don't understand, you can't handle it. (Joanne, age 16, in Murray & Jampolsky, 1982, p. 36)

How a family handles the dissemination of information about the disability or illness will greatly influence a typically developing sibling's adjustment to the condition. Some parents, seeking to protect their children from the sadness they are experiencing, choose to tell their children as little as possible. This, siblings tell us, is to be avoided. When left in the dark about what is happening to a brother or sister, siblings may make up their own stories that will be worse than the truth. They may even blame themselves for their siblings' conditions. Obtaining information, then, can be reassuring, even comforting for a brother or sister. They tell us that they still worry, but their concerns will be easier to manage because they are based on facts rather than fantasies.

> My advice is that doctors and parents ought to give information to the *brothers and sisters straight*! Sometimes, instead of telling them the truth, parents and doctors tell siblings a lot of baloney. It is easier to handle when at least you have all the facts. (Maria, age 15, in Murray & Jampolsky, 1982, p. 43)

Or, as Callahan (1990) noted: "Information, even concerning a painful subject, is preferable to ignorance distorted by imagination" (p. 157).

Traditional sources of information available to parents usually are not available to brothers and sisters. With rare exceptions (such as the resources noted in Appendix A), most books and materials about disabilities and illnesses have been created for adults. In 1991, the Sibling Support Project staff wrote to 112 agencies representing various childhood diseases and disabilities. We specifically requested materials prepared for children, especially young siblings. Only 16 agencies had materials for young readers, and only eight had materials for brothers and sisters.

Siblings are also frequently excluded from another traditional source of information: the teachers, physicians, therapists, nurses, and other providers serving children with special health and developmental needs. Brothers and sisters seldom accompany their parents to clinic visits, or individualized family service plan (IFSP), individualized education program (IEP), or transition planning meetings, and if they do, their opinions, thoughts, and questions are unlikely to be sought. Left "out of the loop" or relegated to waiting rooms, siblings report feeling ignored or isolated.

> I went with Lisa and my mother several times a week to the hospital where Lisa would get finger pokes and sometimes bone marrows (which I thought of as "bone arrows" because the procedure entailed being punctured in the back by a large needle.) . . . She lost all her hair . . . Sometimes she threw up and sometimes she stayed over-night at the hospital. I remember not understanding at all what was happening to my sister, and not receiving any explanations. (Ellis, 1991, pp. 1–2)

> My sister came here for therapy. She got to go on these scooters, but I had to sit in the waiting room with my mom the whole time. Why isn't there something for brothers and sisters to play with while they're there? When you are a kid you don't understand. All your parents are telling you is that she's special and has to go to these special pro-grams. Well, I wanted to be special too! (Fish, 1993)

The isolation, loneliness, and loss some siblings experience will be complicated by a lack of information about their siblings' special needs (Seligman, 1983). In some families, siblings receive a clear (if unspoken) signal that the condition is not to be discussed, leaving siblings to feel alone with their concerns and questions. A friend wrote us about growing up in an extended family in Hawaii:

> Joyce was born soon after me. Joyce, Sharon and I sunbathed to-gether and explored the property between the houses, with cousin Miles as our fearless leader. Then, Joyce got very sick, and didn't "grow up" like the rest of us. . . . Then, Joyce was no longer at home. We would ask: "Where is Joyce? How is she? What's Joyce doing?" Simple questions from children. We received no answers, except: "Don't ask those questions anymore." "Never ask Aunty Florence about Joyce." How were we to know any better? Our friend, our neighbor, our cousin, was no longer in the front house. We were only eight and ten at the time. (A. Tashiro, personal communication, 1992)

However, even when parents are happy to answer questions, some siblings will keep their questions and concerns to themselves. These brothers and sisters are reluctant to ask their parents questions, having witnessed their parents' sadness caused by the disability or illness. "Why would I ask my parents about something which makes them cry?" one sister told us.

Some parents are unaware that their children harbor questions they feel will cause discomfort for either the child or the parent. Often parents will be willing to answer any question their child asks, but when the child does not ask questions, parents may assume that their child has no interest in the topic. Sisters and brothers tell us that par-ents must be proactive in offering information:

> I would like people to understand that children need information, that both handicapped and normal children have feelings and fears. I would like to let people know that they need to be open with their

children, all their children, that just because the sisters and brothers don't ask, it doesn't mean that they don't want to know. (Pat, in Remsberg, 1989, p.4)

PROVIDING BROTHERS AND SISTERS NEEDED INFORMATION

What, then, are the best ways of providing a sibling with information? Siblings, young and not-so-young, recommend a variety of approaches. Few, however, are as important as the family's attitude toward the topic.

Keep the Sibling's Special Needs an Open Topic

Parents have to sit down and talk to the brothers and sisters who aren't handicapped about what the handicap really means. Kids don't automatically understand it by themselves. Maybe the other kids need some help too, understanding that the handicap won't go away, that it will be there and is a fact of life. . . . I love my brother, but I'd like to understand more about his handicap. (Beth, age 16, in Binkard et al., 1987, p. 5)

Although Beth encourages parents to "sit down and talk" to their typically developing children, many siblings report this is an uncomfortable situation for all parties, and have likened it to being told about the "birds and the bees." A far better way, they tell us, is to keep the topic of the special needs open and to offer information frequently, preferably in small doses. If brothers and sisters observe their parents openly discussing the disability or illness, they will learn to do so as well.

Answer Siblings' Questions About the Condition

If children's questions about siblings' special needs are answered in a forthright manner, and if they are made to feel glad that they asked, they will not only gain a growing understanding of their siblings' special needs but will also become confident that they may approach their parents whenever they have questions. Of course, not all siblings will ask questions. Parents need to adopt some strategies that can help all siblings—school-age and older—acquire needed information.

Provide Siblings with Written Materials

Another way to help siblings learn more about their brothers' and sisters' special needs is to utilize materials on the disability or illness. Appendix A lists various books, both fiction and nonfiction, and other materials that can help young readers learn more about various disabilities. Also, parents, family members, and service providers can contact agencies or associations representing the child's disability or illness and request information prepared for young readers. If the agency does not have such materials (and many do not), they should be challenged to create them.

Include Siblings in Visits with Service Providers

> Let him be as involved in the medical side as he wishes to be. Ask him if he would like to visit his brother or sister in the hospital. Let him ask questions and discuss treatments with you and the medical staff. (Schorr-Ribera, 1992, p. 1)

> I wish the doctor had told me his hair would fall out. It surprised me when I saw him bald. It would scare me when he was throwing up because I thought he was dying. Later on, I found out that his baldness and his throwing up were side effects of medicine. . . . My advice to others is to try and get as much information as you can. I was one of the last ones in my neighborhood to find out he had cancer. (Kurt, age 13, in Murray & Jampolsky, 1982, pp. 38–39)

Over the past decade, there has been a growing recognition that a child's disability or illness will affect more than the child and his or her mother. The professional literature today more often refers to the family unit, whereas in the past, the focus was primarily on the mother, or the parents, and the child with the disability or illness. Even when an agency claims to offer family-centered service, brothers and sisters rarely are invited to clinic visits, or involved in the IEP, IFSP, or transition planning process. Service providers who fail to address siblings' concerns squander significant opportunities and resources.

Inviting—but not requiring—siblings to attend meetings with service providers can benefit all parties. When included, siblings can obtain helpful, reassuring information about a sibling's condition (e.g., behavior, schooling, future plans). Brothers and sisters can contribute to the team by providing information and a unique, informed perspective. Their views on issues such as barriers to inclusion with same-age neighborhood peers, or a sibling's ability to accomplish household responsibilities are likely to be insightful—if frequently unsentimental. Parents gain a fresh perspective on the siblings' concerns which can result in improved communication about the child's disability.

Furthermore, when invited to meet with service providers, siblings are brought "into the loop." A message is sent to family members and service providers alike that brothers and sisters are valued members of the child's "team." Including them acknowledges the important roles they currently assume in their siblings' lives and, for many, roles they will have as adults.

Finally, information can promote understanding. Iles (1979) found that when healthy siblings had sufficient knowledge of their siblings' illness and treatment, they had increased empathy for their parents and greater compassion for their ill brothers and sisters (Lynn, 1989, p. 127). To be sure, it will not always be appropriate to invite a brother or sister to a meeting: A sibling may be too young or a meeting may be about delicate issues best discussed first with parents. However, whenever possible, parents and professionals should invite the child's brothers and sisters. At the very least, this will prevent siblings from experiencing the emotional exclusion and limbo of sitting alone in a waiting room.

Determine the Sibling's Knowledge of the Condition

Although the above strategies—keeping the topic open, answering siblings' questions, providing written materials, and inviting siblings to meetings—will go a long way in meeting siblings' informational needs, the only way to be certain siblings understand the disability or illness will be to have them explain it to someone else. One time-tested strategy is for parents to "check in" with their children approximately once per year during the child's school years.

To do this as unobtrusively as possible, parents should choose a time when they are alone with their child, perhaps on the way to soccer practice or play rehearsal. As the child with the special needs naturally enters the topic of conversation, parents pose a hypothetical situation to the typically developing sibling: "If someone asked you, 'What's the matter with Colleen?' what would you say?"

Asking the question like this will provide the parent with a fairly accurate window on the child's understanding of a sibling's disability. Because the question, as asked, is typical of questions asked of most siblings at one time or another, siblings are likely to be interested in discussing what a satisfactory response might be.

Parents then listen carefully to their child's response: If the child seems to have a good grasp for his or her age, he or she is complimented for that knowledge and parents may consider adding a few facts to the knowledge base. If the answer needs some corrections, this will be an ideal chance to improve the understanding of his or her sibling's condition. If the child does not have a satisfactory answer, parents can provide some elementary information. Even a "canned" response will help the child respond when asked this question.

WHEN SIBLINGS THINK ABOUT THE FUTURE

As she grew toward womanhood, fears about the future began piling onto Pat's slim shoulders. "I thought about someday having children of my own," she says. "It seemed like a terrible worry." Late one night, sitting in the kitchen with her mother, she started to brood, then to cry. "I wanted to ask her about it," Pat says, "but I didn't know how." Finally, she just blurted out her question. "If I have children, will they be like Kevin?" (Pat, in Remsberg, 1989, p. 7)

Mother kept repeating that sooner or later I'd have to face my responsibility; that I would have to take care of Connie when she was "gone." At that time I did not equate "gone" with the word "dead." . . . I realized "gone" meant "dead" after several suicide attempts by Mother during my teen years. And I finally understood years later that Connie was ultimately my responsibility after Mother was really "gone." (Royal, 1991, p. 4)

We all have to worry. Who else is going to be there? I will have to worry and it will be my responsibility; I think about it all the time. I think about the person I am going to marry: when I meet someone, they are not going to just marry me, but they are going to have to love my brother and know he is going to be around all my life. (Fish, 1993)

One very difficult topic for brothers and sisters to discuss with their parents is their concerns about the future. A typically developing child may wonder, "Will my own children have disabilities?" and "What responsibility will I have to my sibling when my parents die?"

Childbearing Concerns

Siblings' concerns about their childbearing potential may be rooted in their often unexpressed but nevertheless real fears about the hereditary nature of the handicap (Parfit, 1975). Often these fears are unfounded, but siblings need information and reassurance to that effect. In the event that the condition does have a hereditary basis, older siblings, prior to their childbearing years, need an opportunity to learn about genetic implications of the disability (Murphy, 1979).

> I really don't know what we'd have done if the tests had shown I could pass on osteogenisis imperfecta. I've always loved kids and assumed I'd have some someday. I hadn't really thought about what my mother's and sister's osteogenisis imperfecta could mean for myself. But my husband did bring it up when we were engaged and thought it was something to explore. Luckily, we found out there was no way I could pass it on. (Rachel, age 21, in Binkard et al., 1987, p. 20)

Concerns About Future Responsibilities . . .
School-Age, Teen, and Young Adult Siblings

> My sister and I have this picture of the future, this plan. We are going to buy a house together. Neither of us will get married. When we get jobs, one of us will work days, the other will work nights. That way we can take care of our brother. (17-year-old sister, at a sibling panel)

> I have a lot of fear inside for Allen. I think I have a good future ahead—I work very hard in school and do well—but what will happen to him? I'm sure he'll stay at home with my mom and dad a lot longer than I will, but will he ever be able to get married and have kids? (Beth, age 16, in Binkard et al., 1987, p. 7)

It is not at all unusual for school-age children to express a desire to care for their sibling when they become adults. They may reveal this sentiment in statements such as, "When we all grow up, I want Alicia to come live with me." However, like other children when they reach their teens, it is also common for them to dream of a life beyond their immediate family. Unlike other teens, siblings of people with disabilities or illnesses may feel their future options are limited by their siblings' many needs. Whom they marry and where they may move, they may feel, will be restricted because of the sibling with special needs.

> I just keep thinking that even if I do move away, if I go away to school or if I have a job away, I am going to have to come back to Columbus. Gilbert is only comfortable in certain surroundings. If you take him away from those surroundings, he won't function. So this is going to be my home someday.
> Interviewer: Do you think about this a lot? How much?
> Well—now planning my major—very much. There are only so many jobs in Columbus. (Fish, 1993)

> Right now it's as if I don't have plans for the future. Partly it might be because Jean doesn't either. I guess at some point we all had dreams. I used to have very distinct dreams and goals about an acting career. But right now I'm not strong enough to make a decision and go after something. I'm still too tied in with what's going on at home to break the cycle and reclaim my life. I guess Jean and I are in the same boat. (David, age 29, in Leder, 1991, p. 24)

Siblings' concerns about their own future options will be compounded when they are unaware of their parents' plans for their siblings' adult years. Fish and Fitzgerald's (1980) work with adolescent siblings revealed that 9 of 10 siblings lacked an understanding and awareness of future plans for their brothers or sisters. They reported that they experienced varying degrees of anxiety regarding how the child with the disability would be cared for in the future, and their role in that care.

Siblings tell us that, in many families, the future is often not discussed. Parents, perhaps unaware of their children's concerns, or reluctant to confront their mortality, often fail to make adequate plans for the child's future or to share whatever plans they have made with their typically developing children. Many brothers and sisters assume they will someday shoulder many more responsibilities than their parents actually intend.

> Johnny lives at home and he has been up on the list for a group home at least 6 times, and he has been ready. I keep telling my parents to at least try it. Johnny is very demanding and they have not had a life of their own. "Now Mary," they say "don't worry about it. He's fine here." If something happened to my parents, I always ask them, what then? Are you just going to throw him into the situation? You know, that's going to kill him. I think it will break his heart. (Fish, 1993)

Many families plan for the future, involving siblings in this process. In these families there is a spoken and accepted agreement about the responsibilities that siblings will one day assume. Unfortunately, in other families, there is an unspoken assumption that brothers and sisters will take over the roles previously assumed by the child's parents.

> I don't really know what's going to happen. I don't know if Jean can hold a job to support herself. She's not incapacitated by the illness . . . . But she's very backward socially and doesn't know how to get along with people. She's very demanding and will throw a tantrum if things don't go her way. I hope that she will be able to do something to support herself. . . . My parents are ignoring the issue, denying a potential problem. I have no idea what they plan to do in terms of finances. I know they don't have a lot of money. So when they go, I don't know if there will be a trust or something. I worry about what is going to happen. (David, age 29, in Leder, 1991, pp. 22–23)

Older adult siblings who care for their brothers and sisters with disabilities have an additional concern: What will become of our siblings if we die before they do?

> I think of what if I die first? I am the person he goes to the movies with. Is he going to be all by himself? Sometimes I think it would be

better if he was a little more retarded, because he could fit into a
group home where he would have friends and planned social activities. But he doesn't fit in. If I am not there, who is going to invite him
over for the holidays? (Fish, 1993)

I worry that at my age, I'm not going to be here forever and who is
going to take care of her when I'm gone. I can see if she were worked
with a bit more she could go into a smaller group home or semi-
independent living. I hate the thought of her living with 23 other
adults, on a third floor dorm for the rest of her life. (Fish, 1993)

Unless parents make specific arrangements, responsibility for
support of the family member with special needs may ultimately rest
with the typically developing siblings. When this happens, siblings
can become resentful and may not take adequate measures to meet
their sibling's ongoing needs.

It is like no one else wants to do it. I'm just thrown into the role which,
you know, I don't actually like a lot. I have three brothers and three
sisters. They could help out a little, but they don't, actually. (Fish,
1993)

McCullough (1981), in a study of 23 middle- to upper-class families of children with developmental disabilities, learned that 60% of
the parents said they had not made plans for someone to care for the
special needs child if they could not. However, 60% of the siblings
from these families assumed their parents had made plans. Similarly,
68% of the parents had not made financial arrangements for the child's
future; an equal percentage of siblings had assumed their parents had
made those plans. The picture that emerges from McCullough's study
is one of parents who have not prepared for their children's future,
and, if they have made plans, have not shared this information with
their typically developing children. Various authors (Murphy, 1979;

Parfit, 1975; Powell & Gallagher, 1993) have strongly urged that parents "openly and firmly" face the question of the future, perhaps with the assistance of a specialist, before the need is at hand. Because they can envision a life beyond their parents, teenagers and young adults will require additional information about their siblings' future and what role they will play in that future. If parents have not made plans by this time, it is critical that they begin and encourage the brothers and sisters to be a part of this planning. During their teen years, siblings' perception of their future roles must be discussed with their parents.

When parents plan for their family's future—by writing wills that address the family members' future needs, naming a guardian, setting up trusts—they can reassure their children. They can allay worries by telling them, at an early age, "If you want Alicia to live with you when you grow up that's fine, but if you don't, that's okay too, because Mommy and I are planning for when Alicia grows up."

In other words, brothers and sisters need to know that when they are adults there will be a continuum of ways for them to remain lovingly involved with a sibling with special needs. Parents need to be reassured that many, if not most, siblings will choose to remain actively involved in the lives of their brothers and sisters with special needs.

> They've always told us that Jennifer's problems are theirs to worry about and that Jennifer's future is for them to deal with. I know that they've made plans so that her future can be happy and secure—and left us free to get on with our lives. (Andrea, age 19, in Binkard et al., 1987, p.18)

INFORMATION AT SIBSHOPS

Brothers' and sisters' ongoing need for information creates the rationale for the fourth Sibshop goal (see Chapter 1): to provide brothers and sisters with opportunities to learn more about the implications of brothers' and sisters' special needs.

Ultimately, attempts to provide siblings with information at Sibshops will always be limited: Many serve siblings of children with various disabilities or illnesses, precluding an in-depth look at any single condition. While this type of information is usually best provided by parents and primary service providers, Sibshops can provide participants with overviews of services, therapies, and conditions (as further discussed in Chapter 10). Sibshops can also be a safe place to seek information:

> I never really understood what my sister's sickness was. My mom and dad didn't ever talk to me about it but I knew something was real

unhappy. [At the group] I got to ask things I never asked before. (Forrest, age 10, in Murray & Jampolsky, 1982, p.16)

ADULT SIBLINGS

Mike has only one sibling, a brother Chris. Chris, who has Down syndrome, lives at home with his mom in another state. Mom is in her late seventies; dad died last year. Mike and his parents have never really discussed what will become of Chris after his parents are no longer around to care for him. (Mike figures that because Chris has Down syndrome, his parents always assumed they would outlive Chris.) Mike, who has a young family, worries deeply about Chris's future. Should he bring Chris to live with his family or in his community? What would be the impact on his own family? What services are available for a person with a disability, especially one who is new to the state? (Meyer & Erickson, 1993, p. 1)

Of all the age groups, adult brothers and sisters frequently have the most compelling need for information. Many will find themselves increasingly responsible for meeting the ongoing needs of their siblings. Consequently, adult siblings express a desire to learn more about services for their brothers and sisters. They say they need this information to help their siblings make informed choices and to plan for a future that considers the needs of all family members.

The few programs specifically for adult siblings with special needs all attempt to address participants' need for information. According to organizers of one such program in New Jersey, many members are "apprehensive about what will happen when their parents die" (Meyer & Erickson, 1992, p. 3) and wish to learn about options available for their siblings. The Seattle-area Adult Siblings of People with Disabilities (ASPD) program surveyed 60 adult siblings to determine their informational needs. They identified the following topics, listed in decreasing order of interest: recreation and leisure opportunities; community living and residential options; sexuality, socialization, and friendship; family communications; employment and day program options; eligibility for services; legal issues; advocacy; and respite care options (Meyer & Erickson, 1992). The New York City-based Association for the Help of Retarded Children (AHRC) periodically hosts meetings for local adult siblings on specific topics, including: family teamwork and future planning, guardianship, the caregiver experience, entitlements and benefits, and family and professional partnerships.

Despite their need for information, few agencies serving adults with disabilities reach out to adult siblings. Ironically, many personnel from these agencies have been heard to complain that they have difficulty attracting parents of adults with disabilities to meetings, workshops, and other events. Instead of targeting parents (who may feel they have already attended enough meetings to last several lifetimes), these agencies should be encouraged to market their informational efforts to the family member who will have increasing involvement in the life of the person with the disability.

4
Unusual
Opportunities

When asked to reflect on how their children's needs have changed their lives, most parents will acknowledge that, in addition to the many challenges, there have also been unique, significant, and often unexpected rewards. These parents have told us that, as a result of having a child with special health or developmental needs, they have met the person who is now their best friend or spouse, helped create services for people with special needs, edited a newsletter, written a book chapter, testified at a state legislative hearing, or embarked upon a new career. Having a child with special needs was, perhaps ironically, an opportunity for personal growth.

Earlier research about siblings of people with disabilities, and the families in which they grow up, focused almost exclusively on their concerns, taking a *pathogenic* perspective. The child with special needs was seen as a burden to the family, and the family itself was assumed to be dysfunctional, experiencing chronic sorrow and pervasive guilt. Positive traits, such as optimism, were frequently interpreted as a sign of denial, not as a sign of strength. Families, of course, knew better.

> My experience with my sister has been one of the most important in my life. It has definitely shaped my life and channeled my interests in ways I would not have otherwise pursued. (Itzkowitz, 1990, p. 4)

> My overriding impression of siblings is of amazing resilience. They go through the experience with the same intensity as the patient and the parents, but often on the sidelines. They come out whole, with a maturity, with a different view of things. (Sourkes, 1990, p. 11)

> I continue to be a meaningful part of Martha's life and she is a significant part of mine. I am proud of her and her accomplishments. There are many people with more intelligence than her who cannot hold down a job, practice good grooming habits, and help run a large household. Sometimes I mourn the loss of an ideal sister, but I remind myself that other sisters fight, argue, and even hate each other. I have a much better relationship than that. (Westra, 1992, p. 4)

Parents, especially the growing number of parents who work in social services, medicine, education, and academia, began to challenge this paradigm (see Gerdel, 1986). On a daily basis, in their homes, they witnessed dynamics that apparently had eluded many researchers. They knew that their families and the vast majority of families of children with special needs they knew were—all things considered—doing quite well, thank you.

Researchers (and parents) such as Ann and Rud Turnbull and their many colleagues began to seek a fresh, balanced view of families of people who have disabilities and health impairments. They sought a view that acknowledges the challenges faced by these families, but also appreciates families' many strengths. This view, described as a *salutogenic* perspective (Antonovsky, 1992) has been proposed as an alternative to the pathogenic view of families that has dominated the research and clinical literature.

As described by Turnbull and Turnbull,

> the salutogenic perspective calls for theorists, researchers, families and service providers to identify factors that contribute to families' successful functioning. This perspective assumes that families inevitably will be faced with stressors but have the potential for active adjustment. Accordingly, the role of service providers is to enhance family strengths rather than to focus solely on deficits. For families, the salutogenic perspective implies discovering and learning how best to use one's resources to meet the challenges of life. (1993, p. 11)

Like their parents, brothers and sisters are not the at-risk population described in the early clinical and research literature. Empirical investigations and clinical observations are beginning to substantiate what most family members have believed all along: Siblings of people with disabilities display many strengths and report many opportunities. As Drotar and Crawford (1985) have noted, increasing evidence for psychological strengths among well siblings suggests that future research could effectively focus on the study of competencies among this population (p. 360).

What follows are some of the unusual opportunities reported by brothers and sisters. Since viewing families from a salutogenic perspective is still largely a new research paradigm, this section is briefer than the previous section, and we will rely more upon siblings to speak for themselves. We look forward to more research on brothers and sisters that proceeds from a salutogenic perspective.

Despite its relative brevity, however, this section's topic is no less important than the previous section's topic. If we are to help those families who are truly burdened by the challenges imposed by an individual's disability or illness, it is critical that we understand how so many families adapt and, in fact, thrive. We must learn what strategies, philosophies, and resources have sustained these families during difficult times. Appreciating the family members' many strengths and opportunities for growth should not be viewed as interpreting their lives from a "Pollyanna" perspective. Many of the insights and opportunities, while invaluable, are hard-earned.

MATURITY

> When my sister got sick, I kind of became a big brother. I was younger, but I felt like I had to take some initiative and take care of her myself. (Chad, age 16, in Sourkes, 1990, p. 13)

Brothers and sisters, noted Simeonsson and McHale (1981), are often well-adjusted and characterized by greater maturity and responsibility than typical of their age peers. There are several possible explanations for siblings' frequently observed maturity.

Experiences Different from Peers'

Because of the impact of their siblings' needs, some siblings may feel that their peers' current concerns appear trivial by comparison.

> I have a different outlook on life than many other people my age. I understand that you can't take anything for granted. And you have to be able to look at the positives. . . . With Jennifer, there are negatives, but there's so much more that is good. (Andrea, age 19, in Binkard et al., 1987, p. 19)

> I think after something large like this happens in your family, you feel a lot more mature. When I went back to school after the summer, it seemed like everybody else was so immature. How could they be moaning because they lost a girlfriend or something like that? I felt I had real adult problems now. (Chad, age 16, in Sourkes, 1990, p. 15)

A Loss of Innocence

Like Chad, above, a sibling's maturity may also be coupled with a loss of innocence. This loss is frequently mentioned by parents who have children who have been diagnosed with a serious illness such as cancer or who have experienced a traumatic injury. For these siblings, their maturity will be hard-won: They learn early that life can be unfair, things might not get better in the long run, bad things do not always happen to "other people," and that they, like their brothers and sisters, are not indestructible.

> I have a greater sense of compassion and sensitivity toward people who are different from the norm, but I am acutely aware of ignorance and prejudice through inflictions on my family. I may have acquired

maturity at an early age, but in the process lost a degree of my innocence and childhood. (Cobb, 1991, p. 3)

Increased Responsibilities

A child's special needs are usually synonymous with increased caregiving demands and, as we saw earlier, siblings—especially sisters—
frequently are expected to assume an active role in that care. Successfully handling the tasks assigned them can increase siblings' sense of
maturity and pride:

> I think I matured more quickly than other kids because I felt like I had
> this big responsibility on my hands, taking care of a handicapped
> brother. (Jones, 1991)

Insight

When one has a family member with a special need, insight into the
human condition is inevitable. Siblings' expanded understanding
frequently adds to their mature view of the world.

> Deaf-blindness causes you to look at yourself. You see how much he
> has affected your life; being around you all the time and helping you
> grow up. By dealing with his deaf-blindness, it causes you to become
> more mature. It causes you to deal with life in an "adult" manner. You
> also find out just how much you love your brother and how much a
> part of life he is. (Harkleroad, 1992, p. 5)

As Dudish (1991) has noted, siblings of children with a disability
or illness have multidimensional lives. They see the many sides of life
in a gradual way. From and with their families they learn determina-
tion, patience, and other qualities that can help them grow into mature, sensitive adults.

Although maturity is certainly an attribute desired by parents
(and many siblings we have met have been delightfully mature for
their years), we realize that maturity is an attribute on a continuum:
Early maturity can also be a source of concern. On occasion we have
met young siblings—usually sisters—who have little in common
with their age peers and seem to be very young adults. Most of these
siblings are very involved in many aspects of their siblings' lives,
especially in their care. A reasonable amount of responsibilities, it
seems, can help develop a sibling's sense of maturity; excessive demands can cost a sibling his or her childhood. These children (and
their parents) will need to be encouraged to attend to equally important aspects of their development that have little to do with the sibling
who has the special needs.

> There have been times when I have had to tell my parents, "I am not
> the parent, you are!" Because when I was ten years old, I was proba-
> bly giving them advice on how to help her out and how to raise her.
> (Fish, 1993)

SELF-CONCEPT AND SOCIAL COMPETENCE

Self-Concept

Existing studies on the self-concept of brothers and sisters of children with special needs are inconclusive; however, the majority of recent studies suggest that siblings' self-concepts compare favorably with those of their peers in the community.

For instance, Harvey and Greenway (1984) found that brothers and sisters of children with physical disabilities had lower self-concepts than did controls. However, Coleman (1990) found no significant differences in the self-concept of siblings of children with physical disabilities when compared with siblings of children with mental retardation, and siblings of children with no disabilities.

Kazak and Clarke (1986) compared 8- and 9-year-old siblings of children with spina bifida with a control group. Subjects completed the Piers Harris Self-Concept Scale, which measures their self-concept as well as their perspectives on their own happiness, popularity, level of anxiety, physical appearance, school performance, and behavioral functioning. The authors' results indicated that there were no differences in self-concept between the two groups.

Coleman's (1990) finding that siblings of children with mental retardation were not significantly different from a control group concurs with studies by Dyson (1989), who found that siblings of children with disabilities displayed the same levels of self-concept, behavior problems, and social competence as matched siblings of children with typical development. Other studies (Dyson & Fewell, 1989; Lobato et al., 1987) also have reported that siblings of children with disabilities do not display lower self-concepts.

Studies of the self-concepts of siblings of children with chronic illnesses are similarly inconclusive. Spinetta (1981) found that 4- to 6-year-old siblings of children with cancer had lower self-concepts than did the patients. Tritt and Esses (1988) found that preteen siblings of children seen at three speciality clinics (Diabetes, Juvenile Rheumatoid Arthritis, and Gastrointestinal) had significantly more behavior problems than did controls; however, their levels of self-concept did not differ.

Social Competence

In virtually all studies of the subject, siblings' social competence compares favorably with peers who do not have siblings who have a disability or illness. One study (Abramovitch, Stanhope, Pepler, & Corter, 1987) revealed that both younger and older siblings of children with Down syndrome were significantly more prosocial than children in the normative sample. Ferrari (1984) compared siblings of boys who either had diabetes, pervasive disabilities, or were healthy. Comparing the three groups, Ferrari found no overall group differences in self-concept or teachers' ratings of self-esteem. He found that the siblings of children with diabetes were reported by teachers as displaying the most prosocial behaviors toward other children in the school, and the siblings of children with pervasive disabilities were given the highest ratings of social competence. He concluded that his study fails to support the view that siblings of children with a health impairment or disability are uniformly at greater risk of psychosocial impairment than siblings of children who are healthy.

Gruszka (1988) as reported in Lobato (1990) compared 45 siblings (ages 3–17) of children with mental retardation with a control group of equal size. Mothers of these children were asked to rate the children's behavior problems and social competence and the children completed a standard assessment of their own self-concepts. Gruszka found that the two groups did not differ in their mothers' ratings of their social competence, or number and type of behavior problems. The children held similar positive views of their cognitive and physical abilities and their relationships with their mothers and peers. The way they thought about themselves and the way they thought that others felt about them, concluded the author, was not influenced by the presence of a sibling with mental retardation.

Dyson (1989) also found that children with siblings with disabilities were better behaved, less aggressive and hyperactive, and tended to have fewer acting-out behaviors than did controls.

In a study that compared equal numbers of siblings of children with either autism, mental retardation, or no disabilities, McHale, Sloan, and Simeonsson (1986) found that, as a group, siblings of children with autism or mental retardation were significantly less hostile, less embarrassed, more accepting, and more supportive than siblings of children with no disabilities. The authors did note, however, that there was a much wider variation in the attitudes of the siblings of the children with disabilities than in the control group—that is, some attitudes were extremely positive and others much more negative.

INSIGHT

> Even though Ellen is no longer here on earth, she is ever so alive within me. It is amazing that a person who has never spoken a word or even looked me straight in the eye could have such an influence on my life—but she does. I find my greatest source of strength comes from God and my memory of Ellen. It is a strength to raise my own family with a sense of optimism. For these reasons, I take back the statement that Ellen may not have had anything to do with a "great life" growing up. She had and still has everything to do with it. (Dudish, 1991, p. 3)

Perhaps the greatest of opportunities experienced by any family member of a person with a disability or illness is the insight one gathers on the human condition. Brothers and sisters frequently mention how their siblings have influenced their perceptions and philosophies, giving them reason to reflect on aspects of life that their peers may take for granted.

For instance, young brothers and sisters frequently discuss the meaning of friendship during a Sibshop. A friend, they often say, is not someone who makes fun of a person with special needs. Brothers and sisters, first as grade-schoolers, then as teenagers, and later as adults, may use the treatment of a sibling with special needs as a "litmus test" when screening potential friends, dates, or even spouses:

> I think Gene's having albinism has made me more accepting of people and to look differently at them. If you are exposed to something you *do* change. I tend to look harder and deeper at my friends, at the kind of people they are in handling themselves and treating other people. (Bill, age 16, in Binkard et al., 1987, p. 9)

> When I was in my early 20s I met a girl and fell in love. After a few months I brought her home to meet my family. When my mother went to the kitchen to prepare dinner, I asked the girl, "Would you like to see Oliver?" for I had told her about my brother. "No," she answered.

> Soon after, I met Roe, a lovely girl. She asked me the names of my brothers and sisters. She loved children. I thought she was wonderful. I brought her home after a few months to meet my family. Soon it was time for me to feed Oliver. I remember sheepishly asking Roe if she'd like to see him. "Sure," she said.

> I sat at Oliver's bedside as Roe watched over my shoulder. I gave him his first spoonful, his second. "Can I do that?" Roe asked with ease, with freedom, with compassion, so I gave her the bowl and she fed Oliver one spoonful at a time.

> The power of the powerless. Which girl would you marry? Today Roe and I have three children. (de Vinck, 1985, p. 28)

Appreciating the distinction between mere ignorance and actual rudeness at a young age, many brothers and sisters can be philosophical (and sometimes forgiving) even of those who do not appreciate their siblings' qualities:

> First you have to really know someone like my sister to really understand and appreciate her achievements. (Cassie, age 18, in Binkard et al., 1987, p. 18)

> The people who know him don't tease him. The kids who are my age and my sister's age are more curious than wanting to ridicule. (Bill, age 16, in Binkard et al., 1987, p. 8)

> There are a lot of people who don't understand. The people who are just being "ignorant" I usually don't waste my time with. But people who try to understand, I usually explain the situation. Then they get the full picture and see that he is a person, just slower than others. This taught me to respect people, because I can understand how it feels not to be wanted, held, and cared for. (Jones, August 1991)

Many siblings, realizing how their families differ from others in the community, often express appreciation for things that may go unnoticed or unappreciated by their peers.

Appreciation for Their Siblings' Abilities

Perhaps because they perceive that there is a societal emphasis on their siblings' disabilities, brothers and sisters frequently describe their siblings in terms of their strengths, not their deficiencies:

> The label autism does not cover the breadth of my brother's personality. It does not explain why he prefers contemporary jazz to other types of music, why he will spontaneously initiate verbal games with my fiancee, or why he chooses to bond with certain peers over others. If the word "autism" were the sum total of my brother's personality, would he have learned to be affectionate and communicative? (Shanley, 1991, p. 2)

> Sometimes nothing makes Ray happy and it is frustrating. Then there are days when he is so happy. He can be listening to music or, you think, to your conversations. You really marvel at how your brother copes with deaf-blindness. You appreciate the fact that he "loves" to work as often as he can. (How many people feel this way?) These are some of the things that make me feel he is a very special person. (Harkleroad, 1992, p. 5)

> Peter was the golden thread that held us together. (a sister speaking at a sibling panel)

> Even now, five years after his death, Oliver remains the weakest, most helpless human being I ever met, and yet he was one of the most powerful human beings I ever met. He could do absolutely nothing except breathe, sleep, eat, and yet he was responsible for action, love, courage, insight. (de Vinck, 1985, p. 28)

Life with a sibling with special needs, many say, has profoundly influenced their values. These brothers and sisters claim their siblings have taught them at an early age that there are human qualities to appreciate in a person besides intelligence, popularity, and good looks. Their siblings have taught them about compassion, humor, loyalty, and unconditional love:

> She taught me how to love without reservation; without expectation of returned love. She taught me that everyone has strengths and weaknesses. Martha is no exception. She taught me that human value is not measured with I.Q. tests. (Westra, 1992, p. 4)

> Kevin possesses virtues that I lack. He is not judgmental and he is quick to forgive. He does not expect too much out of people or bear grudges. . . . Although I am the "oldest" in my family, it is his example I follow. He has the virtue of simplicity. It's too bad that simple is often considered a synonym for stupid. They are worlds apart. (Cobb, 1991, p. 3)

> Douglas has a boundless capacity for love which to this day is evident in his smile and affection. His devotion to me has never wavered. For this reason, and many others, my love for him was always stronger than my rage over his actions. (Zatlow, 1992, p. 13)

Appreciation for Their Family

Koocher and O'Malley (1981) reported that while one fourth of the siblings of patients who had been treated for cancer reported feelings of jealousy, others reported feelings of enhanced closeness toward other family members and most appeared to resolve their anger toward the patient once the treatment ended. Brothers and sisters, because they and their families experience challenges unlike those faced by others in the community, often express gratitude for their parents' efforts during difficult times:

> My parents treated us equally—but to be equal Jennifer had to have more direct attention from our parents. We never felt shut out because of her needs though. Our whole family always got attention. (Cassie, age 18, in Binkard et al., 1987, p. 17)

> People tend to think in simplistic terms, not in reality. My mother, for example, is not a saint. In some ways she has still not come to terms with my sister's disability. Yet I see her as a tower of strength. I don't know if I would have that much strength. (Julie, in Remsberg, 1989, p. 3)

> I really admire our family for how well we accept Kim like anyone else. . . . My parents give Kim everything she needs: love, acceptance, understanding, patience, discipline, proper hygiene, entertainment. Everything any other child needs. That's not to say she isn't spoiled, but who does not spoil their children? (Hansen, 1985, p. 6)

Appreciation for One's Health and Capabilities

Many children grow up feeling indestructible. Brothers and sisters who have witnessed their siblings' struggle to learn or simply stay alive are often less likely to take the blessings of good health and abilities for granted.

> Jennifer wasn't going to have all the positive things the rest of us would. I was never jealous. I couldn't be. I have so much, can do so many things and have all the friends that I do. (Cassie, age 18, in Binkard et al., 1992, p. 17)

> I have a greater appreciation for my opportunities and capabilities. Yet, I am painfully aware of what I, and others as fortunate waste. . . . My "special" brother has taught me through his life that my dreams are only as inaccessible as I let them remain. (Cobb, 1991, p. 3)

> Living with Melissa's handicaps makes me so much more cognizant of my own blessings. She provides a constant reminder of what life could have been like for me if I had been my parents' oldest daughter. This encourages me to take advantage of my mental capacities and to take care of my healthy body. (Watson, 1991, p. 108)

TOLERANCE

> Lucy is constantly teaching me stuff. . . . She has taught me to be more patient in accepting people where they are and not putting my expectations on them. (Skrtic, Summers, Brotherson, & Turnbull, 1983, p. 18)

The college-age siblings that Grossman (1972) studied reported that the benefits of growing up with a sibling who has a disability include greater tolerance, understanding of people, compassion, and a dedication toward altruistic goals. Parents, as well as brothers and sisters themselves, have reported that siblings of people with special needs are more tolerant and accepting of differences than their peers are. The siblings of children with chronic illnesses that Tritt and Esses (1988) studied remarked that they had developed more patience, understanding, sensitivity, and awareness about how to deal with someone who is sick.

> In spite of his I.Q., Kevin has taught me many valuable lessons. Growing up with a handicapped brother has fostered perseverance and patience. I am accepting of not only the shortcomings of others, but in those in myself as well. (Cobb, 1991, p. 3)

They are more tolerant, siblings frequently note, because life with their brothers and sisters has made them keenly aware of the consequences of prejudice. Intolerant of intolerance, brothers and sisters bristle when others make assumptions about their siblings based on their physical appearances:

> Sometimes kids at school look at Elizabeth and say 'Is that your sister?' 'Who is she?' They think because she looks different that she's different inside. But she's just like us inside. And she doesn't want to be stared at and laughed at or ignored. ("Jennifer," 1990, p. 2)

> My brother does look kind of different, but that doesn't really affect *him*. If that's a problem for other people, well, that's *their* handicap." (Bill, age 16, in Binkard et al., 1987, p. 8)

PRIDE

With a tendency to focus on their siblings' abilities, brothers and sisters frequently testify to the adaptations their siblings have made to their disabilities or illnesses:

> When my brother had his leg amputated, I wondered if he would ever be able to skateboard or ride a bike again. Then the first day out of the hospital he rode a skateboard. Now he can ride a bike, a horse, and do anything. My brother Tony's ability to deal with the problem helped me to have the strength to deal with it too. (Eric, age 16, in Murray & Jampolsky, 1982, p. 41)

> Jennifer has probably achieved more than I have. She's been through so much. She couldn't even talk when she started school; now she can, and she can understand others. She's really fulfilling her potential. I'm not sure the rest of us are. (Cassie, age 18, in Binkard et al., 1987, p. 17)

> Living away from home, I am able to escape from my label of being "Melissa's sister." I don't have to compete with Melissa for my friends'

attention, and I can avoid unwanted attention from little children staring and pointing at her. My freshman year in college I welcomed this opportunity and purposely neglected to tell my roommate about Melissa. I immediately felt guilty and knew that I was not being fair to myself or Melissa. I am proud of Melissa and I am proud to be her sister. I soon realized that I want everyone to know that I am Melissa's sister. (Watson, 1991, p. 108)

VOCATIONAL OPPORTUNITIES

I have found my upbringing to have been very positive, in spite of the emotional hardship that [my sister's] cystic fibrosis placed on the family. At the age of nine I perceived myself as being a vitally important participating member of the family. My parents encouraged me to assist in the care of my newborn sister and I learned to crush pills and mix them in applesauce, do postural drainage, and clean and fill the mist tent. Through this experience self-esteem was enhanced, responsibility was learned, and maturity was developed. Although I occasionally feel that I grew up too fast, for the most part the experience gave me a personal insight and compassion that I carry with me in my practice as a pediatric specialist. (Thibodeau, 1988, p. 22)

As I plan for my future, I realize how much of my life, of what makes me unique, is the result of having Alison as my sister. My desire to become a doctor, my ability to work well with children, all can be attributed to Ali's presence. (Rinehart, 1992, p. 10)

Authors, as well as brothers and sisters themselves, have noted that siblings of people with special needs frequently gravitate toward the helping professions. Among siblings of people with disabilities, Cleveland and Miller (1977) found oldest daughters most likely to en-

ter helping professions. Grossman's (1972) study of college-age siblings revealed that young adults who grew up with a brother or sister who has a disability were more certain of their own future and about personal and vocational goals than comparable young adults without a similar experience.

Siblings' motivations for entering professions in social services, education, or health are varied. One brother of a person with mental illness noted: "It can be therapeutic to help others if you cannot help your family member" (Dickens, 1991). Another acknowledged that "Part of the reason I've chosen law as my career is to enable myself to deal with some of the problems that Tom will always face" (Mark, age 24, in Binkard et al., 1987, p. 28).

Many siblings have told us that having a brother or sister with special needs has made them feel comfortable with disabilities and appreciate the diversity of the human condition. As a result of their many years of informal education on disabilities, chronic health impairments, or mental illness, these siblings feel that they have much to share. Like the growing number of parents of children with special needs who are assuming leadership roles in education and health care, the brothers and sisters who seek careers in these fields bring a welcome "reality check" to their professions.

ADVOCACY

> Melissa also gives me a sense of responsibility to inform others about the realities of Down syndrome. Although speaking in front of a class usually makes me literally stop breathing and grow dizzy, I have faced large groups without fear, arguing the right to life of babies with Down syndrome. (Watson, 1991, p. 108)

> My parents and I wondered what the purpose of special education might be when it could be suspended so arbitrarily for the crime of growing up. (Zatlow, 1992, p. 15)

Because of the value they place on their siblings' abilities and contributions, and perhaps because they will likely assume increasingly active roles in the lives of their siblings, brothers and sisters often become ardent advocates for people with special needs:

> Today, not because of guilt, but because I genuinely want to, I am helping my mom monitor and coordinate Kim's programs. . . . I think that things go better for people like Kim when service providers know there is a family member on the scene and paying attention. (Marsha, age 28, in Binkard et al., 1987, p. 31)

> We have not fought this hard for Douglas to be thwarted by a termination of programs. Personally, I have not given so much of myself

> and my life to Doug, only to see his existence end in despair. . . . My brother *WILL* have an option. (Zatlow, 1981, p. 2)

Programs that serve brothers and sisters can provide participants with information and preadvocacy skills. New York's Hebrew Academy for Special Children, for instance, encourages siblings of children with severe disabilities to volunteer as camp counselors. Directors believe that as counselors help campers maximize their strengths, counselors view their relationships with their own siblings in a new way. According to one staff member, sibling counselors become "passionate advocates for the rights and needs of special people" (1988 Award Winning Summer Programs, 1989, p. 20).

Similarly, Sibshop discussion activities, such as My Special Dream and Moccasins, and informational activities that acquaint participants with the services, therapies, career and residential opportunities available for adults with disabilities can provide participants with a foundation of information and concepts that will be the basis for future advocacy activities.

LOYALTY

> I'm used to being kind to my brother and sister, so I'm kind to everybody else. But, if someone starts a fight, I will fight. I won't put up with anyone teasing Wade or Jolene. (Morrow, 1992, p. 4)

Like most siblings, brothers and sisters of children with special needs frequently fight and argue within the family. Outside of the family, however, siblings of children with developmental disabilities or chronic health impairments may feel required to defend their brothers and sisters from cruel comments and stares. This loyalty can be a problem for some brothers and sisters.

> When my brother turned four or five years of age, I was a very defensive person. I felt people were treating my brother differently. I used to get into fights with other kids. (Jones, 1991)

> She caused problems for me at school too. I'd get into fights because of her, so I held her responsible for most of my problems. (Marsha, age 28, in Binkard et al., 1987, p. 29)

Yet, for many other brothers and sisters, these incidents can be reason to re-examine the relationship they have toward their brothers and sisters and to reflect on the meaning of friendship and society's tolerance of differences.

> I decided that I had to stop being worried about how friends might react. There were two boys whom I'd met at school and thought were my friends. The first time they met Jennifer though, they laughed. I

told them to leave our house. (Cassie, age 18, in Binkard et al., 1987, p. 16)

My sisters and I can turn into three really big monsters in public if someone makes fun of her when we're around. But we don't want pity for her. She deserves respect as a person. (Andrea, age 19, in Binkard et al., 1987, p. 19)

CONCLUSION

As the brothers and sisters quoted in this chapter make clear, many siblings of people with special needs experience unusual opportunities throughout their lives. We can better appreciate siblings' many strengths and coping strategies if we complement their testimony with research that proceeds from a salutogenic viewpoint. As McConachie (1982) has noted:

Most [scales] do not evaluate positive traits. When the researcher has given parents greater freedom to comment, they tend to demonstrate their strength, resilience, and sense of humor in coping with their own reaction . . . and also with the reactions of their family and neighbors. (p. 161)

In addition to research that respects the complexity of their experiences, siblings deserve more immediate considerations. These considerations should begin when siblings are young and be offered proactively throughout their lives. Parents and providers should become familiar with the wide range of issues siblings may experience growing up. All those who work with people who have disabilities should understand the important roles that siblings play and create policies that include brothers and sisters who wish to be involved in the lives of their siblings with special needs. Programs should be widely available for brothers and sisters who wish to meet and talk with their peers. When brothers and sisters receive these considerations, it is possible to minimize the "unusual concerns" they experience and maximize their "unusual opportunities."

5

Getting Started

In this chapter we discuss the component activities required to create a Sibshop. If the information that follows appears daunting, please remember that any activity—even something as mundane as cleaning a refrigerator or washing a car—can seem surprisingly complex when broken down into component tasks. Use this chapter as a blueprint for planning your Sibshop.

COSPONSORS

Invite Other Agencies to Cosponsor Your Sibshop

As mentioned in Chapter 1, we strongly encourage cosponsorship of Sibshops. When the Sibling Support Project staff respond to requests for training and technical assistance on the Sibshop model, we require that the requesting agency commit to working with other community agencies to cosponsor the Sibshops. We feel that the benefits of cosponsoring Sibshops are many.

First, more siblings are served. Frequently, individual agencies will not have a sufficient number of siblings in the identified age range to create a viable Sibshop. Working with other agencies helps assure that all potentially interested families will learn about the Sibshop and, as a result, more siblings will be registered. An enthusiastic response and a healthy enrollment helps create an exciting program.

Second, costs are shared and resources are pooled. As discussed later in this chapter, cosponsorship allows agencies with limited resources to share costs and pool resources.

Third, there are opportunities for interagency collaboration. Sibshops offer an extraordinary opportunity for collaboration among diverse agencies. Agencies that have worked together to cosponsor Sibshops include: University Affiliated Programs, parks and recreation programs, hospitals, school districts, Parent-to-Parent programs, Arcs, early intervention centers, and Easter Seals programs. We have also witnessed examples of agencies with previously competitive and even acrimonious relationships working together to cosponsor Sibshops. Sometimes, community businesses that donate to a local Sibshop are cosponsors. In Everett, Washington, for example, Sibshops are cosponsored by a community hospital, three early intervention programs, a Parent-to-Parent Program, and a local grocery store!

Of course, any agency or organization serving families of children with special needs can sponsor a Sibshop provided it can offer financial support, properly staff the program, and attract sufficient numbers of participants. Single agency sponsorship may be most appropriate if the Sibshop is to be a component of a large event, such as a statewide conference for families of children with special needs, or if it is for a specific disability, such as a Sibshop for children with hearing impairments, sponsored by a state school for the deaf.

Educate Potential Cosponsoring Agencies About the Need for Peer Support and Education Programs for Siblings

Agency personnel may need to learn more about the need for Sibshops before they will attend a planning meeting. With your letter inviting them to cosponsor the Sibshop, send them information such as the Brief Description of the Sibshop Model found in Appendix C, and follow up with a phone call to answer any other questions they might have.

Ensure Family Participation in Planning for Sibshops

In many communities, Sibshops are spearheaded by what Florene Poyadue of California's Parents Helping Parents program calls "monomaniacs with a mission": people who have a vision of what ought to be. Often, these visionaries are parents. If the representatives of your cosponsoring agencies do not include a parent or sibling of a person with special needs, by all means, invite a family member to be a part of your planning committee.

Ask Agencies to Send Representatives to a Planning Meeting

Once cosponsoring agencies have been determined, the agencies should appoint a representative to be a part of the Sibshop Planning Committee. Ideally, the agencies will send representatives who work closely with family members of people with special needs or are family members themselves. It is recommended that all members of the Planning Committee read this chapter prior to meeting. The committee may find the Sibshop Planning Form in Figure 1 on pages 70 and 71 a helpful tool as they plan your community's Sibshop.

As you and the committee begin, keep in mind that each interagency collaboration resulting in a Sibshop will be unique; the arrangements will reflect the resources each agency has to offer. Often, the arrangements made are somewhat informal, using a "potluck" style, depending on the resources available. For instance, Agency A, while committed to the program, has no funds to support the program. It does, however, have an excellent facility that the Sibshop can use. It agrees to handle the registration. Agency B has a similar lack of money, but is sufficiently committed to the program to offer the services of its staff psychologist, who will take "comp time" for time spent on Sibshops. Agency C has neither staff or space to support the program, but does have $500 in a gift fund to help defray costs, and so on.

PARTICIPANTS

Once the question of sponsorship is determined, it will make decisions about service populations easier. With the planning committee, you will need to identify the brothers and sisters you wish to reach with your Sibshop.

What Are the Special Needs of Siblings of the Children You Will Serve with Your Sibshop?

Will this Sibshop be for siblings of children who have a specific disability (e.g., Down syndrome) or illness (e.g., cancer) or will it be for siblings of children with various developmental disabilities or chronic health impairments? Focusing on a specific disability or illness can offer participants a wonderful opportunity to learn more about their siblings' condition. However, unless you can assure sufficient numbers of participants (at least six), we recommend offering the Sibshop to siblings of children who have various developmental disabilities or chronic illnesses. While there will be some differences in their experiences, there will many more similarities. Besides, differences will afford participants a richer understanding of the diversity embodied in the term "special needs" and insight into their own families.

Will Sibshop Enrollment Be Limited to Siblings from Families Served by the Cosponsoring Agencies?

Will your Sibshop be available for all appropriate brothers and sisters, regardless of where their sibling receives services? Or, is this Sibshop just for the cosponsoring agencies' families? Will they get first priority? Although there is no right or wrong answer, this should be decided upon ahead of time.

What Geographic Area Do You Wish to Serve?

Will your Sibshop be (for instance) for kids from all over the county, or just from a specific school district? This decision may affect (among other things) how you publicize your program and when you host the program.

Sibshop Planning Form

Use this form as you plan for a Sibshop in your community. With your planning committee, discuss the following questions to determine audience, resources, and responsibilities. The format below follows the discussion in Chapter 5, Getting Started.

1. The sponsoring agencies and planning committee.

   What agencies will cosponsor the Sibshop?

   Who are the identified representatives from these agencies on the planning committee?

   What members of the planning committee are also parents or siblings of people with special needs?

2. Identifying the brothers and sisters you wish to serve. Please define your population with regard to:

   The special needs of the siblings of the children you wish to serve.

   The ages of the children who will attend your Sibshop.

   The geographic area you wish to serve.

   The maximum number of children you wish to serve.

   Will enrollment be limited to families served by the cosponsoring agencies?

3. Identifying resources. Please discuss what financial or other resources may be available to support your Sibshop for the following areas:

   Potential costs:

   Sibshop facilitators

   Materials and food

   Facility

   Other (postage, stationery, printing, photocopying, processing registrations, etc.)

(continued)

Potential sources of income:
Registration fees

Grants, gifts, and other sources of income

4. Identifying Sibshop facilitators
   What is your desired facilitator-to-participant ratio?

   Who will be your Sibshop facilitators?

5. Where will your Sibshop be held?

6. When and how frequently will your Sibshop meet?

7. Who will publicize the program and recruit participants?

8. Who will register participants and manage the Sibshop budget?

What Will Be the Ages of the Children Who Will Attend Your Sibshop?

Avoid the temptation to offer a Sibshop for children of all ages. Sibshops that are hosted for children ages 4–16 will confuse the 4-year-olds and bore the 16-year-olds, and the confusion and boredom can adversely affect the flavor of the Sibshop for the children in between. Although Sibshops can be adapted for younger and older children, they were designed with children ages 8–13 in mind. Restricting the age range ensures that the siblings share common interests and levels of emotional maturity that make Sibshops successful.

By 8 years of age, most brothers and sisters know a little about their siblings' disability and can talk about their life, their feelings, and other people. Children younger than 8 may not even be aware that their sibling has special needs, and often have a difficult time grasping the topics discussed by the older children. The typical 4-hour Sibshop will also be too long for children younger than 8.

It is far easier to expand the target range of 8–13 to include older siblings. Many programs have successfully incorporated older siblings by meeting with them prior to the Sibshop, offering them a junior leadership role, and seeking their advice and help in modeling the discussion and sharing desired during Sibshop activities.

If the committee determines that what they want is a program for siblings other than the target range of 8–13 years of age, there are alternatives. First, they may wish to stretch the target range by holding two Sibshops, one for younger siblings (i.e., 7–10 years) and another for older siblings (i.e., 11–14 years). Second, the committee may wish to sponsor a Sibshop specifically for younger children (i.e., 4–8 years) or for teenagers. Chapters 7–10 include activities that will be helpful with younger children and teens. Sibshops for younger children will need to be shorter in duration than typical Sibshops. (Committees wishing programs for younger children may want to consult Debra J. Lobato's *Brothers, Sisters, and Special Needs: Information and Activities for Helping Young Siblings of Children with Chronic Illnesses and Developmental Disabilities*, 1990, Paul H. Brookes Publishing Co., which describes a curriculum for younger brothers and sisters.)

How Many Children Do You Wish to Serve?

Sibshops should be large enough to offer participants a vital, exciting program, yet small enough to assure that everyone gets to participate in the discussion activities. Ideally, there will be enough children in the group that a child will be likely to find another child—a future friend, perhaps—of the same sex and close in age.

With a recommended ratio of one facilitator per five or six participants (more with younger children; slightly less with older), the number of facilitators you have—as well as the space available in your facility—will influence how many siblings you can serve.

FINANCIAL ISSUES

Most communities, organizations, and agencies have limited funds for services for families, regardless of how valuable they may be. This is true for traditional "family" programs (i.e., programs for parents), and especially true for nontraditional programs, such as Sibshops. Consequently, most programs for brothers and sisters have budgets and funding bases that can be considered both "creative" and individualistic.

Sibshops rarely exist because of readily available funds. They exist because individuals and agencies share a deeply held belief that brothers and sisters deserve peer support and education opportunities despite a lack of earmarked funds. This encourages agencies to seek innovative approaches to funding. While a typical Sibshop budget may be elusive, many local programs utilize similar strategies.

Agencies' abilities to share costs and pool resources will greatly affect a Sibshop budget. Some programs, relying on volunteers and donated foods and materials, have achieved a zero-based budget. Others pass on all costs to participants. Most fall somewhere in between. A discussion of costs associated with hosting Sibshops follows.

Costs

Facilitators According to a survey of existing sibling programs (Meyer & Erickson, 1992), a majority of facilitators lead the programs as a part of their jobs, although many volunteer, and a minority are hired to conduct the programs. Although volunteers can be a wonderful asset to a program, volunteers—because they donate their time—may be less reliable than paid staff. Hiring staff to conduct the Sibshop can help assure reliability and accountability, assuming funds are available. Some programs have "paid volunteers," where facilitators receive a small stipend.

Committing staff to conduct sibling programs is perhaps the best option. No new funds need to be identified and staff conducting Sibshops frequently take "comp time" during the week for their involvement in a weekend Sibshop. Many agencies profess a commitment to serving people with special needs *and their families*, when, in practice, they may simply be serving the client and his or her parents. By committing staff to facilitate sibling programs, agencies acknowledge siblings' critical role in the family.

Materials and Food In creating the Sibshop model, an effort was made to select activities that do not rely greatly on materials. There are two reasons for this: to reduce costs and to streamline planning. Many times Sibshops are conducted by personnel who do not work at the facility where the Sibshop is being held. Consequently, facilitators will need to "import" all materials or, at the very least, seek permission to use the facility's materials. Food, we have found, is an essential part of Sibshops. When facilitators' time and the facility are donated, Sibshop registration fees can cover materials and food.

Facility   Frequently, use of a facility will be a contribution of one of the cosponsoring agencies. Later in this chapter is a further discussion on preferred locations for Sibshops.

Other   Postage, stationery, printing, photocopying, and processing registrations are all miscellaneous costs that vary greatly from program to program. Generally, one program assumes responsibility for all of the above.

Income

Part of the costs associated with presenting Sibshops may be offset by registration fees. Many agencies charge a nominal, nonrefundable registration fee for their Sibshops; most also make provisions for families who cannot afford the fee. Charging a small fee helps defray costs and assures regular attendance.

Other local Sibshops have successfully applied for grants from community mental health boards, developmental disability councils, fraternal organizations, local private benefactors, and city block grant programs.

Sibshop Budgets

There is no typical Sibshop budget. However, Tables 1–3 are sample budgets for three different Sibshops. For the purposes of comparison, each example Sibshop uses four facilitators and has a 4-hour meeting once a month for 5 months. The first two Sibshops serve 20 children; the third serves 10.

Table 1.   Budget for Sibshop A

Facilitator 1	Services donated by Agency 1 (employee)
Facilitator 2	Adult sib "paid volunteer" services donated by Agency 1 ($140—$7/hour × 4 hours per session × 5 sessions)
Facilitator 3	Volunteer, works for Agency 2
Facilitator 4	Services donated by Agency 3 (employee)
Food	$300 ($3 × 20 participants × 5 meetings)
Materials	$100 ($1 × 20 participants × 5 meetings)
Facility	Donated by Agency 3
Other (e.g., registration, stationery, mailing, printing)	Donated by Agency 1
TOTAL	$400
INCOME	$450 registration ($5 per session × 18 paying participants × 5 sessions. Two additional participants received scholarships.)

Table 2.   Budget for Sibshop B

Facilitator 1	Community volunteer
Facilitator 2	Community volunteer
Facilitator 3	Services donated by Agency 1 ($250—$50 per session × 5 sessions)
Facilitator 4	Services donated by Agency 1 ($250—$50 per session × 5 sessions)
Food	Donated by local grocery stores and individuals ($400—$4 × 20 participants × 5 meetings)
Materials	Donated by Agency 1 ($150)
Facility	Donated by Agency 2
Other (e.g., registration, stationery, mailing, printing)	Donated by Agencies 1–4
TOTAL	$0
INCOME	N/A (no registration fee)

FACILITATORS

We believe that Sibshops are best facilitated by at least two people. Ideally, one facilitator will be an adult sibling of a person who has a special need similar to the siblings of the participants. The involvement of an adult sibling can keep the program "honest," credible, and focused on issues important to the participants.

The other member of the team will be a service provider (such as a social worker, special education teacher, professor, psychologist, or nurse) who will be aware of issues, resources, and services. This person, frequently employed by one of the cosponsoring agencies, can also serve as the liaison between the facilitators and the planning committee.

Parents, of course, can be excellent facilitators, but they should not facilitate Sibshops that their own children attend. Parents are

Table 3.   Budget for Sibshop C

Facilitator 1	$90 ($18 per session × 5 sessions)
Facilitator 2	$90 ($18 per session × 5 sessions)
Facilitator 3	$90 ($18 per session × 5 sessions)
Facilitator 4	Volunteer, works for Agency 2
Food	$200 ($4 × 10 participants × 5 sessions)
Materials	Donated by Agency 1
Facility	Donated by Agency 2
Other (e.g., registration, mailing, stationery, printing)	Donated by Agency 1
TOTAL	$470
INCOME	$600 ($15 × 8 paying participants × 5 sessions. Two additional participants received scholarships.)

often the driving force for creating community-based Sibshops: They appreciate the value of peer support, and witness, on a daily basis, the concerns experienced by brothers and sisters. Even if they are not facilitators, there are many behind-the-scenes contributions parents can make to ensure a successful Sibshop.

Based on years of conducting programs for siblings, we believe that Sibshop facilitators should share some varied core skills. Both facilitators, for instance, should be as comfortable leading discussions as they are organizing a game of Ultimate Nerf or a cooking project for 14 children.[1] It is strongly desired that Sibshop facilitators:

1. Have a working knowledge of the unusual concerns and unusual opportunities experienced by brothers and sisters of children with special needs. At the very least, future Sibshop facilitators should read Chapters 2, 3 and 4 of this book. They were written with them in mind. However, facilitators and the planning committee should not stop there. The sibling panel and the books, videotapes, and newsletters discussed in Chapter 11 are excellent ways to learn more about sibling issues.

2. Have personal or professional experience with people who have special needs and their families. They should also possess knowledge of the "special needs" represented at the Sibshop. Therefore, a special education teacher, despite her experience with children with developmental disabilities, may not be the best candidate for a Sibshop for brothers and sisters of children who have cancer.

3. Be familiar with active listening principles. These skills will be valuable throughout the Sibshop and especially during discussion activities.

4. Have experience leading groups, preferably groups of children.

5. Convey a sense of joy, wonder, and play. Having fun is an important component of a successful Sibshop. Even though we learn at them, Sibshops are not school. Even though we talk about our feelings, Sibshops are not therapy. All potential facilitators should truly enjoy the company of children. A self-deprecating sense of humor helps too!

6. Be available to meet at the times and dates identified by the planning committee.

7. Be somewhat physically fit. Sibshops are lively, exciting events, with many high-energy activities. Facilitators will be expected to model and participate in these activities.

---

[1]During training on the Sibshop model, we promise future facilitators at least three things. First, if they do it right, they will have at least as much fun as the participants; second, they will need no further exercise on the day of the Sibshop; third, they will sleep very well that night.

8. Appreciate that the Sibshop participants, not the facilitators, are the experts on living with a brother or sister with special needs. One of the rewards of facilitating the program is what we can learn from the kids we serve.

LOCATION

An ideal facility will be centrally located and kid-friendly, and have a gym or large multipurpose room for games, a quiet meeting place for discussions, and a working kitchen that accommodates all participants. Ironically, while public schools may seem the best choice (as they certainly meet the above qualifications), they can also be the most problematic. Although some districts will donate the use of a school, others will charge fees to cover general rental or to pay for a custodian. In some instances, stringent contracts with food-service unions will prevent use of a school kitchen without paying an employee overtime (in which case you may wish to inquire whether the district has a living-skills classroom with a kitchen). It may be easier (and less expensive) to meet in a church hall, community center, early intervention program, and so forth.

TIMES AND DATES

When

Although many Sibshops are held on Saturdays from 10 A.M. to 2 P.M., it is not a time that will be ideal for all parties. Many programs have found that this time slot is simply the "least worst time" for most families, participants, facilitators, and agencies. Smaller communities often have greater flexibility with regard to times than larger communities. If all the participants attend the same school district, Sibshops can be held on teacher inservice days. In communities where Friday afternoon traffic is not a nightmare, Sibshops are sometimes held on Friday evenings.

How Often

How often your Sibshops meet will be determined by the needs and resources in your community. Examples of how frequently Sibshops have been offered by various agencies follow.

Annually   Some Sibshops meet only once a year. Examples of this are a 6-hour Sibshop that is a part of a national conference for families who have children with a specific disability or illness and a 4-hour Sibshop that is a part of a statewide conference for families who have children with various disabilities. Another example is the

Sibshop that is a component of a camp for children or families who have disabilities or illnesses.

Every Six Months In rural communities, where the long distance traveled would prohibit meeting more frequently, some Sibshops are offered once every 6 months. Sometimes a simultaneous program is offered to parents.

Every Other Month Some communities like the flexibility offered by open enrollment. Families do not have to commit to a series of meetings (such as the monthly model described below) and children can attend throughout the year if they wish. The drawback is that, for planning purposes, there must be a registration (if only phone registration) for each event. Another drawback is that the "cast of characters" will change somewhat from Sibshop to Sibshop. If your planning committee would like the flexibility that open enrollment affords, offering Sibshops every other month may be a workable solution, as it allows time to send letters announcing an upcoming Sibshop to all members on your mailing list as well as time for them to respond.

Monthly Some Sibshops meet monthly, often during school months only. This may be a series of three or five monthly 4-hour Sibshops held in an urban or suburban community. One community did it this way: Series One (September, October, and November) was for siblings ages 7–10; Series Two (January, February, March) was for siblings ages 11–14; Series Three (April, May, June) was again for the 7- to 10-year-olds. (December was avoided due to the often-hectic holiday season.) The advantage of this model is that group identity is formed, even during three meetings. The drawback is that some families and participants may have difficulty committing to all the scheduled dates.

Weekly Some Sibshops are held weekly. Usually, these are much shorter in duration (1–1½ hours) and are often held after school.

Other Of course, there are many variations on the theme. As noted earlier, some Sibshops are held on teacher inservice days, and still others are held during the summer, perhaps every day for 3 days or even 1 week.

Finally, when deciding how often to meet, remember this rule of thumb: We think it is better to meet less frequently and have Sibshops that are well planned, exciting, and meaningful events than to meet often and have programs that become routine.

PUBLICITY

Making parents, brothers and sisters, agencies, organizations, and the general public aware of your services for brothers and sisters is not a one-time effort. How often you will need to publicize your program will depend on how frequently the program is offered. If you offer your sibling program in a series (e.g., one meeting a month for 5 months), expect to publicize your program prior to each series. If your program is an ongoing program (e.g., quarterly meetings with open enrollment), plan on publicizing the program once per year and sending letters to parents on your mailing list announcing each meeting. If you hold the program infrequently or as a one-time event, plan on publicizing your sibling program prior to each event. See Chapter 6 for a further discussion of awareness activities, sample awareness materials, and timelines.

REGISTRATION AND BUDGET MANAGEMENT

To plan ahead for your sibling audience, you will require more information on your sibling participants than you can easily gather over the phone. Consequently, we recommend that parents call the agency handling registration to reserve a "slot" for their child. A registration form can be sent to parents (see Figure 2 for a sample registration form) to complete and return with registration fees (if any). Registration is usually handled by the agency that manages the Sibshop budget or donates the facility where the Sibshop will be held.

CONCLUSION

Once you have answered the questions posed on the Sibshop Planning Form and discussed in this chapter, you should have a clear idea of:

Who your cosponsors are
Who will be served by your Sibshop
What your financial and other resources are
Who will facilitate your Sibshop
Where your Sibshop will be held
How frequently it will meet
Who will publicize the program
Who will register the participants

If you can answer all or most of the above questions, congratulate yourself and your planning committee. If you can't, hang in there! There's a good chance that no one in your community has ever tried anything like a Sibshop before. As pioneers and history-makers you and your colleagues will be expected to be creative, resourceful, and occasionally monomaniacal. If you get stuck, seek the counsel of other Sibshops in your state. An Arc, Parent-to-Parent program, Parent Training and Information (PTI) center, or the Sibling Support Project may be able to help you locate the nearest program. When the logistics are resolved, the fun begins. In the next chapter, we provide detailed information on planning your first Sibshop.

Sibshop Registration Form

Date: _____

Child's name: _____

Date of birth: _____ Age: _____

Gender: _____

School: _____ Grade: _____

Does this child receive any special services (e.g., counseling, speech-language
therapy, special education)? _____

_____

_____

_____

Parent(s) name(s): _____

Home address: _____

_____

Home telephone: _____

Name of brother or sister with special needs: _____

Date of birth _____ Age: _____

Gender: _____

Nature of disability or illness: _____

_____

_____

_____

School: _____

What kind of related special education services (e.g., speech, occupational, or
physical therapy, counseling) does this child receive? _____

_____

Other siblings

Name	Date of birth	Age	Gender

(continued)

Figure 2.   A sample Sibshop Registration Form. (For the reader's use, this material may be reproduced.
From Meyer, D.J., & Vadasy, P.F. [1994]. *Sibshops: Workshops for siblings of children with special
needs.* Copyright © 1994 Paul H. Brookes Publishing Co.)

What are your reasons for enrolling your child in the Sibshop program? _____
_____
_____
_____
_____

Do you have any concerns about enrolling your child in the Sibshop? _____
_____
_____
_____

Do you have any particular topics that you would like addressed during the Sibshop?
_____
_____
_____
_____

Does your child have any food allergies or restrictions?
_____
_____
_____

Please provide any other information that you feel will make this an enjoyable and educational experience for your child:
_____
_____
_____
_____
_____

I assume all risks and hazards of the conduct of the program and release from responsibility any person providing transportation to and from activities. In case of injury, I do hereby waive all claims or legal actions, financial or otherwise, against Children's Hospital, Seattle Public Schools, or The Arc of King County, their elected and appointed officials and employees, the organizers, sponsors, supervisors, or any volunteer connected with the program. In absence of signature, payment of fees and participation in the program shall constitute acceptance of the conditions set forth in the release. I grant full permission to use any photographs, videotapes, motion pictures, recordings, or any other record of this program for any purpose.

_____   _____
Signature of Parent or Guardian   Date

Please return this form and the registration fee* (a check for $25 made out to the Sibling Support Project) and mail to:

The Sibling Support Project, CL-09
Children's Hospital and Medical Center
4800 Sand Point Way N.E.
Seattle, WA 98105

*If you would like your child to be considered for a scholarship, please call the Sibling Support Project at 206-368-4911. Donations to the Sibshop Scholarship Fund are gratefully accepted!

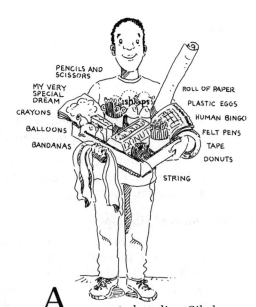

6

Putting It All Together

As we noted earlier, Sibshops are logistically no more difficult to organize than other groups for kids, such as Camp Fire, Cub Scouts, or Brownies. They may, in fact, be easier! In this chapter we guide you as you plan your first Sibshop. We provide you with a timetable for publicizing your program and provide you with sample awareness materials. Furthermore, we give you and your colleagues a tested, detailed Sibshop schedule that can help you plan your very first meeting. At the end of this chapter, we suggest ways of evaluating parents' and participants' satisfaction with your program.

In providing the information in this chapter, we are assuming that:

1. You and your planning committee have read Chapter 5.
2. Representatives from cosponsoring agencies and family member representatives have been identified and have met.
3. The population of children you wish to serve has been defined.
4. Needed financial resources have been identified.
5. A site for your Sibshop has been identified.
6. Facilitators for your Sibshop have been identified, meet the qualifications discussed in Chapter 5, and are ready to hop into their sneakers and have some fun.
7. Dates for your Sibshop have been set.

AWARENESS AND RECRUITMENT ACTIVITIES

Timeline

Once resources, dates, facility, and facilitators have been identified, you'll want to develop a suggested timeline for awareness and recruitment activities. We suggest the following:

8 Weeks before—Create and print flier.
6 Weeks before—Send fliers and letters to agencies.
5 Weeks before—Send fliers and letters to parents of children served by cosponsoring agencies.
4 Weeks before—Send press releases to local media.

2–6 Weeks before—Send registration forms to parents who have phoned requesting registration materials.

This chapter contains sample awareness materials you may use to publicize your upcoming Sibshops. You may, of course, adapt these in any way you see fit.

Expanding Awareness of Sibshops

A very effective way to create awareness of your Sibshop program in general is to present information at local programs for parents of children with special needs. You may wish to request a chance to speak to parents at support groups sponsored by Arcs, early intervention centers, schools, hospitals, or Parent-to-Parent programs. This need not be a lengthy discourse. Remembering the dictum to "be brief, be bright, and be gone," you can "plug" your program in 15 minutes or less. You may use the Brief Description of the Sibshop Model (in Appendix C) as a basis for your talk and as a handout.

Publicizing Your Sibshop

A Sample Press Release   According to Dean Forbes, Media Relations Coordinator for Children's Hospital and Medical Center (Seattle), press releases should be sent no later than 3 weeks prior to the event or registration deadline for maximum impact (sample copy is shown in Figure 3).

If your agency does not already have a list of contacts and addresses for local media, consider asking "well-connected" colleagues in the community for their lists.

A Sample Flier   Included in this chapter is a "blank" flier with empty boxes that you may use to publicize your program (see Figure 4a). The box on the left may be filled in with information about the sponsoring agencies and the box on the right may be filled with contact phone numbers, as shown in Figure 4b. This flier then may be used in several ways. As long as it does not mention dates, it may be distributed to agencies for children with special needs and their families to post indefinitely. It may be photocopied on the back of the letter you send to parents, or included with your press release.

A Sample Letter to Parents   The letter you send to parents provides them with details pertaining to the "who, what, when, where, and how much" of the program (see Figure 5). It also reassures parents about the program in which they will be enrolling their children. The letter to parents, like the flier, should present the program as a positive, fun experience for a deserving population. One common way of disseminating these letters is to send them home with children who attend special education programs.

Other ways of distributing the letter include obtaining mailing lists of families from Parent-to-Parent programs, Arcs, and other parent-

---

FOR IMMEDIATE RELEASE   [date]

Contact: Don Meyer, Sibshop director, [phone]

Participants Wanted for Sibling Support Group

Brothers and sisters of children with disabilities now have a chance to meet and talk with other kids whose brothers and sisters have special needs. They'll have an opportunity to talk about the good and not-so-good parts of having a sibling with a disability. They'll also have fun!

Sibshops are an exciting new support, information, and recreation opportunity for siblings ages 8–13. They are cosponsored by Children's Hospital and Medical Center, Seattle Public Schools, and The Arc of King County. Sibshops will be held at Olympic View Elementary School, 504 NE 95th, Seattle. Cost is $25 for five meetings. For more information and to register, call Children's Sibling Support Project at 368–4911.

The first meeting is Saturday, February 22, from 10 A.M. to 2 P.M. Additional meeting dates are March 21, April 25, May 16, and June 13, 1995.

Besides peer support, Sibshops provide participants with an opportunity to learn more about their sibling's disability. Most important, Sibshops are fun! Participants play new games, cook lunches, and make new friends.

Brothers and sisters may have feelings that are difficult to express, even to a friend: sadness that a sister can't learn things that others take for granted, anger when a brother's behavior problems prevent the family from doing things other families do, or the special pride when a sibling with a disability learns a basic but important life skill after months or years of practice. At Sibshops, siblings will share these feelings with others who truly understand.

Figure 3. Sample press release.

driven organizations, or requesting that these organizations include a copy of this letter in their routine mailings to families.

A Sample Letter Announcing the Next Meeting of an Ongoing Sibling Program   Ongoing programs that have open enrollment can use a letter similar to the one in Figure 6 to announce the next meeting. It would be sent out to parents, agency personnel, and others, such as school counselors, psychologists, and social workers who have requested to be on your mailing list.

A Sample Letter to Agencies Announcing Upcoming Sibling Workshops   The letter in Figure 7 may be used to send to other agencies serving people with special needs. It asks agencies to post a flier and offers further information on your program. An alternative to sending this letter is to send agencies a press release and a flier.

PLANNING FOR YOUR VERY FIRST SIBSHOP

The information below is designed to assist the planning committee and especially the facilitators in planning a Sibshop for 8- to 13-year-old brothers and sisters of children with special health or develop-

Sibshops: A program just for brothers and sisters of kids with special needs!

Sibshops are a celebration of the many contributions made by brothers and sisters.

Here's what kids say about Sibshops:

"At **Sibshops** you get to meet other brothers and sisters of kids with special needs."

"**Sibshops** have outrageous games!"

"At **Sibshops** you can talk about the good and not-so-good parts of having a brother or sister who has special needs."

"**Sibshops** are a place to learn about cool things."

"**Sibshops** have great cooking activities!"

"**Sibshops** have some of the greatest kids in the world!"

"**Sibshops** are fun!"

Sibshops are for kids who have a brother or sister with special health or developmental needs. **Join us!**

Figure 4a.   "Blank" Sibshop flier. (For the reader's use, this material may be reproduced. From Meyer, D.J., & Vadasy, P.F. [1994]. *Sibshops: Workshops for siblings of children with special needs.* Copyright © 1994 Paul H. Brookes Publishing Co.)

Sibshops: A program just for brothers and sisters of kids with special needs!

Sibshops are a celebration of the many contributions made by brothers and sisters.

Sibshops are co-sponsored by: Children's Hospital and Medical Center, the Arc of King County, and Seattle Public Schools.

Here's what kids say about Sibshops:

"At **Sibshops** you get to meet other brothers and sisters of kids with special needs."

"**Sibshops** have outrageous games!"

"At **Sibshops** you can talk about the good and not-so-good parts of having a brother or sister who has special needs."

"**Sibshops** are a place to learn about cool things."

"**Sibshops** have great cooking activities!"

"**Sibshops** have some of the greatest kids in the world!"

"**Sibshops** are fun!"

Sibshops are for kids who have a brother or sister with special health or developmental needs. Join us!

For information and registration call 368-4911.

Figure 4b.   Sample Sibshop flier.

Dear Parents,
It gives us great pleasure to announce Sibshops, an exciting program just for brothers and sisters of children with special needs. At a Sibshop, brothers and sisters will:

- Meet other brothers and sisters of children with special needs;
- Have fun;
- Talk about their brothers and sisters with others who really know what it's like to have a sibling with a disability;
- Make new friends;
- Learn more about disabilities and the services that people with disabilities receive; and
- Have some more fun!

There will even be a meeting just for parents to talk about sibling issues.

Whom are Sibshops for? Sibshops are for 8- to 13-year-old brothers and sisters of children who have special needs.

Who sponsors Sibshops? Sibshops are a collaborative effort of Children's Hospital's Sibling Support Project, The Seattle Public Schools, and The Arc of King County.

Who runs Sibshops? This spring the Seattle area Sibshops will be run by:

Erica Lewis—Erica is the program assistant at the Sibling Support Project. She has an older brother with Down syndrome.

Jennifer Newman—Now a student at University of Washington, Jennifer was a Sibshop participant when they were first offered at the UW's Experimental Education Unit. Jen has a sister who has Down syndrome.

Leslie Collins—Leslie will begin work on her Master of Social Work degree at UW this fall. She works for The Arc as an Independent Living Instructor and was a facilitator at the Fall/Winter Sibshops with Erica and Jen.

Grant Hiraoka—A social work intern from UW, Grant works with Seattle Public Schools' Family Services Program. Grant has a brother who has special health needs.

Billie Butterfield—Billie wears two hats for Seattle Public Schools: She works as a teacher for kids with hearing impairments and is a school psychologist.

What are Sibshops? Sibshops are a lively mixture of new games, discussion, and guest speakers. Participants should dress comfortably and be ready for action! We'll also make and eat lunch!

When and where are Sibshops? Sibshops will be held from 10:00 A.M. to 2:00 P.M. on the following dates: February 22, March 21, April 25, May 16, and June 13. We want all who register to attend each session! Each Sibshop will be held at Olympic View Elementary School, 504 NE 95th, Seattle.

What is the cost of Sibshops? A $25 registration fee covers all five Sibshops, including lunch. A limited number of scholarships are available. Donations to the scholarship fund are accepted!

Sounds great! How do I register? Call the Children's Sibling Support Project at 368-4911 for more details. Hurry, as space is limited!

Figure 5.   Sample letter to parents.

mental needs. The annotated schedule describes, in detail, Sibshop discussion, recreation, and food activities; component tasks; and materials that will need to be purchased or gathered. We are confident that, after you have conducted a Sibshop using this schedule, you will

Dear Brothers, Sisters, and Parents,

We are happy to announce that on Saturday, May 30, from 10:00 A.M. until 2:00 P.M., the Family Support Program of Cascade County will host its next Sibshop. Like previous Sibshops, this will be held at Evergreen Community Center and is open to brothers and sisters—ages 8–13—of children with special needs.

As usual, we'll feature a combination of fun, information, surprises, discussion, and more fun for everyone who attends. There is no charge for Sibshop but *phone registration is a must.* Let us know if you're attending by calling the Family Support Program, no later than May 26th.

We're looking forward to seeing you on the 30th!

Take care and see you soon,

Mike Martison   Margaret Newman

Figure 6.   Sample letter announcing the next meeting of an ongoing sibling program.

Dear Colleague,

We are pleased to announce that Children's Hospital's Sibling Support Project, Seattle Public Schools, and The Arc of King County are cosponsoring Sibshops for 8- to 13-year-old brothers and sisters of children with special needs. Sibshops offer brothers and sisters the opportunity to meet other siblings of people with special needs, share common joys and concerns, and learn more about the implications of their siblings' disability—all in a lively, recreational setting.

We are enclosing a flier on the Seattle-area Sibshops and ask that you post it where parents and other interested professionals might see it. A letter to parents describing the program is also enclosed. Please feel free to photocopy it and distribute it to families. On February 22 we will begin our second series of Sibshops that will meet monthly through June of this year.

If you would like further information about any of these programs or the Sibling Support Project, please call us at 368-4911.

Sincerely,

Donald J. Meyer
Director
Sibling Support Project

Figure 7.   Sample letter to agencies announcing upcoming sibling workshops.

have no problem planning subsequent Sibshops. At the end of this chapter, we discuss a planning sheet that will simplify planning for future Sibshops.

The schedule shown in Table 4 is intended to make your first Sibshop as smooth and successful as possible. Set a time to meet with the other cofacilitators to work through the packet and assign responsibilities as needed. **It is critical that you and your cofacilitators read the Annotated Sibshop Schedule carefully.** You and your team, of course, can feel free to substitute other activities of your choice.

AN ANNOTATED SIBSHOP SCHEDULE

What will happen during the first Sibshop is explained, in some detail, in this section. You are asked to photocopy some materials, gather others, and decide who will present activities.

With Regard to Times . . .

The times listed on the Sibshop schedule and this annotated schedule assume that your Sibshop will run from 10 A.M. until 2 P.M. If necessity dictates that your Sibshop occur during different hours, adjust the schedule. In any event, the times listed are approximate. You may not have time for all activities or you may try a game suggested by a brother, sister, or cofacilitator.

Please note: This schedule does not include a guest speaker or other learning activity. During the first Sibshop, we usually spend extra time getting to know one another. If you are hosting your Sibshop at a conference for a specific population (e.g., siblings of children

Table 4.   Sibshop schedule

Time	Activity	Materials needed	Lead person
9:15	Set Up	Signs, tape Coffee?	
10:00	Trickle-In Activity Parents: Enrollment Sibs: Facetags	Enrollment form Facetags Felt-tip pens	
10:10	Introductory Activity Strengths and Weaknesses	S and W sheet Pencils	
10:35	Knots		
10:45	Lap Game		
11:00	Stand Up!		
11:10	Group Juggling	Balls	
11:30	Triangle Tag	Wristbands	
11:40	Sightless Sculpture	Handkerchiefs Chairs	
11:50	Lunch prep		
12:00	Lunch		
12:20	Lunch clean up		
12:30	Dear Aunt Blabby	Letters, envelopes	
12:55	Pushpin Soccer	Balloons 2 push-pins	
1:15	Blob Tag		
1:30	Sound-Off	Sound-Off Sheet	
1:55	Closure		
2:05	Debriefing and Planning for next Sibshop		

with spina bifida), you may wish to amend the schedule to make room for an informational activity (e.g., Ask Dr. Bob!).

All facilitators will need a copy of the schedule for Sibshop day. **Who will photocopy the schedule?**

9:15 A.M. Set Up

It is a good idea for all facilitators to arrive 45 minutes before kids are scheduled to arrive. This provides time for staff to assure that the building and rooms are as you wish (i.e., open and clean), arrange furniture, post directional signs (e.g., Welcome to SIBSHOPS! Use front door →), assure that all materials have been gathered, and confer briefly before the festivities begin.
Materials: Signs, paper, tape, coffee
Who will gather materials?

10:00 A.M. Trickle-In Activity: Enrollment

Invariably, some participants will be early, some will be late, and a few might even arrive on time. It is always helpful to have a few activities available while kids are trickling in. Examples include group juggling, a pickup basketball game, or helping the facilitators set up the food activity for the day.

However, because this is the first day, you will ask parents for information during the trickle-in time. If the participants' parents have not completed and returned the Sibshop Registration Form (Figure 2, p. 80), ask them to do so when they drop off their children. Participants will make Facetags (see Chapter 7).

At every Sibshop at least one facilitator should be available to welcome kids and parents and help participants with nametags. For this, your first Sibshop, have all staff on hand to welcome parents and participants.

Materials: Sibshop Registration Forms, pens, pencils, felt-tip pens, and Facetag sheets.

Who will make photocopies of Registration Forms and Facetags?
Who will gather materials?

10:10 A.M. Introductory Activity: Strengths and Weaknesses

See p. 111.

For our first Sibshop, we will get to know one another using a simple activity called Strengths and Weaknesses. In addition to introductions, this activity gives participants permission—from the start—to say flattering and not-so-flattering things about their brothers and sisters with special needs.

Materials: Photocopies of Strengths and Weaknesses for each participant and facilitator, pencils

Who will make photocopies? and gather materials?
Who will present Strengths and Weaknesses?

10:35 A.M. Knots

See p. 113.

The entire group ties itself into one big knot. Can it be untied? You'll find out!

Materials: None

Who will present Knots?

10:45 A.M. The Lap Game

See p. 170.

This game doesn't require anyone to run laps, nor does it hail from Lapland. This lap refers to (as the dictionary defines it) "the front region or area of a seated person extending from the lower trunk to the knees." In short, participants and facilitators will attempt to sit on each other's lap—all of them, at the same time. Can it be done?

Materials: None

Who will present the Lap Game?

11:00 A.M. Stand Up!

See pp. 178–179.

Pairs of equal heights sit back to back, reach back, lock elbows and attempt to stand up. Lots of variations on this activity

Materials: None

Who will present Stand Up?

11:10 A.M. Group Juggling

See pp. 106–108.

While it can be difficult to juggle three balls by oneself, it's easier with a little help from your friends. Or is it? In a circle, we pass a ball and establish a pattern. Once established, we add another ball. And then another. Then we'll try it a different way entirely.

Materials: Three to four soft balls (not softballs!) for each group of five to six

Who will gather materials?

Who will present Triangle Tag?

11:30 A.M. Triangle Tag

See pp. 179–180.

A geometrical twist on Tag. Three players hold hands to make a triangle. One wears a wristband or a bandana around the wrist to identify her as the "target." A fourth player attempts to tag the target while the triangle moves around to protect the target.

Materials: One wristband or bandana for each group of four.

Who will gather materials?

Who will present Triangle Tag?

11:40 A.M. Sightless Sculpture

See pp. 177–178.

Can a person who is blind be an artist? Sure she can, even a sculptor. This activity requires three participants: one who will be a model, one who will be a blob of clay, and one who will be a blindfolded sculptor. This can be done in groups of three. It is even better when groups of three sculpt in front of the rest of the Sibshop.

Materials: Bandanas or blindfolds, chairs (optional)

Who will gather materials?

Who will present Sightless Sculpture?

11:50 A.M. Lunch: Super Nachos

We suggest Super Nachos for the first lunch. Most kids love nachos and, compared to other food activities, they require little in the way of equipment and preparation. After you use the kitchen and get to know its strengths and shortcomings, you can attempt something more adventurous. Despite their relative ease, even nachos can be difficult to prepare if an important ingredient or piece of equipment is forgotten. You will need:

Food
Tortilla chips
Yellow cheese (in blocks, so kids can grate)
Mild salsa
Black olives (optional)
Sour cream (optional)
Tomatoes (optional)
Green pepper (optional)
Mild onion (optional)
Refried beans (optional)
Juice, cider, or other beverage
Fruit or dessert (optional)

Equipment
Working oven
Hot pads
Metal spatula
Bowls for salsa, etc.
Cheese graters
Can opener
Cutting boards
Kid-friendly knives
Cookie sheets
Pan for heating refried beans (or a microwave and a suitable bowl)
Cups
Paper or other plates
Napkins
Cleaning equipment and soap

Who will shop?
Who will visit the kitchen to determine equipment needs?
Who will gather the remaining equipment?

12:30 P.M. Discussion Activity: Dear Aunt Blabby

See pp. 141–154.
A visit with Dear Aunt Blabby puts the participants in a rarely recognized role: as an expert on what it is like to live with a brother or sister who has special needs. Write out five to seven letters from Appendix D and place them in individual envelopes addressed to Dear Aunt Blabby.
Materials: Dear Aunt Blabby letters in envelopes
Who will copy the letters and place them in envelopes?
Who will present Dear Aunt Blabby?

12:55 P.M. Pushpin Soccer

See pp. 175–176.

Soccer with a point, and a caution: this game requires goalies to use pushpins! Teams swat balloons toward their goalie who pops the balloon. For safety's sake, goalies cannot reach outside of the goal box and other players cannot reach inside. If the thought of participants plus pushpins is more than you can bear, substitute an equally lively activity such as Ultimate Nerf (p. 180), Tag-O-Rama (p.179), or something outrageous, like Body Surfing (pp. 162–163) or The Dangling Donut Eating Contest (p. 165).

Materials: 30 balloons (more for big groups); two pushpins; 1-inch masking tape to mark boundaries and goal boxes

Who will gather materials?

Who will lead Pushpin Soccer?

1:15 P.M. Blob Tag

See pp. 161–162.

This is a great game in an open gym. One person is "it." When "it" tags someone, they both become "it." They hold hands and go after a third. The three, holding hands, go after a fourth and so on until all players are "it" except for one fast-moving individual.

Materials: None

Who will lead Blob?

1:30 P.M. Discussion Activity: Sound-Off

See p. 124.

Sound-Off provides participants with an open ended structure to hypothetically tell a friend, teacher, parent, or the whole world whatever they wish about being the brother or sister of a person with special needs. Responses generally cover a wide range of experiences.

Materials: Sound-Off Sheet, pencils.

Who will photocopy the Sound-Off Sheet?

Who will lead Sound-Off?

1:55 P.M. Closure

Closure is a good time to check in with participants. You may wish to ask: "If your friends ask you what you did today, what would you tell them?" (Inevitable answers: "We played games!" "We ate nachos!" Continue to rephrase the question; eventually they will mention that they had a chance to talk about their brothers and sisters.) An alternative question might be: "You know, there are probably some brothers and sisters who knew about the Sibshop but weren't sure whether they wanted to attend. What would you say to them to encourage them to come to the next Sibshop?"

Finally, closure is a good time to ask participants to suggest food activities, recreational events, or guest speakers. Accommodating the group's wish to, say, make pizza or play freeze tag at the next Sibshop can encourage continued participation. At the very end, you may wish to have a group cheer. If this is to be your only meeting, it is also a great time to take a group picture, or to hand out the Official Sibshop Certificate (see Figure 8). (Group pictures are a wonderful way of extending the Sibshop experience. We know participants who were involved in Sibshops 10 years ago who still have their Sibshop group picture and can still identify many of the kids in the group. If you are holding a series of meetings, plan on taking a group picture during your next-to-last meeting. At your last meeting hand out copies, along with a list of the names, addresses, and phone numbers of all the participants.)

Who will lead closure?

2:05 P.M. Debriefing and Planning for Subsequent Sibshops

This is an opportunity to discuss what went on while it is still fresh in your mind. Even though you will have had a long day, spend a few minutes planning for the next Sibshop. A few minutes spent at this time may mean that the group will not need to meet again before the next Sibshop. The Activity Planning Form (Figure 9) will help you plan subsequent Sibshops in short order.

USING THE ACTIVITY PLANNING FORM

The Activity Planning Form can greatly simplify the process of coming up with the next meeting's agenda. For each activity, the form asks you to estimate time and identify a leader, materials needed, and materials that may need to be purchased. Here is how it is done:

1. Flipping through Chapter 8, identify the Peer Support and Discussion activity you want to try at your next Sibshop. For a 4-hour Sibshop, two will be plenty; one may be enough.
2. Decide on information activities or guest speaker, either one proposed in Chapter 10 or as identified by the facilitators. Of all activities, planning this activity should get top priority; potential guest speakers need as much lead time as possible. You may wish to identify a back-up speaker or activity. Also, the times that a guest speaker is available may influence the rest of your schedule.
3. Select an Introductory Activity (Chapter 7).
4. Select a food activity from Chapter 9 or, better yet, create one of your own. Do think through the ingredients, materials, and equipment you will need.
5. Select three or four high-energy activities and two or three quieter recreational activities from Chapter 9.

Figure 8. Sibshop certificate. (For the reader's use, this material may be reproduced. From Meyer, D.J., & Vadasy, P.F. [1994]. *Sibshops: Workshops for siblings of children with special needs.* Copyright © 1994 Paul H. Brookes Publishing Co.)

SIBSHOP ACTIVITY PLANNING FORM

Planning for a Sibshop need not be difficult or time-consuming. Use the following form to record the activities you select for your next Sibshop. After deciding upon your "core" (discussion and information) activities, decide upon complementary recreational activities. Once completed, use this information to build a schedule.

Date: _____

Discussion/Peer Support Activity: _____
Estimated time to complete activity: _____
Activity leader: _____
Materials needed: _____
Shopping list: _____

Information Activity/Guest Speaker: _____
Estimated time to complete activity: _____
Activity leader: _____
Materials needed: _____
Shopping list: _____

Introductory/Warm-Up Activity: _____
Estimated time to complete activity: _____
Activity leader: _____
Materials needed: _____
Shopping list: _____

Food Activity: _____
Estimated time to complete activity: _____
Activity leader: _____
Materials needed: _____
Shopping list: _____

High-Energy Recreation Activity #1: _____
Estimated time to complete activity: _____
Activity leader: _____
Materials needed: _____
Shopping list: _____

High-Energy Recreation Activity #2: _____
Estimated time to complete activity: _____
Activity leader: _____
Materials needed: _____
Shopping list: _____

High-Energy Recreation Activity #3: _____
Estimated time to complete activity: _____
Activity leader: _____
Materials needed: _____
Shopping list: _____

Quieter Recreational Activity #1: _____
Estimated time to complete activity: _____
Activity leader: _____
Materials needed: _____
Shopping list: _____

(continued)

Figure 9.   Sibshop Activity Planning Form. (For the reader's use, this material may be reproduced. From Meyer, D.J., & Vadasy, P.F. [1994]. *Sibshops: Workshops for siblings of children with special needs.* Copyright © 1994 Paul H. Brookes Publishing Co.)

Figure 9.   (*continued*)

Quieter Recreational Activity #2: _____
Estimated time to complete activity: _____
Activity leader: _____
Materials needed: _____
Shopping list: _____

Special Event: _____
Estimated time to complete activity: _____
Activity leader: _____
Materials needed: _____
Shopping list: _____

Other #1: _____
Estimated time to complete activity: _____
Activity leader: _____
Materials needed: _____
Shopping list: _____

Other #2: _____
Estimated time to complete activity: _____
Activity leader: _____
Materials needed: _____
Shopping list: _____

NOTES: _____
_____
_____
_____
_____
_____
_____
_____
_____
_____

6. If you are having special events or other activities, include the estimated time, activity leader, and materials needed on the Activity Planning Form.

7. Using the completed form, begin to build a schedule around timed activities such as introductory activities, lunch, and perhaps your guest speaker. Discussion activities are often best held after lunch, when full tummies predispose participants toward quiet conversation and contemplation. Follow high-energy activities with a quieter activity.

Materials: Activities Planning Form
Who will photocopy the Activities Planning Form?
Who will develop the schedule for the next Sibshop (based on activities suggested on the Activities Planning Form)?

EVALUATING YOUR PROGRAM

After you have held two or three Sibshops, seek feedback from participants and their parents. Completed anonymously, they will provide you with invaluable information and allow you to adjust and improve your program. At the end of a session, distribute pencils and a consumer evaluation sheet such as the Official Sibshop Feedback Form (Figure 10). As parents pick up their children, hand them a consumer satisfaction survey, such as the Parent Evaluation Questionnaire shown in Figure 11. To increase your chances of having the questionnaires returned, also provide a self-addressed, stamped envelope.

CONCLUSION

In the chapters that follow, we provide detailed descriptions of favorite Sibshop introductory, discussion, recreational, food, and informational activities. As you plan your fist Sibshop, be sure to read the introductions to each of these chapters. They contain information that will help you plan and present Sibshop activities for the first time.

THE OFFICIAL SIBSHOP FEEDBACK FORM

Date: _____

Your age: _____

Name of Sibshop leaders: _____

Your name (optional): _____

1. What do you like most about Sibshops? _____
   _____
   _____
   _____

2. What don't you like about Sibshops? _____
   _____
   _____
   _____

3. Please tell us what you think about the Sibshop activities.

		Good	So-so	Not-so-good	Don't remember
a.	Warm-up activities ( )	1	2	3	4
b.	Games ( )	1	2	3	4
c.	Discussion activities ( )	1	2	3	4
d.	Cooking activities ( )	1	2	3	4
e.	Information activities ( )	1	2	3	4
f.	Guest speakers ( )	1	2	3	4

4. Are the Sibshop leaders: Helpful? _____
   Interesting? _____
   Boring? _____
   Other? _____

5. Is there something you want to know that we could learn during a Sibshop?
   _____

6. Is there something you would like to talk about with the other kids? _____
   _____

7. How can we make these Sibshops better? _____
   _____

8. Do you think other kids whose brothers and sisters have special needs would like to go to a group like this? Yes   No   Why? _____
   _____

9. Do Sibshops make you think of your brother or sister? How? _____
   _____

10. Is there anything else that you want to say about the Sibshops? _____
    _____
    _____
    _____

Figure 10. The Official Sibshop Feedback Form. (For the reader's use, this material may be reproduced. From Meyer, D.J., & Vadasy, P.F. [1994]. *Sibshops: Workshops for siblings of children with special needs.* Copyright © 1994 Paul H. Brookes Publishing Co.)

PARENT FEEDBACK FORM

Please take some time to answer each of the following questions about your child's participation in the Sibshop series. Be as honest and open in your answers as possible. Thank you for your time and attention.

Date: _____

Sibshop leaders: _____

Meeting time and location: _____
_____

Your name (optional): _____

Rate your satisfaction with the following aspects of the group on a scale from 1 (very dissatisfied) to 5 (very satisfied). If you have no opinion or the item is not applicable, circle N.

1.	Meeting time	1	2	3	4	5	N
2.	Location	1	2	3	4	5	N
3.	Length of Sibshop	1	2	3	4	5	N
4.	Group composition	1	2	3	4	5	N
5.	Communication and contact with Sibshop leader	1	2	3	4	5	N
6.	Sibshop format	1	2	3	4	5	N
7.	Sibshop activities/content	1	2	3	4	5	N
8.	Opportunities for parent input	1	2	3	4	5	N
9.	Impact on your child's knowledge of disabilities or illness	1	2	3	4	5	N
10.	Impact on your child's feelings toward his or her brother or sister	1	2	3	4	5	N
11.	Impact on your child's feelings toward other family members	1	2	3	4	5	N
12.	Impact on your child's self-image	1	2	3	4	5	N
13.	Impact on your concerns about your child	1	2	3	4	5	N
14.	Impact on your knowledge/awareness of your child's needs	1	2	3	4	5	N
15.	Quality of the Sibshop series, overall	1	2	3	4	5	N

16. Comments regarding above items (please note item number)
_____
_____
_____

17. Has your child talked about what has happened during the Sibshops?
Yes   No
Comments: _____
_____
_____

18. Has your child seemed to enjoy the Sibshops?   Yes   No
Comments: _____
_____
_____

(continued)

Figure 11   (*continued*)

19. Was there any particular activity that your child seemed to have really enjoyed?   Yes   No
     Comments: _____
     _____
     _____

20. Has your child seemed upset by any meeting?   Yes   No
     Comments: _____
     _____
     _____

21. Has any activity made a strong impression on your child?   Yes   No
     Comments: _____
     _____
     _____

22. What do you think your child has learned from the Sibshops? How has he or she benefited so far?
     Comments: _____
     _____
     _____

23. Is there any way in which you feel your child may have been harmed by the Sibshop activities?   Yes   No
     Comments: _____
     _____
     _____

24. Overall, are you glad your child participated in the Sibshop series? Yes   No
     Comments: _____
     _____
     _____

25. Is there anything we should consider for future Sibshops to make them more enjoyable or informative?   Yes   No
     Comments: _____
     _____
     _____

26. Any other comments? _____
     _____
     _____

Please return this questionnaire to:

7

Introductory Activities

When we help start a new Sibshop, one question we often ask participants is, "Not counting your own brothers and sisters, how many of you have ever met other brothers or sisters of kids with special needs?" It still surprises us to find out that usually only 20% have ever met another sibling. The introductory activities presented in this chapter will help you and your colleagues accomplish the first Sibshop goal:

Goal 1: Sibshops will provide brothers and sisters with an opportunity to meet other siblings of children with special needs in a relaxed, recreational setting.

This seemingly simple opportunity—to meet their peers—may be the most important experience that Sibshops provide.

How we introduce ourselves to the participants and the participants to each other will set the tone for the day. Be prepared for the day's events so you can attend to participants as they arrive. Remember that for many first-time participants, attending your Sibshop was their parents' idea, not theirs. Consequently, from the moment they walk through the Sibshop door, your young participants should feel that the adults who are running the program are happy to see them, interested in who they are, and ready to have fun.

The activities you offer at the very beginning of a Sibshop can help break the ice and introduce participants to the facilitators and each other. "Trickle-in" activities are good to use as participants are arriving. These activities can be as simple as inviting participants to join a pick-up basketball game or volleyball. If participants arrive during preparations, enlist their help to blow up balloons or prepare for the day's cooking project. We begin some activities, such as Facetags, as soon as participants walk through the door.

Once most of the participants arrive, it will be time for slightly more organized introductions. Some of the activities described in this chapter, such as Strengths and Weaknesses, will introduce participants to one another. Others, like Knots, will warm up a group by putting them in close physical proximity.

NAMETAGS; FACETAGS

Materials: Standard stick-on nametags, bright, water-soluble markers; for Facetags, copies of facial silhouettes

Nametags are standard issue at most Sibshops, so why not make them fun to design and wear? As participants arrive, give each a nametag and access to a wide array of colorful markers. Facilitators can model artistic license by creating and wearing an outrageously designed nametag.

Facetags, suggested by Fay Morgan of Pittsburgh, allow participants to draw a humorous self-portrait as a part of their nametags. As participants arrive, they select a silhouette that most looks like their own face. They then fill in and color the face to resemble themselves. Once completed, the silhouettes can be affixed to their clothing using a regular stick-on nametag on which the participant's name has been clearly written. See Figure 12.

GROUP JUGGLING

Materials: Three to four *soft* balls, such as Nerf balls, Gertie balls, or beanbags for each group of six. (Gertie balls, available at toy stores, are good to have on hand for a variety of activities. They inflate easily without the use of a pump; deflated, they are easy to store. Because they are soft, although fairly tough, kids cannot be hurt by them even

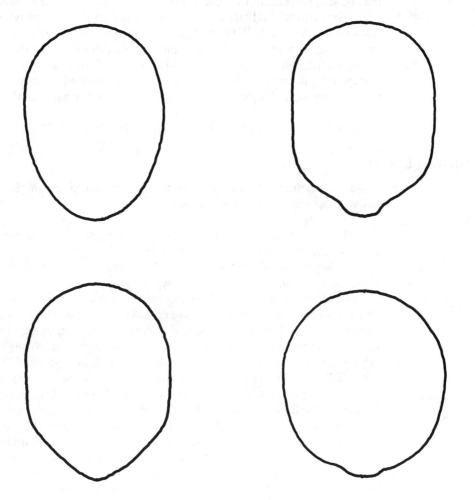

Figure 12. Facetags activity sheet. (For the reader's use, this material may be reproduced. From Meyer, D.J., & Vadasy, P.F. [1994]. *Sibshops: Workshops for siblings of children with special needs.* Copyright © 1994 Paul H. Brookes Publishing Co.)

if they are accidentally hit in the face—which can happen during Group Juggling.) Water balloons are optional!

While it can be difficult to juggle three balls by yourself, it is easier with a little help from your friends. Or is it? A group of five or six participants, standing in a circle, gently toss a ball back and forth, establishing a pattern: Bob throws to Ashley, Ashley throws to Sam, Sam throws to Gina, and Gina throws to Bob. Two helpful strategies may be suggested: Call the name of the person to whom you are throwing as you throw the ball, and keep your eyes on the person who always tosses you the ball. Once this pattern is perfected with one ball, another ball is added. And then another ball. And then another. For younger children, it may be easier to sit on the floor in a circle, with feet spread out, and to roll the balls instead. A wonderful warm-weather Group Juggling variation is to use softball-size water balloons!!

Source: Adapted from *More New Games* (Flugelman, 1981, p. 61)

HUMAN BINGO

Materials: Human Bingo sheet, pencils. Optional: three small, silly prizes (e.g., glow-in-the-dark slugs)

This is a great introductory activity for a group of school-age siblings. It is guaranteed to warm things up in a hurry!

To begin, ask the participants who knows how to play Bingo. Have these participants describe how, in Bingo, you win by completing a horizontal, vertical, or diagonal row of boxes. Distribute Human Bingo sheets (Figure 13) but not pencils. Ask how they think Human Bingo is played. Using hypothetical examples, let participants know that a box is completed by filling in the name of a person in the group who meets the conditions or can perform the actions specified in the box. "If I asked Maurice if he likes blue cheese, and he answers yes, I would write his name in the blue cheese box." Explain that, like regular Bingo, the first person to complete a horizontal, vertical, or diagonal row is the winner and should yell "Bingo" when they think they've won. Pass out pencils, say, "Ready, Set, Go!", and stand back! Kids asking questions, wiggling ears, imitating elephants, and writing simultaneously create a funny, friendly, if chaotic, scene. You can stretch this activity by having three winners: one who wins by the above means, another who fills in the four corners first, and a third who is able to assign names to all 16 boxes.

FAVORITES I

Even though participants will share the "common denominator" of having a brother or sister who has special needs, they will be different

HUMAN BINGO

Find someone (besides yourself) who . . . .

Has a bird for a pet. NAME_____	Can name the last four U.S. Presidents VAN HALEN? JACKSON? NAME_____	Has four kids in their family NAME_____	Can imitate an elephant NAME_____
Likes anchovies on their pizza NAME_____	Has been to the Statue of Liberty NAME_____	Has a dog for a pet NAME_____	Can do the splits NAME_____
Has visited their special sib's school NAME_____	Can wiggle their ears NAME_____	Can roll their tongue NAME_____	Likes blue cheese NAME_____
Was born in another state U. S. A NAME_____	Has been to Disney World or Disneyland NAME_____	Knows why their sib has a disability NAME_____	Can pat their head and rub their tummy for 10 seconds NAME_____

Sibling Support Project · Seattle, Washington

Figure 13.   Human Bingo sheet. (For the reader's use, this material may be reproduced. From Meyer, D.J., & Vadasy, P.F. [1994]. *Sibshops: Workshops for siblings of children with special needs.* Copyright © 1994 Paul H. Brookes Publishing Co.)

from one another in many ways. One small way of celebrating these differences is to try an activity such as Favorites I or II. Favorites II is especially good with younger participants.

Materials: A slip of paper as described below, pencils

Favorites I creates a flurry of activity and warms up a crowd quickly. At the very beginning of the Sibshop, participants are instructed to fill in a slip of paper providing the following information:

What is your favorite food? _____
What is your favorite hobby? _____
What is your favorite television show? _____
IMPORTANT—DON'T WRITE YOUR NAME ON THIS PAPER!!

The completed slips are collected, mixed up, and redistributed at the beginning of the activity. Participants then must find the person who wrote on their piece of paper by asking others what their favorites are (e.g., "Is your favorite hobby *skateboarding*?"). Because participants are simultaneously seeking the writer of the paper they are holding *and* being sought, the activity creates mild confusion, but don't worry—it is a pleasant, constructive commotion. Once everyone finds the person they are seeking, participants introduce their "partners" to the group and announce their favorites.

FAVORITES II

Materials: 5″ × 7″ index cards, felt-tip pens, safety pins

Favorites II is especially fun with younger groups (6- to 8-year-olds). At the beginning of the Sibshop, instead of nametags, give each participant a 5″ × 7″ index card and a felt-tip pen. Have available as a model two posters illustrating index cards. One poster will describe the information you wish:

favorite TV program		favorite pastime
	name	
	word that describes me	
favorite food		favorite color

A second will have an illustration of the card as it might be completed by a participant:

Ducktales	Jump rope
Belinda	
Silly	
Pizza!	Purple

Help participants fill out a card that describes their favorites. Use a hole puncher and a safety pin or tape to attach nametags. At the beginning of the Sibshop, ask participants and facilitators to share the information on their tags.

Source: Adapted from *Child Support* (Landy, 1988)

STRENGTHS AND WEAKNESSES

Materials: Strengths and Weaknesses activity sheet, pencils

Strengths and Weaknesses interviews take introduction activities one step further: They help participants begin to think in terms of their sibling with special needs. Strengths and Weaknesses also serves two other purposes: First, it acknowledges that everyone has strengths and weaknesses; and second, it provides participants permission—from the start—to say flattering and not-so-flattering things about their brothers or sisters with special needs.

Introduce the activity this way. Ask the group if they believe that everyone has strengths—things that they do well. The answer, of course, will be yes. Ask them about people who have disabilities or illnesses: Do they have strengths also? Then ask them whether most people also have weaknesses—things they do not do so well. As you introduce this activity, model the sharing you would like to see from the participants. If you are a good cook but a truly awful singer, describe, with gusto and detail, how bad and good you are at these activities.

Have participants pair off with someone whom they have not met before and, using the activity sheet shown in Figure 14, interview each other on their strengths and weaknesses and the strengths and weaknesses of their brothers and sisters with special needs. Distribute pencils and the activity sheet and dispatch participants to various corners of the room. Allow approximately 5 minutes for the interviews.

When the interviews are completed, regroup in a circle and have participants introduce their partners and describe their partners' and

STRENGTHS & WEAKNESSES

Everybody has strengths – that is, things they do well.

Everybody has weaknesses – things they don't do so well.

Turn to the person next to you, interview him or her and find out ONE strength they have and ONE weakness.

Also, find out ONE strength and ONE weakness for their sibling with special needs.

Take good notes. You'll introduce the person you interviewed!

Name of person you interviewed:

_____

One strength: _____

_____

One weakness: _____

_____

Name of person's brother or sister with special needs: _____

His or her strength: _____

_____

His or her weakness: _____

_____

Your Name: _____

Figure 14.   Strengths and Weaknesses activity sheet. (For the reader's use, this material may be reproduced. From Meyer, D.J., & Vadasy, P.F. [1994]. *Sibshops: Workshops for siblings of children with special needs.* Copyright © 1994 Paul H. Brookes Publishing Co.)

their partners' siblings' strengths and weaknesses. This can be a good time to ask the person being introduced if they know the name of their siblings' disability. It is also a good time to explore common experiences (e.g., "Does anyone else have a brother or sister who can't talk?" or, "Sounds like we have a few musicians here. Who else is good at music?" or, [in mock horror] "Oh no, not you too! How many people do we have here who have a hard time keeping their room clean?").

KNOTS

Materials: None

In Knots, a group of six to eight players tie themselves together into one big knot. To begin this activity, players stand, shoulder to shoulder, in a circle facing inward. Players extend their hands and grab two hands, observing two rules: 1) do not take both hands of the same person, and 2) do not take the hands of a person next to you. Once knotted, players gently try to untie the knot, stepping over and under arms and pivoting handholds without breaking their grip. Can it be untied? There is only one way to find out! This game is guaranteed to get participants close in a hurry!

Source: Adapted from *New Games Book* (Flugelman, 1976, p. 69)

INSTANT REPLAY

Materials: None

Try this decidedly silly name-learning game after a warm-up activity such as Knots, Group Juggling, or Human Bingo. In a circle, each group member says his or her name while making an extravagant

motion. For instance, Mike may choose to hop around in a circle on one foot (or do a forward roll, or slap his knees, etc.) ending by shouting, "Mike!" After Mike demonstrates, everyone else does an "instant replay." That is, they simultaneously perform the same silly act and say, "Mike!" Going around the circle, encourage participants to introduce themselves with dramatic gestures.

Source: Adapted from *More New Games* (Flugelman, 1981, p. 71)

GO STAND IN THE CORNER!

Materials: Sheets of large (8″ × 14″) paper, markers; or two chalkboards, chalk, and erasers

In Go Stand in the Corner, we vote with our feet. To prepare, have two assistants stand in opposite corners of the room or gym. One assistant will have pieces of paper with the words from Column A written in large letters. The other assistant will do the same except with words from Column B. Alternatively, both assistants can stand at chalkboards and write the choices on their boards for each round. Have participants join you in the center of the room and dispatch them to corners based on the preferences listed below.

Ask participants: Which describes you best?

Column A	or	Column B
Baseball		Football
Orange juice		Tomato juice
Burger King		McDonalds
Cereal		Bacon and eggs
Donald Duck		Daffy Duck
Potato chips		Taco chips
Get up early		Sleep in
School, thumbs up		School, thumbs down
Pizza, pepperoni		Pizza, extra cheese

Have several pieces of blank paper on hand so participants can privately suggest other choices.

Source: Adapted from *More New Games* (Flugelman, 1981, p. 71)

THE NAME GAME

Materials: None

The Name Game, like Telephone, is a game that will be known to many readers. Although we constantly are on the lookout for innovative games, we have learned that games that we might consider old war-horses are still enjoyed by young participants who have never experienced them before. The Name Game helps participants and facilitators learn names; it also lets the group know that the program has begun and their attention is required. If you have many participants, you may wish to break into two or even three circles for this activity.

To play, the group sits in a circle. The first person says, "My name is Michelle." The person to her left says, "My name is Sean and that is Michelle." The person to Sean's left says, "My name is Terese, that is Sean and Michelle." Continue adding names as you go around the circle.

SIBSHOP ACTION ART

Materials: White or light-colored mural butcher paper (2–3 yards), scissors, crayons or markers

Sibshop Action Art is a great warm-up activity that gives each kid a chance to "fit" his or her individuality into the group! It was developed by Karen Mataya and Erica Lewis Erickson, lead facilitators at the Seattle-area Sibshops.

Prior to the Sibshop, decide on a word or phrase applicable to the group and draw it in big bubble letters on the butcher paper. Then cut the paper in puzzle-like pieces, one for each member of the group. Remember to cut *through* the letters, so that each piece has just a part of one or two letters.

As participants arrive, give each a piece of the puzzle, and explain that it may be decorated however he or she wishes. Colors, shapes, and tones will vary with each child's emotions and feelings. When each participant is finished, or the time is up, explain that it is now time to fit all of the individual pieces together into a whole. Guesses are welcome as to what the finished word or phrase will be!

Tape the pieces together as they are fitted correctly . . . and hang the puzzle on the wall for all to see as you begin your group circle or full group activity.

TELEPHONE

Materials: A bag containing sayings, such as those described below, written on slips of paper

Kids love this chestnut. Line up the participants in a straight line. Explain that the first child will be handed a slip of paper with a message on it, such as:

Loose lips sink ships.
A bird in the hand is worth two in the bush.
An apple a day keeps the doctor away.
Early to bed, early to rise, makes a man healthy, wealthy, and wise.
What we've got here is a failure to communicate.
People who need people are the luckiest people in the world.
The rain in Spain stays mainly in the plain.
Toto, I've a feeling we're not in Kansas anymore.
Cleanliness is next to godliness.
When the well's dry, we know the worth of water.
Little strokes fell great oaks.
Yellow cat, black cat, as long as it catches mice, it is a good cat.
Dreams are necessary to life.
It don't mean a thing if it ain't got that swing.
The trouble with a kitten is that eventually it becomes a cat.
Without justice, courage is weak.
Water, water, everywhere, but not a drop to drink.
Live simply so that others may simply live.
The corn is as high as an elephant's eye, An' it looks like it's climbin' right up to the sky.
I yam what I yam and that's all that I yam!
In like a lion, out like a lamb.
There is only one success—to be able to spend your life in your own way.

The first child turns to his or her neighbor and, whispers the message. This participant whispers it to the next person and so on. Challenge the group to be as accurate as possible. By the end of the line you will likely have a garbled phrase. Have the last person announce the phrase as he or she understands it or, even better, write it on a chalkboard. Have the first participant announce the original sentence.

If desired, have the group discuss where the breakdown occurred and what this activity teaches (miscommunication can cause disagreements and even hurt feelings). A nonverbal variation of this game is to have the first player make a face that represents an emotion, and "pass along" that face to other players down the line.

THE WEB

Materials: A ball of heavy yarn

Build cohesiveness in your group by spinning a web of shared thoughts and experiences! To begin, have participants sit in a circle. Hold a ball of yarn in your hands and state: "If I were an animal, I would like to be a _____." Hold the end of the yarn and gently toss the yarn ball to a participant. Ask this participant: "If you could be an animal, what would it be?" Once this player answers, he or she holds onto the yarn, but gently tosses the ball to someone else. This continues until all have shared and a web has been created. Other possible topics include:

1. What do you enjoy doing in your spare time?
2. What is your favorite color, song, place, or food?
3. Who is someone important to you and why?
4. What is one thing you always wanted to do?

Source: Adapted from *Belonging* (Devencenzi & Pendergast, 1988, p. 32)

WHEN YOU'RE HOT, YOU'RE HOT!

Materials: "When You're Hot, You're Hot" activity sheet, pencils

Like Strengths and Weaknesses, this activity acknowledges that we all have different talents and limitations. With this activity, participants fill out the sheet shown in Figure 15 and share a sample of their findings with the group. As the participants share their results, celebrate the diversity of the responses and acknowledge similarities.

By the end of the first half-hour of your Sibshop, your young participants will have been properly greeted and introduced to one another, and may even be "warmed up" to a point of light sweat! Now you're ready to try other Sibshop activities, such as those described in the following chapters.

Source: Adapted from *We All Come in Different Packages* (Konczal & Petetski, 1983, p. 13)

WHEN YOU'RE HOT, YOU'RE HOT . . .

. . . and when you're not, you're not! Nobody does everything well. Things that are easy for some folks are difficult or even impossible for others. That is okay. Life would be pretty boring if we all did the same things well. And pretty tough if we all had problems doing the same thing! Indicate how well you can do each of these things by putting an X in one of the boxes beside it.

	For me it is . . .			
	Easy	Hard	Impossible	Never tried it!
Adding numbers "in your head"				
Ballet				
Braiding hair				
Chin-ups				
Climbing a rope				
Cooking a whole meal				
Dancing				
Doing a head stand				
Doing a magic trick				
Doing cartwheels				
Doing science projects				
Drawing				
Flying a kite				
Jumping rope				
Looking up words in the dictionary				
Memorizing a part for a play				
Painting				
Playing a musical instrument				
Playing chess				
Riding a horse				
Rollerblading				
Saving money				
Shooting baskets				

(continued)

Figure 15.   When You're Hot, You're Hot activity sheet. (For the reader's use, this material may be reproduced. From Meyer, D.J., & Vadasy, P.F. [1994]. *Sibshops: Workshops for siblings of children with special needs.* Copyright © 1994 Paul H. Brookes Publishing Co.)

	Easy	Hard	For me it is . . . Impossible	Never tried it!
Singing				
Skateboarding				
Skipping				
Sleeping in				
Spelling				
Swimming				
Swinging on monkey bars				
Telling a joke				
Tossing a football				
Typing				
Using a computer				
Using a yo-yo				
Whistling				
Writing a story				

Figure 15.   (*continued*)

8

Sibshop Discussion and Peer Support Activities

Peer support and discussion among participants occur throughout a Sibshop. Often, discussion is incidental to another activity, such as the introductory activities described in Chapter 7. Frequently, the discussion and peer support are informal: One of the reasons we like cooking activities is because of the sharing that takes place while grating cheese for pizza or Super Nachos. Sometimes the support is unspoken, with participants taking comfort in the knowledge that they are among peers:

> *Interviewer:* "Your mom told me you go to Sibshops. Do you like them?"
>
> *Justin, age 12:* "Yes. I don't have to worry about the kids teasing me about my brother and I don't have to feel that much different there because I'm not the only kid around who has a mentally delayed brother."
>
> *Interviewer:* "Do you guys talk to each other about it?"
>
> *Justin:* "Sometimes, but not too much—we just feel it there." (Morrow, 1992, p. 1)

Support and discussion are also encouraged by more formal Sibshop activities designed to invite/encourage participants to reflect on their experiences with their siblings with special needs. These activities offer a counterpoint to the lively recreational activities. Whether it is formal or informal, planned or incidental, the support offered at a Sibshop seeks to accomplish two Sibshop goals:

Goal 2: Sibshops will provide brothers and sisters with opportunities to discuss common joys and concerns with other siblings of children with special needs.

> Goal 3: Sibshops will provide brothers and sisters with an opportunity to learn how others handle situations commonly experienced by siblings of children with special needs.

The majority of activities presented in this chapter are designed to allow brothers and sisters—perhaps for the first time—a chance to discuss their lives with others who share similar experiences. Other activities are designed to encourage discussion on a variety of topics. Although these activities may make reference to the sibling with special needs, "sibling issues" are not the sole focus. Providing discussion activities on other topics acknowledges that participants are more than a "brother-or-sister-of-a-person-with-special-needs."

Sibshop peer support and discussion activities are *not* a form of group therapy, nor are they an adequate substitute for a child who needs intensive counseling, although they may be "therapeutic" for some siblings. Children who may need to be referred for other services include:

Children showing signs of depression as demonstrated by reports of decreased appetite, sleep disturbance, chronic fatigue, apathy, loss of interest in previously enjoyed activities, changes in behavior or personality, or preoccupation with the subject of death
Children who display outbursts of anger or emotional lability
Children who demonstrate low self-concept or describe themselves as worthless or not appreciated by anyone
Children who are extremely withdrawn or noncommunicative
Children who act out in the group or are markedly defiant
Children who report a lot of stress symptoms or physical complaints (Usdane & Melmed, 1988, p. 13)

When in doubt, facilitators should always err in the direction of safety and consult the child's parents about the child's possible need for further assistance.

The following sample Sibshop discussion activities will help get you started.

TIME CAPSULES

Materials: Slips of paper (as described below), aluminum foil, "capsules" (e.g., film canisters, paper tubes, plastic eggs), a small box

In Time Capsules, brothers and sisters get to talk about various "times" in their lives. To prepare, write the times, listed below, on individual pieces of paper. Then place the papers in individual "time capsules" listed above, wrapped in aluminum foil to give them a fu-

turistic look. An alternate method is to place the slips of paper in a shoe box that is made to look like a time capsule. Participants then select a capsule or a piece of paper from the capsule for the group to discuss. Examples of times could include:

A time when I was really proud of my brother or sister
A time when I was really proud of something I did
A time when I really was embarrassed by my brother or sister
A time when my brother or sister caused problems with a friend
A time when I helped my brother or sister in a special way
A time when my brother or sister helped me in a special way
A time when my brother or sister really made me mad
A time when my brother or sister made me laugh
A time when I was confused about my brother's or sister's disability

MOCCASINS

Materials: None

Moccasins asks participants to see the world from their siblings' point of view. Share with the group the Native American proverb: "Do not judge a man until you have walked a mile in his moccasins." Discuss what this means. Each member of the group then gets to "try on the moccasins" of his or her brother and sister. Acknowledge that while no one can really speak for another person, brothers and sisters are as qualified as anyone to imagine what their brothers and sisters who have disabilities might say. Discuss questions such as:

What would your sibling say about having a disability?
What would your sibling say about having you as a sibling?
What would your sibling say about his or her life?
What would your sibling say about school?
What would your sibling say about his or her friends?

SOUND-OFF

Materials: Sound-Off activity sheet, pencils

Sound-Off is an open-ended activity that gives participants permission to air their feelings about life with a sibling who has special needs. To begin, hold up the Sound-Off sheet (Figure 16) and announce that "during Sound-Off we'll have a chance to tell others how we feel about having a sibling with special needs. Everyone will probably fill out this sheet differently. For instance, someone might write, 'If I could tell the *whole world* just one *great* thing about having a brother or sister with special needs it would be: *He's a really neat guy even though he has a hard time learning.*' Someone else might write, 'If I could tell *the kids on the school bus* just one *bad* thing about having a brother or sister with special needs it would be: *I hate it when they pick on my brother.*' "

Distribute the workshop sheets and pencils, and give participants 5 minutes to complete them (and illustrate them if they wish). At the end of 5 minutes, encourage participants to read their Sound-Off sheet. There is frequently a wide range of responses, including some very personal comments. Respect the wishes of those who do not wish to share.

DEAR AUNT BLABBY

Materials: Letters to Aunt Blabby in individual envelopes, addressed to Dear Aunt Blabby (See appendix at the end of this chapter.)

Since it was first presented over 10 years ago, the most durable of Sibshop discussion activities has been Dear Aunt Blabby. Aunt Blabby, a bogus advice columnist, receives letters from brothers and sisters who have concerns similar to those the participants may expe-

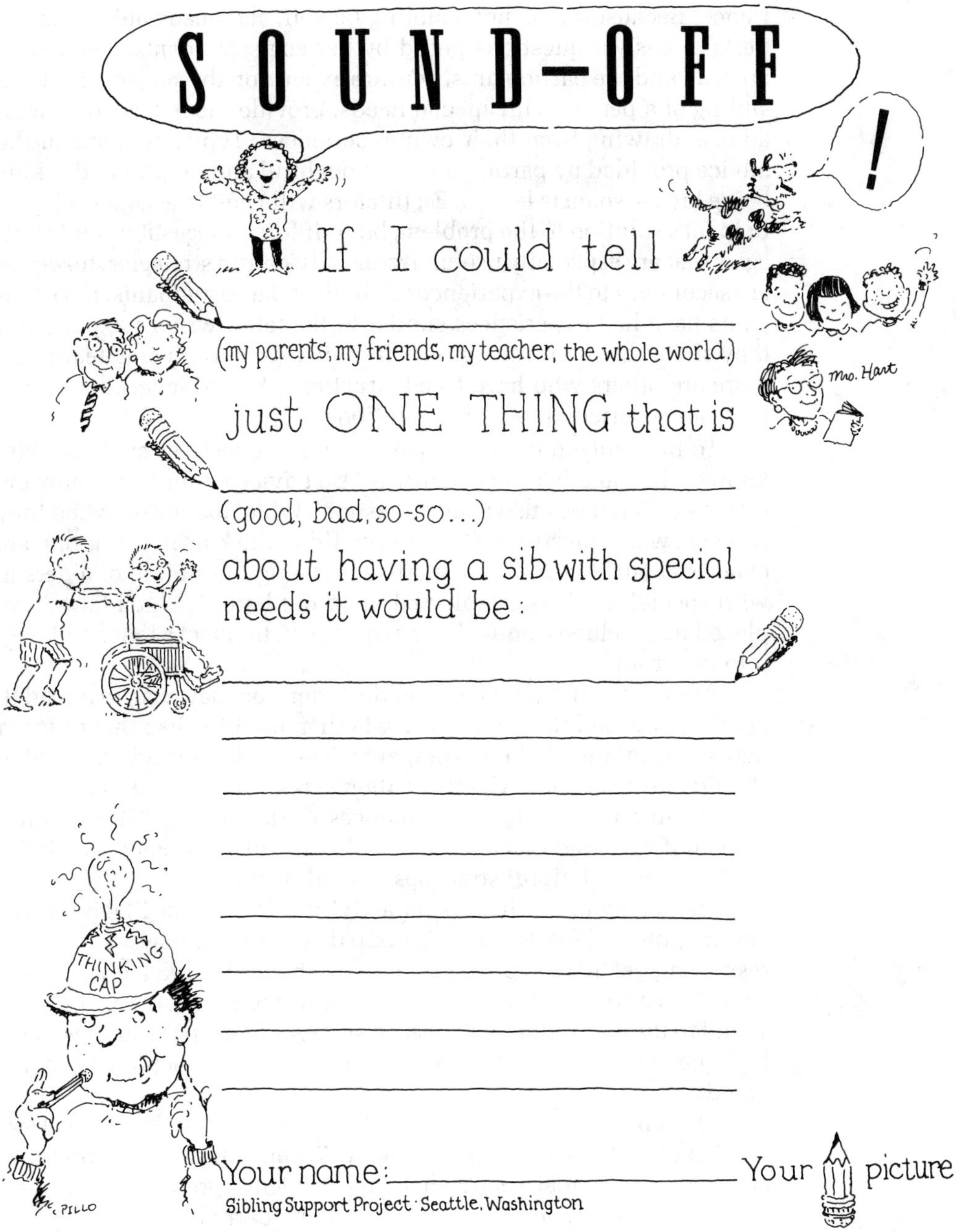
SOUND-OFF
!
If I could tell
(my parents, my friends, my teacher, the whole world.)
Ms. Hart
just ONE THING that is
(good, bad, so-so...)
about having a sib with special needs it would be:
THINKING CAP
Your name:
Your picture
Sibling Support Project · Seattle, Washington

Figure 16. Sound-Off activity sheet. (For the reader's use, this material may be reproduced. From Meyer, D.J., & Vadasy, P.F. [1994]. *Sibshops: Workshops for siblings of children with special needs.* Copyright © 1994 Paul H. Brookes Publishing Co.)

rience. Because she is not a sibling herself, she needs help from experts to answer questions posed by her correspondents. The letters are read and the participants, who are experts on the subject of being a sibling of a person with special needs, provide the letter writer with advice, drawing from their own experiences. Typically, some of the advice provided by participants is thoughtful and helpful and—kids being kids—some is less so. Facilitators will want to accept each participant's solution to the problem, but reinforce suggestions and strategies that are especially useful. Actual advice and strategies, however, are secondary to the experiences shared by the participants. If participants have had experiences similar to the letter writer's experience, they share them with the group. In doing so, participants learn that there are others who have faced situations they have faced and that there are a variety of possible solutions.

To introduce the activity, ask the group questions such as: Who knows what an advice columnist is? Do advice columnists know everything? Can they answer any question? What do they do when they can't answer a question? What do you think the kids in this group are experts about? Once their expertise on being the sibling of a person with special needs is established, hold out letters (which have been placed in envelopes) and allow a participant to select a letter and read it to the group.

After the participant has read the letter, you may wish to reread it, pausing now and then to inquire whether anything like this has ever happened to any of the participants. Then ask their advice: "What should Perplexed do?" Gently challenge responses by asking the participant to consider the consequences of the advice: "What would happen if you tried that approach?" End the discussion of each letter by restating the helpful strategies offered by the group.

Like many other discussion activities, Dear Aunt Blabby works best in groups of five to eight. A group this size encourages a variety of responses, yet allows each participant a chance to talk. Although it is a good idea to have six or seven letters in reserve, you may only respond to three or four letters in each session. To keep the interest level high, be sure to move on to a new letter before participants become bored.

The appendix to this chapter contains sample letters to Dear Aunt Blabby for you to use or adapt. When selecting, adapting, or creating letters, make sure that the problems presented are sufficiently common to allow discussion among participants.

GOOD NEWS/BAD NEWS

Materials: Activity sheet (see Figure 17) and pencils

Good News/Bad News gives participants permission to harbor the ambivalent feelings most people have about their siblings, special

---

Good News/Bad News

Many brothers and sisters say that having a brother or sister with special needs is sort of like a good news/bad news joke. Sometimes it's great and sometimes it's not so great!

Find a partner to interview. Find out what the bad news and the good news is for this person. Then switch and let this person interview you.

Allow 5 minutes for each interview.

Your name: _____

Name of person you are interviewing: _____

The good news is: _____

The bad news is: _____

The good news is: _____

The bad news is: _____

The good news is: _____

The bad news is: _____

The good news is: _____

The bad news is: _____

Figure 17.   Good News/Bad News activity sheet.

needs or not. Introduce this activity by saying: "A lot of kids say that having a brother or sister with a disability is sort of like a good news/bad news story," and share the following story:

> I've got some good news and bad news about your brother.
>
> The good news is: Your brother got to ride on an airplane!
>
> The bad news is: Your brother fell out of the plane.
>
> The good news is: He was wearing a parachute!
>
> The bad news is: The parachute didn't open.
>
> The good news is: He landed in a haystack!
>
> The bad news is: There was a pitchfork in the haystack!

Present participants with a workshop sheet such as the one shown in Figure 17. Divide your group into pairs and instruct them to interview each other. At the end of 10 minutes, have the pairs share their findings with the group.

WORD PORTRAIT

Materials: Lined paper or index cards, pencils, butcher paper, and tape or chalkboard

Sibling programs provide participants with a chance to talk to other brothers and sisters about the good and not-so-good parts of living with a sibling who has a disability. Word Portrait allows siblings to discuss their ambivalent feelings in a novel way.

Word Portrait helps provide participants with words for the wide range of emotions about their siblings with special needs. To begin, tell the group that they are going to create portraits of their siblings who have special needs. Explain that instead of using paints, these portraits will be created using single words.

Give participants a piece of lined paper or an index card and a pencil with an eraser. Explain that to create a word portrait, each participant should write down as many single words as possible that describe his or her brother or sister.

To get the group started, ask a few participants to give examples of words they could use to describe their siblings (i.e., brave, loving, goofy, a pain). Acknowledge that all the words do not have to be flattering.

Give participants 5 minutes to complete their individual word portraits. Next, have the participants share them with the group. (Participants can change their lists as they listen.) To create a "group portrait" of brothers and sisters who have special needs, transcribe words on a chalkboard as they are read, or simply tape the cards or papers to a wall.

20 QUESTIONS

Materials: Butcher paper and markers; or chalkboard and chalk

Having a sibling with a disability is only one part of the lives of the children in your group. This variation of 20 Questions will give participants opportunities to talk about their emotions as they pertain to the many facets of their lives.

On butcher paper or a chalkboard, list emotion words such as *happy, sad, angry, afraid, surprised, curious, worried, embarrassed,* and *proud.* Encourage participants to add emotion words that they think should be included. Have one participant select an emotion (e.g., *surprised*) for the first round. Then, ask a volunteer to *think* of a time she was surprised, but not *tell* anyone. The group, then, tries to guess what made her feel surprised using only yes or no questions ("Were you surprised on your birthday?"). Count questions asked. If the number of questions reaches 20, have the person reveal the time. If a person correctly guesses before that time, that person becomes the next "guessee." You may continue with the same emotion for the next round or elect to change it.

Source: Adapted from *Learning to Care* (Feshback, Feshback, Fauvre, & Ballard-Campbell, 1983)

OPPOSITES

Materials: Index cards and a small box or bag

The Opposites activity considers two sides of familiar events. It can be a fine introduction to role playing. On one side of an index card, write one reaction to the event; on the other side, the opposite reaction. Events and reactions could include:

Coming home from a fun day
Coming home from a rotten day

Eating something new—and you like it
Eating something new—and you hate it

Going somewhere you *love* to go with your parents
Going somewhere you *hate* to go with your parents

Listening to beautiful music
Listening to horrible, screechy music

Listening to someone praise you
Listening to someone criticize you

Reading a book that is funny
Reading a book that is boring

Smelling something delicious
Smelling something awful

Touching something that feels nice and soft
Touching something that feels slimy

Watching a movie that makes you laugh
Watching a movie that makes you cry

Being told good news
Being told bad news

Place cards in a bag or box. Inform participants that during this activity they will be actors. Explain that in the bag or box are cards that describe different situations for them to act out. When a person selects a card, he or she should read only the side that is up when pulled from the bag or box. The person then acts out what the card says until told to stop. Then the card is handed to another person who acts out what is described on the other side of the card. After both situations have been acted out, the audience guesses what was acted out.

During the activity, you may wish to discuss with the group how they guessed what was being acted out and how the person demonstrated the situation.

Source: Adapted from *Learning to Care* (Feshback et al., 1983)

MY VERY SPECIAL DREAM

Materials: Pencils, crayons, or felt tip pens, and workshop sheet

A well-run Sibshop provides participants with a safe place to share, to wonder, and to dream. Try this activity once your members have developed trust in one another. It will provide participants with a chance to share the dreams they have for themselves and for their brothers and sisters.

Ask the participants, "When you were little, what did you want to be when you grew up?" As participants respond, acknowledge their responses as dreams: "You wanted to be an astronaut." "You dreamed that you would be a famous movie star."

Ask participants whether only "little kids" have dreams about the future. Comment that everyone can have dreams, even grown-ups. Ask, "What do you think your parents' dreams are for you?" Tell them that they are going to have a chance to dream about themselves and about their brother or sister who has special needs. Hand out drawing instruments and workshop sheets and tell them that they can draw the dreams they have for themselves and for their brothers and sisters who have special needs. See Figure 18 for a sample dream sheet.

If they need further clarification, let them know that they can illustrate any dream they want. You can suggest: "Your dream can be about what you wish will happen when you grow up or what you wish will happen next week or year." After participants complete their drawings, have them share the results with the group.

Source: Adapted from KIDPOWER (Burton, 1991)

WHEEL OF FEELINGS BEANBAG TOSS

Materials: One beanbag and a sheet of poster board on which to draw a feelings wheel. When completed, the wheel should be at least 2 feet in diameter.

Have the group sit in a circle on the floor, with the feelings wheel in the center, several feet from the participants. Explain what will happen in the first round and demonstrate by taking the first turn.

During Round 1, each player takes a turn tossing the bag onto the wheel. The feeling word on which the beanbag falls determines the feeling the player will describe. The player then provides an example of when he or she felt that way. Thank each person in turn for sharing his or her feelings. Complete the first round before explaining Round 2.

During Round 2, each player again tosses the beanbag. This time each player talks about one time he or she felt that way about his or her

Figure 18.   Sample sheet: My Very Special Dream. (For the reader's use, this material may be reproduced. From Meyer, D.J., & Vadasy, P.F. [1994]. *Sibshops: Workshops for siblings of children with special needs.* Copyright © 1994 Paul H. Brookes Publishing Co.)

brother or sister *with a disability.* If a cofacilitator has a sibling with a disability, he or she may wish to go first, modeling the type of response he or she wishes from the participants. This round frequently sparks discussion, as participants share similar experiences. Cofacilitators may wish to prompt participants with comments such as, "I wonder if anyone else ever felt that way?" At the end of each turn, be sure to return to the comment of the "tosser" and thank him or her for sharing before passing the beanbag.

Source: Adapted from *Child Support through Small Group Counseling* (Landy, 1988)

SAME AND DIFFERENT

Materials: Photos of participants and their siblings with special needs (as described below), butcher paper and markers, or chalkboard and chalk

Especially good with younger brothers and sisters, this activity reinforces what many brothers and sisters know intuitively—people with disabilities are more like their family members than they are different. Consider it a preadvocacy activity! Prior to the Sibshop, send a note home requesting that participants bring two photos (e.g., school pictures) to the next Sibshop: one photo of the child with special needs and one of the child who attends the Sibshop.

To begin, select one pair of photos and post them where participants can see them. On a piece of paper or chalkboard, make two columns, *Same* and *Different*. Say to the participants: "Here are Melinda and Michael. How are they the same?" Have the group brainstorm as many ways as possible that Melinda and Michael are the same (same hair color, same family, etc.) before asking Melinda. Then ask Melinda to help the group out by telling other ways that she is the same as Michael (both like same television shows, both like the color blue). Record the ways that they are the same in the appropriate column. Repeat this for differences.

Finally, ask, "Is one of these kids better than the other?" Briefly discuss how *different* does not mean better. Ask the group, "Who would like to go next?"

STRENGTHS AND WEAKNESSES, JR.

Materials: Chalkboard and chalk

Try this activity with younger brothers and sisters who may not have the writing skills to accomplish easily the Strengths and Weaknesses activity found in Chapter 7. Divide a long chalkboard as shown in Figure 19, with participants' names on the top and their "special needs" siblings' names on the bottom. Announce to the group: "Everybody has strengths—that is, something they do well. And everybody has weaknesses—things they do not do so well." Provide dramatic examples of abilities of which you are proud and equally dramatic examples of things at which you are truly awful. Then ask the group: "Do you think that people who have special needs have strengths—things they do really well? How about weaknesses—things they don't do so well?"

Tell the group that they will now have a chance to tell about their strengths and weaknesses and the strengths and weaknesses of their brothers and sisters with special needs, and that you will list these on the board. Let them know that they can add to their lists of strengths and weaknesses as you go along. Frequently, participants will be "inspired" to add another strength or weakness after hearing another participant's contribution.

Sibshop Kids!!			
Tony's strengths	*Brian's strengths*	*Tashina's strengths*	*Danielle's strengths*
Basketball Videogames	Soccer Math Pizza making	Jump rope Science Singing	Keeping my room clean Spelling
Tony's weaknesses	*Brian's weaknesses*	*Tashina's weaknesses*	*Danielle's weaknesses*
Making his bed Spelling	Jump rope Saving money	Spelling Homework	Cooking Telling jokes

Our Sibs Who Have Special Needs			
Allison's strengths	*Rachel's strengths*	*Tracey's strengths*	*Kelly's strengths*

Funny
Learning to
  walk
	Soccer
	Likes to cook
		Can't think of
		  any
			Very curious
			Learning to
			  sign

Allison's weaknesses	*Rachel's weaknesses*	*Tracey's weaknesses*	*Kelly's weaknesses*

Has temper
  tantrums
	Math
	Gets in Brian's
	  stuff
		Embarrasses
		  me
			Gets into
			  Danielle's
			  stuff
			Can't talk

Figure 19.   Sample chart of Strengths and Weaknesses, Jr.

THINGS I LIKE TO DO

Materials: Activity sheet and pencils

This activity gives participants an opportunity to share and discuss things they like to do with their brothers and sisters who have special needs as well as with other family members. Do not use this activity if a parent of any of the participants is deceased. Distribute pencils and an activity sheet such as Figure 20.

Have participants share what they wrote, spending a little extra time discussing what they like to do with their brothers and sisters with special needs.

Source: Adapted from *Child Support* (Landy, 1988)

SOMETHING

Materials: Index cards, as described below

If your young sibling group has a flair for the dramatic, try this dramatic play game. Write, on index cards, "somethings" such as:

Things I Like to Do

My Name: _____

I like to do different things with different people.

Something I like to do with my brother   Something I like to do with my mother:
or sister with special needs:

Something I like to do with my father: Something I like to do with my other
                                           brothers and sisters:

Something I like to do with just one   Something I like to do with a group of
friend: friends:

Something I like to do all by myself!:

If you have extra time, draw a picture of one of the above ideas on the back of this
sheet!

Figure 20.   Things I Like to Do activity sheet (Adapted from Landy, 1988.)

Something I do well
Something I hate to do
Something I like to do
Something I like to do alone
Something I like to do with my brother or sister
Something I like to do with my friend
Something my brother or sister did that embarrassed me
Something my brother or sister does that bugs me
Something my brother or sister does that makes me proud
Something that I do every summer
Something that scares me

Place cards in a box. One by one, give participants a chance to select a card and read it to the group. The participant then pantomimes what the card says as the group guesses. Before selecting another card, ask, "Who else would like to try this card?" Throughout, emphasize participants' uniqueness.

Source: Adapted from *Child Support* (Landy, 1988, p. 78)

HOW YA FEELIN'?

Materials: List of feeling words

During this activity, a participant pantomimes actions that demonstrate an emotion or feeling word while the group guesses the word. To begin, tell the group to guess the feeling word you will act out. If, for instance, you wish to demonstrate "yucky," you might pantomime reaching into your pocket only to find a wad of gum. Or watch a mushy television show—something many grade schoolers find truly yucky. After the demonstration, ask for volunteers. Whisper the feeling word to the volunteer, choosing easier words for younger players. The participant then moves in a way that demonstrates the feeling or emotion. The group attempts to guess the word being demonstrated. Continue with a new volunteer.

Here is a list of feeling words to get you started:

Amazed	Embarrassed	Nervous
Angry	Encouraged	Pleased
Annoyed	Excited	Proud
Anxious	Frustrated	Puzzled
Ashamed	Gloomy	Relaxed
Bored	Grumpy	Resentful
Burned-out	Guilty	Restless
Cheerful	Happy	Sad
Contented	Hateful	Satisfied
Critical	Indifferent	Scared
Delighted	Interested	Silly
Depressed	Irritated	Surprised
Disappointed	Jealous	Tense
Discouraged	Left out	Thankful
Disgusted	Loving	Tired
Dissatisfied	Miserable	Worried
Eager		

GRAFFITI WALL

Materials: A long sheet of butcher paper, markers, and crayons

Graffiti Wall provides participants with a chance to express and discuss a wide range of feelings that they may have toward their brothers, sisters, and parents in a novel way. To prepare, line a long wall (e.g., a hallway) with butcher paper and make vertical lines with a marker to create columns 2 feet wide. At the top of each column, print, in large letters, a word from the array of ambivalent feelings your participants may have for their brothers and sisters, for example,

proud, angry, left out, inspired, embarrassed, and *confused.* Leave two columns blank. The number of columns you have will depend, in part, on the number of participants in your Sibshop: You should have at least one column for every two participants, with a minimum of eight columns.

In an area or room away from the wall, ask participants to close their eyes and think of their brother or sister for a short while, perhaps 30–45 seconds. Then, with their eyes still closed, ask them to volunteer a feeling word that describes how they feel when they think about their sibling. After this have them open their eyes. Explain to the group that most brothers and sisters have mixed feelings about their siblings, regardless of whether they have special needs or not. Tell the group that, in Graffiti Wall, they will have a chance to express this mixed bag of feelings in a new way. Hand the participants one felt-tip pen each (preferably each a different color) and lead them to the wall that you have prepared. Review the feelings listed on the wall, noting that these are feelings that brothers and sisters sometimes have about one another. Ask if they have any other feelings that should go into the two blank columns. Explain that they are to choose a column and in that column write about or illustrate a time when they had that feeling about their sibling with special needs. For participants who have poor writing skills, facilitators can help by serving as scribes. After participants have finished one column, they are free to move to another column and contribute an additional story or picture. At the end, review the stories and pictures in each column with the group.

OPEN DISCUSSIONS

Open group discussions may be used successfully with older siblings or with articulate younger participants who do not require the structure of a Dear Aunt Blabby or Time Capsule activity to talk about their lives. They may also be valuable for siblings who have participated in some of the above activities and are ready to participate in a more in-depth or personal discussion.

Open discussions follow a facilitated group discussion format. Although participants select the topics for discussion, the discussion is not without structure. Facilitators introduce the activity, establish a few ground rules, probe for topics of common interest or concern, and facilitate and close discussion when appropriate.

Below is an example of how one facilitator introduced a discussion and established ground rules. He adapted his opening remarks from those given by Ken Moses at a 1982 conference offered for high school–age brothers and sisters:

All of you are different from one another in hundreds of ways: what you like to eat, the way you look, the clothes you choose, and so on.

But there is an important way that you are the same: you are all brothers and sisters of children with special needs.

We've learned a lot about kids with special needs, but very little about their brothers and sisters. We don't know whether having a special sib is a good thing, a bad thing, or a little of both. Today, we'll have a chance to switch roles. In a way, you'll be the teacher and I'll be the student, although we'll all be learning from one another. We'll have a chance to learn what you think and how you feel about your special sib, your parents, your family, your friends, and yourself.

There are a few rules. First, I'd like you to talk about yourself and how you feel rather than guess how others feel. Second, I'd like you to feel free to disagree with one another and me. If someone says something that doesn't ring true to you, speak up! Third, I'd like us to maintain confidentiality. That usually means not telling anyone outside of the group what was said inside the group. I'd like it to mean that we are kind to one another. That means not laughing when someone shares something personal. It also means that when we talk about what we say outside the group, we protect one another and do not use names.

Now, I'd like you to introduce yourself, and tell us what brings you here today. If there is something you'd like the group to talk about, please mention it.

Going around the circle, siblings introduce themselves and share why they came. Facilitators will wish to acknowledge and accept all responses, including the inevitable, "My parents made me come." As participants introduce themselves, facilitators may ask a question or make a comment. Throughout the introductions, participants may need to be reminded that they can ask each other questions, make comments, or suggest topics for discussion.

When a sibling offers a problem or topic for discussion, the facilitator will want to find out if it is a concern that is shared by other participants. The facilitator may wish to "check in" with the other siblings and ask, "I wonder if other brothers and sisters have ever experienced anything like this." This will not only give the facilitator an idea of how widespread the concern is, it will also make the participants reflect on their lives and think about their common experiences. The facilitator should list the topics the siblings suggest and note how many siblings indicate interest in each topic.

Look over the topics the siblings mention (we recommend that you write them down), and select a topic for discussion. The topic you choose will depend on the siblings' relative interest in the topic and its appropriateness for discussion. Some topics may not be appropriate—they may be too specific for general discussion. Some topics may be requests for specific information. Of course, you should not ignore these topics or questions, but rather try to address them individually.

To begin the discussion, ask the participant who suggested the chosen topic to share some further thoughts on the subject, and then open it up to the group for discussion. For instance, if the siblings want to talk about what to do when strangers stare at their sibling, the facilitator may wish to guide the discussion to elicit a wide range of problem-solving strategies for responding to people's stares. Below is an example of questions that can be used to facilitate a group discussion of effective strategies. Remember to use questions that begin with *what*, *why*, and *how*, because those are most likely to elicit discussion.

Step 1.   What is the problem?

Ask the person who brought up the topic to expand on it. For example: "Shannon, tell us some more about what happens when people stare at your brother."

Step 2.   Who else has the problem?

You probably know from the siblings' introductions who else has experienced this problem. Present the concern to the group. For example: "Other people said that people sometimes stare at their sibs. I'm interested: What happens to the rest of you?"

Step 3.   Why does the problem exist?

This can help the group explore the issues underlying the problem. For example: "Why do you think people stare at people who have disabilities? Why does this bother you?"

Step 4.   What have you tried?

This will help draw out the array of strategies participants have used. "What do you do when people stare at your brother or sister?" The facilitator should acknowledge all responses but give special attention to those that are appropriate, creative, or workable.

Step 5.   Has it worked?

An important follow-up question to Step 4. For example: "What happens when you do that or say that?"

Step 6.   What are some other ways of solving this problem?

Drawing on what the group has learned in Step 3 (*Why does the problem exist?*) and the strategies that worked in Step 4 (*What have you tried?*), the group, under the facilitator's guidance, searches for additional creative solutions. For example, say, "A moment ago we said that people who stared at people with disabilities did so because they probably do not know anyone who has a disability. What are some other ways that we can help people get to know people with special needs so they will not stare at them?" (A most creative solution to this problem was volunteered by a sibling whose mother says to staring strangers: "You seem to be interested in my daughter. Would you like to meet her?")

Remember that these are only guidelines for group problem-solving; not all discussions will follow this outline exactly. Also, discussion may not always focus on problems siblings experience. Participants may also wish to express their thoughts and opinions on a wide variety of subjects related to their experiences as siblings of a child with special needs.

CONCLUSION

Well run, Sibshops discussion activities are among the richest and most memorable experiences we can offer participants. During these activities, participants share knowing laughs, discuss the good times and the tough spots, and trade war stories and helpful strategies. When they learn that their agemates sometimes feel the same way they do, participants experience camaradery, their feelings are validated, and they are less likely to feel alone with their concerns. These activities can be potent experiences for the people who lead them as well. The insight and wisdom expressed by these young participants often stay with facilitators for a long, long time.

Appendix
The Dear Aunt Blabby Letters

$$T$$ he first collection of letters to Dear Aunt Blabby are from brothers and sisters of children who have developmental disabilities. The second collection, starting on page 148, are from siblings of children who have cancer or other chronic illnesses. No matter which type of sibling group you are working with, be sure to read all the letters. You will likely find letters you can easily adapt for the participants you serve.

Many thanks to Kim Armer, Marcia Bloom, Cathy Bonner, Terri Dawson, Carol Ferreir, Martha Grady, John Grove, "Jennifer," Gail Karp, Kathy Kelker, Doug Krieger, Donna McGlaughlin, Barbara Papanestor, Paul Polisbo, Sarah Potter, Beverly Powanda, Robin Read-Giase, Paula Recchia, Becky Takemoto, Ann Verbanac, Pam Vose, N. Weiner, and Richard Wheland who each contributed a letter to Dear Aunt Blabby. All 71 letters have been rewritten to achieve an overall third-grade reading level (Flesch-Kincaid) as measured by Grammatik 4 software. (The Flesch-Kincaid grade level scores are readability scores based on a subroutine of the Grammar Check function contained in Microsoft Word for Windows, 6.0.)

Dear Aunt Blabby,

Sometimes I feel like the invisible man. My brother has Down syndrome. He has a lot of needs that seem to take up all my parents' time. It seems like the only time my parents pay attention to *me* is when I get into trouble. How do I let them know that they have *two* kids instead of one?

(signed)
The Invisible Man

Dear Aunt Blabby,

Maybe you can help me with my problem. My big sister has a disability. Sometimes, my friends ask me what's the matter with her and how she got that way. Once my teacher even asked. I never know how to explain it. Any suggestions?

(signed)
Speechless

Dear Aunt Blabby,

Boy, am I mad! For the fifth time tonight my sister has bugged me while I'm trying to do my homework. She is always bugging me! Especially when my friends come over. Help!

(signed)
Fuming

Dear Aunt Blabby,

I have a problem. My brother Michael has a disability. I hate to admit it, but sometimes he embarrasses me. Don't get me wrong—in a lot of ways Mike is a great guy. He can really do a lot for himself, even with all of his special needs. My problem is that I get embarrassed when he acts up in church or has a temper tantrum at the shopping mall. What can I do?

(signed)
Embarrassed

Dear Aunt Blabby,

I hope you can help. My brother has a lot of problems, and I have a lot of questions! My mom never really told me what happened to Josh. I feel funny asking her. Can you give me some tips on how to ask my mom about what happened to Josh?

(signed)
Need to Know

Dear Aunt Blabby,

Maybe you can help me. I really like my sister. She has a lot of special needs, but I love her a lot. My problem is that I get bored just going for walks and watching TV with her. What else can I do with her that will be fun for both of us?

(signed)
Curious

Dear Aunt Blabby,

I have a problem that maybe you can help me with. Just because my brother has a disability and I don't, my parents expect me to be a "Superkid." They expect me to get perfect grades in school. Does that seem fair to you? What can I do?

(signed)
I'm No Superkid

Dear Aunt Blabby,

I'm really worried. If I don't get an A in history, I won't get in the honor society. My parents have so many problems with my sister. I'd really like to make them happy with my schoolwork. Do you think they will be disappointed if I don't get in the honor society?

(signed)
Worried

Dear Aunt Blabby,

Is it O.K. to tease your sister? I mean, I tease my other brothers and sisters, but when I tease my "special" sister, my grandma yells at me. I'm not doing it to be mean or anything—it's just teasing. Is it O.K. or not?

(signed)
To Tease or Not to Tease

Dear Aunt Blabby,

I don't know what to do. My little brother Mark has lots of problems learning. In September, Mark started going to my school. Some kids at my school make fun of the special education kids. I even heard them call my brother names and laugh at things he does. Aunt Blabby, what should I do?

(signed)
Perplexed

Dear Aunt Blabby,

I'm not sure what I should do. I have a new friend, Tom. We have a lot of fun together. We like the same sports and video games. My problem is that when Tom is joking around, he will say things like "cut it out, you retard!" I hate it when he says that because my baby sister, Jamie, has Down syndrome. How can I get him to stop using that word?

(signed)
Still Want to Be Friends

Dear Aunt Blabby,

My brother uses a wheelchair. When we go to the mall, people are always looking at him. I never know what to do. Sometimes people look at him and smile. But sometimes people just stare. Do I stare back at them or just pretend I don't see them? What can I do?

(signed)
Tired of Rude People

Dear Aunt Blabby,

My little sister is deaf. Our whole family is learning sign language. It is *fun* to be able to talk in a secret language! But I feel funny about using signs when I'm with my family in the mall or something. Sometimes kids make fun of us. They will flap their hands or make weird noises. Even adults stare at us sometimes and use words that are wrong like "deaf and dumb." Mom tells me I have to be polite to adults. How can I tell them to use the *right* words without sounding rude?

(signed)
Kid Teacher

Dear Aunt Blabby,

I am beginning to feel like Cinderella. My parents make me take care of my little brothers and sisters, especially my little sister who has autism. Also, I spend every Saturday helping my mom clean the house. I never get to do anything! Does that seem fair to you?

(signed)
Where's My Fairy Godmother?

Dear Aunt Blabby,

My sister is driving me nuts. Melissa is 4 years old and has Down syndrome and everybody thinks she's so cute. Wherever we go, it's Melissa this and Melissa that. It's like I'm not even there! What can I do?

(signed)
Look at Me Too!

Dear Aunt Blabby,

My brother Jason has a hard time at school. My dad says he has a learning disability. School is pretty easy for me, except for last week when I really bombed out on a math test. Do you think that I might have a learning disability too?

(signed)
Worried

Dear Aunt Blabby,

My brother gets away with murder. He never has to do anything around the house just because he has a disability. I know he can do things. It's just that my parents won't make him.

(signed)
Ripped Off

Dear Aunt Blabby,

I feel kind of bad. Next month I will turn 16 and my mom says that I can take driver's ed. My sister is 18 and has a disability. My mom says she won't ever be able to drive. Should I feel bad that I can do things that my sister can't?

(signed)
Confused

Dear Aunt Blabby,

Lately, I've been thinking about the future. Our family lives in Ohio, but I think it would be neat to live in California someday. When I grow up, will I have to stay in Ohio to take care of my brother who has a disability?

(signed)
California Dreamin'

Dear Aunt Blabby,

Help! No one seems to understand! When I tell my friends about my little sister, they don't understand what a neat kid she is and all the things she can do. All they see is her wheelchair and floppy arms. Am I the only one with this problem? What can I do?

(signed)
I Like My Sister!

Dear Aunt Blabby,

I wish I knew someone who has a sister with problems like Amy's. I have friends, but they don't understand what it is like when your little sister has seizures and gets sick and goes to the hospital all the time. My friends don't understand the good stuff either. I was really proud when Amy (who is 6) finally learned to go the bathroom by herself! Are there other kids who know what it's like to have a sister like Amy?

(signed)
Who Knows?

Dear Aunt Blabby,

I wish I was like my friend Jenny. She has a big sister and they do lots of things together. They borrow each other's clothes, put on plays, yell at each other, and laugh a lot too. My sister, Melinda, has lots of problems. I love her, but we're not like Jenny and her sister at all. I wish we were.

(signed)
Only Sort of a Sister

Dear Aunt Blabby,

I have an older brother and sister with special needs. My parents and teachers expect me to do everything right. They call me "the lucky normal one." I know my parents have lots of problems, so I want to make them happy. But sometimes I feel under so much pressure! Do other kids feel this way?

(signed)
Not So Lucky

Dear Aunt Blabby,

When my sister does not cooperate in school, the teachers come to me to get some help. I feel sorry that my sister is having such a hard time, but can't they deal with it? How can I get the teachers to stop coming to me?

(signed)
Not My Job!

Dear Aunt Blabby,

My mother dresses my brother like a nerd. I want him to look cool like a normal kid. What can I do?

(signed)
Joe Cool

Dear Aunt Blabby,

My brother has Down syndrome. When our family goes to the mall, he is very friendly with people. Even if he doesn't know someone, he will give them a hug! He's 10 years old and it's sort of embarrassing. What can I do and not hurt my brother's feelings?

(signed)
Sensitive

Dear Aunt Blabby,

I always have to baby-sit for my sister. She has problems and my parents say I am the only one they can trust. I want to get a job after school but I'll feel bad if I leave them empty-handed. What should I do?

(signed)
Penniless

Dear Aunt Blabby,

My brother always wants to play with my friends and me. He can't hit the ball. He can't catch the ball. He doesn't understand the rules. My friends get mad. This is more than I can take!

(signed)
Caught Between

Dear Aunt Blabby,

I just started a new school. My mom said that I can invite two friends to spend the day at my house on Saturday. I'm really excited about them coming over. I'm also a little worried about Tonya. Tonya has a lot of special problems, and my new friends don't know a thing about her. When should I tell them about Tonya? Before they come over? Or should I wait until they get to the house? What should I say?

(signed)
Anxious

Dear Aunt Blabby,

I got in trouble at school and almost got suspended because I punched a kid who was staring at my sister. He stared and said something to his friends, and then they all laughed and pointed at her. I admit, she looks different, but she is my sister and I love her. What should I do?

(signed)
Jake the Rake

Dear Aunt Blabby,

My sister has epilepsy. Last week, at my birthday party, my sister had a seizure in front of my friends. Yesterday, when my friends came over to play, my sister ran upstairs to her room, locked her door, and started to cry. How can I make her feel O.K.?

(signed)
The Pits

Dear Aunt Blabby,

I have a younger brother who has Down syndrome. He is not at school yet. Sometimes I see my school friends teasing other kids with Down syndrome. I feel like I should make them stop, but I want them to like me. What should I do?

(signed)
Soon It Will Be *My* Brother

Dear Aunt Blabby,
    My brother has Down syndrome. When we are together, people ask *me* questions for *him*. How can I get people to ask him—not me?
                                            (signed)
                                            He's Got Answers

Dear Aunt Blabby,
    I have a terrible secret. When my mom was pregnant with Jamie, I had this huge temper tantrum. My mom got real mad at me. Later that day, she went to the hospital and had Jamie. Now Jamie has all these problems. Dear Aunt Blabby, I think Jamie's problems are all my fault!
                                            (signed)
                                            Guilty

Dear Aunt Blabby,
    I have this problem. Yesterday, two people I know were talking about my brother and making fun of the noises he makes. They didn't see me, but I didn't stop them or stick up for my own brother! I feel bad and don't understand why I didn't stick up for him.

                                            (signed)
                                            Torn-Up Inside

Dear Aunt Blabby,
    My sister doesn't get asked to friends' houses or birthday parties like I do. She gets mad at me or Mom when I get to do something she can't. What should I do?
                                            (signed)
                                            Need a Life of My Own

Dear Aunt Blabby,
    My sister always complains to me about her spina bifida. She then upsets me by saying, "Why do you think God made me different?" I really don't know what to answer.
                                            (signed)
                                            Feeling Guilty

Dear Aunt Blabby,
    When I was little, I used to tell my parents that I wanted my sister Jenna to live with me when we grew up. Aunt Blabby, now I think I don't want her to always live with me. Is that O.K.? Where would she live? By the way, I love my sister a lot!
                                            (signed)
                                            Don't Know

Dear Aunt Blabby,

My brother is always getting into my room and totally trashing it. My mom doesn't make him clean it up. She says he can't clean it the way it is supposed to be cleaned. Mom says she doesn't have time to do it by herself. What do I do with him? And what do I do about my room?

(signed)
Miss Compulsively Neat

Dear Aunt Blabby,

My older brother Andrew has epilepsy. His seizures started when he was 10. I'm going to be 10 soon. Do you think I'll have seizures like my brother?

(signed)
A Little Worried

Dear Aunt Blabby,

You would think that the only kid that mattered in our family is Evan, my brother with Down syndrome. Whatever our family does, we do for Evan. On our vacations we go to these Down syndrome meetings. At dinner it's always Down syndrome this, Down syndrome that. My parents are always at some meeting about Evan or Down syndrome. Evan is an O.K. brother, I guess, but I'm sick of everything always being for him.

(signed)
Too Much

Dear Aunt Blabby,

My summer is ruined!! I was looking forward to sleeping in every morning and having fun and goofing off. My brother, who has autism, still has to go to school all summer. My mom makes me go with her when she drops him off. We have to get up at 7:00 A.M. and drive for an hour! Mom says I'm not old enough to stay by myself. There goes my time off. What can I do?

(signed)
Tired of Traveling

Dear Aunt Blabby,

I'm 11 years old and my brother is 14. My brother has lots of seizures even though he takes his medication. My parents don't want to leave him alone at home so we never get to go anywhere like the mall, the movies, or out to dinner. Mom can't find anyone to baby-sit for my brother because everybody is afraid of his seizures. Why do I have to suffer and not have any fun like all my friends?

(signed)
Feeling Trapped

Dear Aunt Blabby,

My sister has something called ADHD. My mom says sugar makes her jump around. Just because she can't have sugar, we have no candy, pop, or cookies in our house. Mom says if I have it then she will want it too. That's not fair!

(signed)
Sweet Tooth

Dear Aunt Blabby,

This will sound weird, but I wish my brother had Down syndrome. Some of the kids at our Sibshop talk about how cool their sibs are even if they have Downs. My brother has ADHD and is a pain. All the time! It is hard to find anything positive to say about him.

(signed)
Jealous

Dear Aunt Blabby,

I have a younger brother who has a disability. We go to the same school. Whenever I want to go to a school basketball or football game with my friends, my parents make me take my brother with me. Aunt Blabby, I love my brother, but I don't think this is fair. Does that seem right to you?

(signed)
This Sister Needs Help

Dear Aunt Blabby,

My sister who has Down syndrome never gets punished like me. My mom is unfair and gives in to her moods and stubbornness too much. What can I do?

(signed)
Miss Treated

Dear Aunt Blabby,

Sometimes I feel like I'm chained to my younger brother. He always wants to go where I go and play with *my* friends. My brother has cerebral palsy, uses a wheelchair, and can be a real pain. Why won't my mom let me go by myself?

(signed)
Chained

Dear Aunt Blabby,

I'm really frustrated. My sister is always kicking. I know it is part of her disability because she is really hyper. But what can I do? She just gets me so angry!!! Help!!!

(signed)
Frustrated! GRRR!

Dear Aunt Blabby,

I'm confused. My sister has many behavior problems. I love my little sister and I'd like to play with her, but I'm afraid of her because she sometimes hurts me. She bites me and punches me. My mom says I shouldn't hit her back and I should play with her. What should I do?

(signed)
Want to Play

Dear Aunt Blabby,

My brother, who has autism, sometimes hits kids when we are at the playground. These kids get mad and want to hit him back. What should I do?

(signed)
All Mixed Up

Dear Aunt Blabby,

My brother has mental retardation. Sometimes, he gets very angry and throws things. Now that he is bigger, I am afraid he might hurt me or someone else. What should I do?

(signed)
Tired of Ducking

Dear Aunt Blabby,

My sister has autism. She wakes me up all night and breaks all my toys and I can't even have friends over because she's so mean to them. What can I do?

(signed)
What's the Limit?

Dear Aunt Blabby,

Sometimes I can't understand my friends. They complain when their little brothers or sisters bug them. I don't see what the big deal is— they should try living with my sister Mary. Mary has autism! Then they wouldn't complain! Know what I mean?

(signed)
Life Is Not So Bad

Dear Aunt Blabby,

Most people probably wouldn't think that Michael could teach you much—he has so many problems and can't even talk. But he has really taught me a lot about caring and love and stuff like that. Do you think that is weird?

(signed)
Learned a Lot

Dear Aunt Blabby,

Sometimes kids look at Lisa and say, "Is that your sister?" "Who is she?" They think that because Lisa looks different that she is different on the inside. But she is just like us inside. She doesn't want to be stared at and laughed at or ignored. Am I the only one who feels this way?

(signed)
Cut It Out!

Dear Aunt Blabby,

My friends say my brother can't do very much, but you should see what he did at Special Olympics! Wow! I didn't know he could run so fast! It may sound funny to some people but I am really proud of what my brother can do!

(signed)
One Proud Brother

Dear Aunt Blabby,

To tell the truth, my brother Mark is a butt most of the time, but I hate it when kids pick on him because of his disability. Sometimes I have to defend him. Am I the only one?

(signed)
Somebody Has to Stick Up for Him!

The following Dear Aunt Blabby letters are for siblings of children who have cancer or other chronic illnesses.

Dear Aunt Blabby,

I'm 14 years old, and I have an 8-year-old sister with medical troubles. I'm always expected to "understand" and "know better" and "act like an adult" and "think of what your sister's been through." I'm just 14! Does that seem fair to you?

(signed)
Give Me a Break

Dear Aunt Blabby,

   Kids at my school know that my sister has cancer. Most of them are pretty nice about it, except for the jerks who ask, "Is your sister going to die?" Aunt Blabby, what can I say to them?

(signed)
They're So Rude!

Dear Aunt Blabby,

   It seems like everything has changed since Jennie got leukemia. My friends won't even come to my house anymore. They say they don't want to catch her leukemia and die. What can I do?

(signed)
Home Alone

Dear Aunt Blabby,

   Michael, my little brother, has a brain tumor. He needs to spend a lot of time in the hospital. When he does, I have to stay over at my aunt's house. I'm sick of staying there. None of my cousins are even my age. Any suggestions?

(signed)
I Wanna Go Home

Dear Aunt Blabby,

   My brother has cancer and is on these drugs. They are supposed to help him, but they made him lose most of his hair and now he's really fat. People stare at him when they see him. I know I shouldn't be embarrassed about how he looks, but I am. What can I do?

(signed)
Embarrassed

Dear Aunt Blabby,

   I am sick of my sister being sick. I know she has cancer, and I know cancer is serious, but I am tired of it. We can't go on a vacation because my sister might get sick. I can't bring friends over because they might make her sick. Everything is for her. What about me?

(signed)
Sick of It!

Dear Aunt Blabby,

I know this sounds weird, but sometimes I wish I had cancer too. You should see all the stuff people give my brother! He gets Nintendo systems, videos, expensive drawing sets, you name it. Every once in a while they'll give me and my sister a little something, but nothing like the stuff our brother gets.

(signed)
It's Not Fair

Dear Aunt Blabby,

My sister has cancer and it's really hard on all of us, especially my mom and dad. I try not to bother them with my troubles. They have enough problems with Michelle. I'm glad I can write to you when I have a problem, but I'd rather talk to my parents.

(signed)
Don't Know Where to Go

Dear Aunt Blabby,

Since we learned that my brother has a tumor, I worry all of the time. I worry that my brother might die in the middle of the night. I worry that the doctors or my parents are keeping secrets from me about David. It is getting hard to do schoolwork! Aunt Blabby, what should I do?

(signed)
Really Worried

Dear Aunt Blabby,

My sister has cancer and I think I have cancer too. A year ago, her legs hurt a lot and we took her to the hospital. That is when we found out that she has cancer. When I woke up this morning, my legs hurt. Can you catch cancer?

(signed)
Scared Stiff

9

Sibshop Recreational and Food Activities

$\mathbf{I}$n 1992, the Sibling Support Project conducted a phone survey of 97 Sibshop participants from programs across the United States. Among the open-ended questions we asked was: "What did you like best about Sibshops?" Ninety-three percent responded that they liked the games and activities best. Sixty-seven percent said they liked the opportunity to meet other brothers and sisters and 40% mentioned that they liked making and eating lunch together.

Although Sibshops are intended to provide participants with peer support and education, we could not have been more pleased with the participants' endorsement of our games and activities. The spirited games and activities—which account for over half of the time spent at a Sibshop—are an essential element of a successful program and critical to accomplishing the model's first goal:

Goal 1: Sibshops will provide brothers and sisters of children with special needs an opportunity to meet other siblings in a relaxed, recreational setting.

Recreational events are key in providing peer support from a kid's-eye view.

Recreational activities promote informal sharing and friendships among participants. The friendships begun during Sibshops are frequently continued outside the program, offering siblings ongoing sources of support that may last a lifetime. We recall watching several preteen girls playing in the gym at the close of a Sibshop held in a small New England city. The girls had just met that day, but had become fast friends, having spent the previous 4 hours playing, cooking, and talking about their lives, families, and interests. Their parents, who had arrived to pick up their children, were struck by how well the girls were playing and how reluctant they were to leave. One parent noted, "You know, these girls will probably know each other as adults."

Recreational events also make Sibshops appealing to the young participants. We are never surprised to learn that a brother or sister is reluctant to attend a Sibshop for the first time. After all, a sibling might think, "Why should I give up a Saturday to hang out with a bunch of kids I don't know, just because they have a sibling with a disability?" A Sibshop's games and activities can encourage a participant to return and benefit from the program's discussion and information activities. In short, recreation is essential to a Sibshop. The games, activities, and food projects reflect the model's emphasis on siblings' strengths and wellness. They are an indispensable component in a program that seeks to celebrate the many contributions made by brothers and sisters.

GAMES—NEW AND OTHERWISE

Many of the Sibshop recreational activities have been borrowed from various sources, most notably the New Games Foundation. If New Games are new to you, you are in for a treat. They are offbeat, fun, and sometimes silly games designed to appeal to a wide range of ages and abilities. (New Games, while ideal for school-age children, were originally developed by and for playful adults. Consequently, most of the activities we present will also work well with teenagers.) Some are competitive, but most are not. In any event, playing, not winning, is what is fun and important. Most New Games require little equipment but a lot of energy.

In the next section, we provide capsule descriptions of some of our favorite games and activities. We have purposely selected activities that have minimal equipment needs. Most activities have been adapted, with permission, from the books listed below. These books are highly recommended; plan on purchasing as many as your program can afford. Besides providing you with enough Sibshop recreation activities so you need not ever repeat an activity (although you will want to!), the activities described in these books are also enjoyed by adults at picnics, retreats, and staff development events.

The New Games Book (Flugelman, 1976)
More New Games! (Flugelman, 1981)
The Incredible Indoor Games Book (Gregson, 1982)
The Outrageous Outdoor Games Book (Gregson, 1984)
(Other useful activity books are listed in Appendix B.)

Of course, you will want to customize and enrich these games with your own skills and ideas. If you have musical, artistic, or dramatic talents, be sure to share your gifts with the participants. The Sibshop model is sufficiently flexible to allow facilitators to express their own creativity.

PRESENTING SIBSHOP RECREATIONAL ACTIVITIES

As noted in Chapter 5, Sibshop facilitators will need diverse skills. On the one hand, presenting Sibshop discussion activities requires facilitators to model the thoughtfulness and reflection we desire from the young participants. Sibshop recreation activities, on the other hand, call upon the facilitators to be exuberant, dramatic, and "on."

Below are some general tips on how to make your games and activities successful:

Before the Sibshop, decide who will "pitch" the activity. This person will be responsible for gathering materials (if any), and deciding what assistance he or she may need from the other facilitators. Will everyone do the activity together, or will we break into groups with a facilitator assigned to each group?

Become familiar with the activity you will present. Sibshops are safe places to try a game or activity that is new to you and the group, and even to make mistakes. However, do not wait until a Sibshop has begun to read the directions for an activity. It will be difficult to inspire adventurous, imaginative play if you have to read the instructions to the group. As the Boy Scouts advise: Be prepared.

When explaining the activity, place yourself at the edge—not the center—of the circle, so everyone can see you. For large groups, have participants sit in a semicircle. They can watch you demonstrate the activity with a small group of volunteers, before being dismissed to do the activity in smaller groups.

Explain the rules and the structure of the activity as simply and clearly as possible. After you explain the activity, ask for questions, but do not get involved with needlessly lengthy answers: Often, just playing the game will answer most questions.

When explaining the activity, first describe it in general way ("Who knows how to play Tag? Let's play Blob Tag—Tag with a twist!"). Demonstrate as you explain the object of the game, with volunteers if appropriate: (standing behind three volunteers) "Let's pretend Sarah's It. She chases Jason and tags him." (Take Sarah's hand and tag Jason.) "Now they're both It!" (Join their hands.) "Holding hands, they chase Michael and tag him and then all three are It!" (Have one participant tag Michael.) "They keep tagging and the Blob keeps getting bigger and bigger until there is only one very fast person left! Are there any questions?"

Present the activity in a style that encourages participation and playfulness. The New Games Foundation recommends inviting participants to play by saying: "Let's try. . . . " instead of "You're going to. . . . "

Encourage variations. Sibshop participants and their energetic facilitators can always come up with variations on games and activities. Think of your Sibshop as a Game Lab: Some of the ideas will work and some will not. Regardless, a Sibshop is an environment where playful invention and experimentation are indulged.

Be certain to make all safety issues painfully clear! Make sure that all participants understand any warnings before proceeding with an activity. If necessary, ask them to repeat the warnings and why they are being made. Most of the activities described below can be played in a gym or large multipurpose room. Make sure that the environment is as free as possible of objects that might injure participants or facilitators as they zoom across the room in a spirited round of Tag-O-Rama.

Be sensitive to mood and energy changes. Like a stand-up comedian who gauges laughter before going on to the next joke, assess the energy and interest remaining in an activity to determine when to move on to the next. Provide occasional low-energy activities to allow participants to catch their breaths between the high-energy activities.

Sometimes, you will be able to make a connection between the recreation activity you are presenting and some aspect of having a special need. An example would be Sightless Sculpture and artists who have disabilities. If you can make a connection, great—just don't overdo it.

Have fun! This isn't school! Model your ability to laugh at yourself and forgive yourself for making mistakes. One of the perks of facilitating a Sibshop is an opportunity to get in touch with your playful self. Your obvious enjoyment of the activities you present will set the tone for your young participants.

Below are recreational activities that we have enjoyed. It is not an exhaustive list by any means. If you have a favorite that you would like to share with a wider audience, we hope you will let us know.

A WHAT?

—A novel way of making the painfully obvious totally confusing

Energy level: Low
Environment: Indoor
Materials: Two small common objects such as a key, a comb, a spoon, a pencil

Directions: The object of A What? is to pass two common objects in opposite directions around the circle. To begin, players sit on the floor in a circle. The person leading the activity displays two common objects and gives each an imaginary name, such as Fribon or Moolee. He then hands one object to the player #1, on his right, saying, "This is a Fribon." Player #1 responds, "A what?" The leader says, "A Fribon" and passes the Fribon to Player #1. Player #1 now shows the object to Player #2, stating again, "This is a Fribon." Player #2, naturally, asks, "A what?" Player #1, instead of answering, turns to the leader and also asks, "A what?" whereupon the leader answers, "A Fribon." Player #1, now informed, turns to Player #2 and announces, "A Fribon." Now it is #2's turn. She shows the object to Player #3 and announces, "This is a Fribon." Player #3 asks, "A what?" and the "A whats?" continue all the way back to the leader, who provides the answer, which is again passed along.

Now, if this is not confusing enough, the leader, after starting the Fribon around the circle to the right, starts a Moolee around to the left. At some treacherously confusing juncture, the objects will cross paths and chaos may reign! But, be bold, and see if you can keep going until the objects go all the way around the circle and return to the leader.

Sources: *The Incredible Indoor Games Book*, p. 51, and *More New Games*, p. 73

AURA

—Can you see a person's aura? We can't either, but it's fun to try to feel a partner's "energy," even with our eyes closed. This is a good activity to demonstrate with two people before having the whole group try it.

Energy level: Medium
Environment: Open space
Materials: None

Directions: Have pairs of participants stand and face each other. Tell the group to reach out to their partner, touch palms, close their eyes, and "feel the connection." Next, with eyes still closed, participants drop their arms to their sides, circle once in place, and try to relocate their partner's "aura" and touch palms again. If this is too easy, try turning two or three circles instead of just one!

Source: *The New Games Book,* p. 37

BACKLASH

—This makes for a great relay race variation, once partners can manage a few steps in their new form!

Energy level: High
Environment: Gym
Materials: Balloons

Directions: To begin this relay race variation, divide the participants into two (or more) teams, and then divide each team into pairs who are of similar height. Instruct the partners to stand back to back and link arms. The leader then places a balloon between the pair's backs.

To begin the race, one pair from each team runs to the end of the gym and back in the balloon-in-the-middle, back-to-back, linked-arms position. The object—to keep the balloon between them—is not so hard while just standing, but running is something else! Players will likely try push-me/pull-you techniques until they realize that side-stepping is probably the best approach. Once back at the starting position, they unlink and wedge the balloon between the backs of the next pair, and the race continues.

There are at least two variations of Backlash. First, instead of wedging the balloon between their backs, each person can hold a balloon in his or her hands while running in the same linked, back-to-back position. When it comes time to transfer the balloons, the pair may not unlink arms. Second, for a truly wild version, try this variation with water balloons—outside, of course!

Source: *The Outrageous Outdoor Games Book,* p. 105

BALLOON DUO

—Another cooperative partner balloon race

Energy level: High
Environment: Field or gym
Materials: Balloons

Directions: To play, partners stand side by side and link arms. The leader gives each team one balloon. After the leader announces, "Go," partners bat the balloon forward with their free arms, keeping it in the air while racing toward a finish line. If a balloon hits the ground, players may scoop it up, but may not unlink arms.

Source: *The Outrageous Outdoor Games Book,* p. 106

BEHAVIOR MODIFICATION

—A crash course in shaping behavior.

Energy level: Medium
Environment: Indoor
Materials: None

Directions: Two volunteers are asked to leave the room. While they are gone, the rest of the group decides what physical position (not too difficult or detailed) they would like the volunteers to assume once they are back. The group also decides on how they will let the volunteers know whether they are getting close to the desired pose. Among the signals we have used are clapping loudly or softly, cheering or booing, or humming high or low. The volunteers then re-enter the room and attempt to replicate the pose.

Source: *More New Games,* p. 63

BLOB TAG

—A tag game that grows on you

Energy level: High
Environment: Field or gym
Materials: None

Directions: This is a great game in an open gym. One person is It. When It tags someone, they both become It. They hold hands and go after a third. The three, holding hands, go after a fourth, and so on until all players are It except for one very fast-moving individual.

Source: *The New Games Book*, p. 107

BODY SURFING

—This unique, if slightly goofy, form of surfing is as popular in Iowa as it is in Hawaii.

Energy level: Medium
Environment: Grassy field or inside on mats
Materials: None

Directions: With the exception of the surfer, everyone lies face down, sardine-style, with a one-foot space between each person. The surfer gently lies down, arms extended, crossways over several bodies. Everyone simultaneously rolls in one direction to propel the surfer toward the end.

Source: *More New Games*, p. 133

CATERPILLAR

—This "caterpillar" has more to do with heavy construction equipment (the kind that move on large treads) than with future butterflies.

Energy level: Medium
Environment: Grassy field or gym mats
Materials: None

Directions: Have the entire group lie face down and side by side. Pack everyone really close together, with any tiny people squeezed between two larger ones! Begin by having the person at one end roll over onto a neighbor, and continue rolling down the whole line-up. When reaching the end, the roller lies on his or her tummy and the next person begins rolling from the other end. Before you know it, this human treadmill will have advanced its way across the gym or field!

Source: *The New Games Book,* p. 117

CENTIPEDE

—A real wiggle

Energy level: Medium
Environment: Open grassy area or gym
Materials: None

Directions: Divide the group into two teams of at least five similar-size players. (If your group has fewer than 10, don't worry—just stay as one team.) Instruct teams to line up behind each other at the starting line and sit down. Once seated, team members wrap their legs around the waist of the person in front of them, forming the body of a centipede. At "Go," players lift with their arms and wiggle the centipede across the field. If any centipede segments separate, they must reconnect en route. The winning centipede is the one who first makes it completely over the finish line with all segments connected.

Source: *The Outrageous Outdoor Games Book,* p. 97

CHALK DRAWING

—Drawing on the ground is one of the oldest—and most rewarding— methods of expressing oneself artistically.

Energy level: Medium
Environment: Blacktop playground or sidewalk
Materials: Colored sidewalk chalks

Directions: This activity can be as structured or unstructured as fits the group. Try starting with the name of your group or SIBSHOP in big bubble letters and having everyone fill in different parts with their own designs or decorations. Or, have participants write their own names in big letters and decorate their names with pictures that say something about themselves. Kids will not want to stop, so be sure to have lots of chalk on hand!

Source: *The Outrageous Outdoor Game Book*, p. 74

COMMONS

—A game wherein group members determine what they have in common—even if it is just a silly action

Energy level: Medium
Environment: Indoor
Materials: None

Directions: Groups of three decide on three nonsensical actions that can be performed quickly, that is, thumb on nose with raspberry sound; a scary face with a lion's roar; or thumbs in ears, wiggling fingers and a turkey gobble. Once each group has determined their sounds, players turn back to back. After a count of three, groups turn around and perform one of the three actions. If all members choose the same action, they "win," and play continues until all groups have won.

Source: *More New Games*, p. 25

COPY CAT

—There is probably a moral in this game; we just don't know what it is!

Energy level: Medium
Environment: Open area
Materials: None

Directions: Have participants stand in a circle. Instruct participants to secretly pick a person to mimic. Have players spin around once, and then begin to mimic the movements, slightly exaggerated, of the person they have chosen. The movements of the group will get larger and larger and usually everyone will end up doing the same movements without even knowing who started it!

Source: *The Outrageous Outdoor Games Book*, p. 64

DANGLING DONUT EATING CONTEST

—As much fun to watch as it is to play, the Dangling Donut Eating Contest is sure to appeal to all Sibshop gourmands.

Energy level: Low
Environment: Indoor hallway with beams or ceiling to which tape will stick; or outside, perhaps under monkey bars on a playground
Materials: Yarn, tape, broom (or dropcloth for the many crumbs), and a cake donut (powdered sugar is even better) for each player

Directions: Prepare for this activity by threading a piece of yarn through each donut, making sure that the yarn is long enough so that when taped to the ceiling, or tied to the monkey bars, the donut will dangle at the mouths of the players. To begin, line up the contestants, have them keep their hands behind their backs, and attach their donuts at proper height. At the "Go" signal, participants race to see who indeed is the most capable dangling donut eater. There are sure to be crumbs, so have a broom or shakeable dropcloth on hand. (If you are in a smaller area, this race can be done in heats.)

Source: *The Outrageous Outdoor Games Book*, p. 69

DOT'S DOT

—An opportunity to stretch the imagination, often with impressive results

Energy level: Low/trickle-in
Environment: Tables and chairs

Materials: Sheets of blank paper, pencils, crayons. Optional: ¼" circular color coding dots, available from office supply stores.

Directions: Have participants cover a sheet of paper with 20–25 randomly scattered dots. These papers are collected and redistributed or simply traded with a neighbor. Have players concentrate on the dots to imagine a picture, and then connect the lines so the picture emerges. If some are having difficulties, have participants turn the paper in different directions to imagine other possibilities.

Source: *The Incredible Indoor Games Book,* p. 91

FINGERPRINT PICTURES

—It is amazing the amount of art that is available at one's fingertips!

Energy level: Low/trickle-in
Environment: Tables and chairs
Materials: Paper, washable ink pads, thin markers or crayons, paper towels, and a bar of Lava soap for cleanup!

Directions: Place a sheet of paper at each seat, and place enough ink pads and markers around so materials are within easy reach of each artist. Once participants' sleeves are rolled up, the finger inking can begin. Show participants how to press their fingers and thumbs into the ink pad and then firmly onto paper. Encourage them to experiment with different forms and different techniques, such as rolling the fingertip or even printing the sides or heels of their hands.

Once participants have finished making their fingerprints, have them wipe their hands with a paper towel and use markers to give their blotches some character. Ask for some ideas to get imaginations rolling. For further inspiration, consult *Ed Emberley's Great Thumbprint Drawing Book* (Emberley, 1977), which is all about fingerprint illustrations. A super cleanup of hands will be necessary at the finish.

Source: *The Incredible Indoor Games Book,* p. 98

HOG CALL

—An activity as refined and subtle as its name suggests

Energy level: High
Environment: Field or gym
Materials: Blindfolds (such as bandanas) for everyone, and a list of "pairs" to assign partners, such as salt and pepper, dogs and cats, ba-

con and eggs, sugar and spice, horse and carriage, peanut butter and jelly, cops and robbers, track and field, milk and cookies, and hugs and kisses. (The group, of course, can generate its own list.)

Directions: Divide the group into pairs and have them choose a pair of things to be. Each player then chooses one part of the pair that he or she will "call." Players then scatter across the field or opposite ends of the gym and are blindfolded. The object is for partners to reunite by shouting their calls and listening for their "mate." Hog call is over when the last pair has been matched and unblindfolded.

Source: *The Outrageous Outdoor Games Book,* p. 91

HUG TAG

—Try out this new form of tag after you have warmed up with a round or two of Knots (see p. 113).

Energy level: High
Environment: Field or gym
Materials: None

Directions: Use the same rules you are accustomed to for Tag, only now a player is "safe" only when hugging another player! After playing for a bit, change the rules so players are safe only when three people are hugging.

Source: *The New Games Book,* p. 115

HUMAN PINBALL

—Everyone gets to be a flipper in this huge people-powered pinball machine.

Energy level: Medium
Environment: Field or gym
Materials: One rubber gym ball

Directions: Set up this activity by having all participants (except one) stand in a circle, facing outward. Have participants spread their legs as far apart as comfortable. Their feet should touch their neighbors' on both sides. Everyone bends down and swings their arms (now flippers) between their legs. (The upside-down view of everyone's backside will be good for a laugh.) The one non-flipper enters the circle as the target and the flippers try to hit her or him with the gym ball by knocking it back and forth across the circle. Whoever hits the target gets a point and becomes the new target. The target gets a point any time the flippers get wild and the ball escapes the confines of the pinball machine. Being a flipper can be quite exciting, but watch out for human head rushes!

Source: *The New Games Book*, p. 51

HUMAN SPRING

—A counterpart game to Stand-Off (see p. 178). In this game, players cooperate to keep each other balanced upright.

Energy level: Medium
Environment: Grassy area or indoor on mats
Materials: None

Directions: Two players stand with feet spread, facing each other at an arm's distance. Hold arms up in front, palms forward. Keeping bodies as rigid as possible, partners gently lean forward and catch each other

with their palms and rebound to a standing position. Too easy? Take a short step back and try again. This works best on a soft surface!

Source: *More New Games*, p. 17

INSTANT REPLAY

—Try this decidedly silly name-learning game after a warm-up activity such as Knots, Group Juggling, or Human Bingo (see p. 113, pp. 106–108, and p. 108, respectively).

Energy level: Medium
Environment: Indoor
Materials: None

Directions: Standing in a circle, each group member announces his or her name while making an extravagant motion. For instance, Mike may say his name while hopping into the circle on one foot (or turning circles with his hands raised, or slapping his knees). After Mike demonstrates, everyone else does an "instant replay." That is, they simultaneously perform the same motion and say, "Mike!" Going around the circle, encourage participants to introduce themselves with dramatic gestures.

Source: *More New Games*, p. 71

ISLANDS

—Akin to Musical Chairs and contrary to Hug Tag (see p. 167), if you make contact in this game, you are out!

Energy level: High
Environment: Field or gym
Materials: Paper or plastic plates (one for every three or four participants); recorded music (optional).

Directions: Scatter plates on the ground. Instruct participants to begin wandering around the "islands." When the referee calls, "Islands," everyone runs to touch a plate. While more than one person can touch a plate, the last person to get to a plate is "out." In a departure from typical Sibshop activities, Islands does not promote contact—in fact, if any two people touch at all while scrambling for the plates, they are "out"! Continue to reduce the number of plates as the group grows smaller, until there are just a few people ready to pounce on a single island. A variation is to play music while participants wander about the islands, stopping the music to signal that the land rush is on.

Source: *The New Games Book*, p. 127

THE LAP GAME

—What is the one thing that disappears every time you stand up? Your lap, of course. In the Lap Game participants attempt to sit on each other's laps—everyone, at the same time. Can it be done?

Energy level: Medium
Environment: Indoor
Materials: None

Directions: Have all participants stand shoulder to shoulder in a very tight circle. Each player then turns to the right and places his or her hands on the waist of the players directly in front. When signaled by the leader, all players simultaneously guide the players in front of them to sit on their knees. If done correctly, all players are sitting in the laps (or, more correctly, on the knees) of the person behind them. If not done correctly, the players create a human—if ridiculous—representation of the domino theory. If all goes well and everyone has a lap to sit on, the group may try to lift their arms in the air and applaud themselves. Or, if players are feeling especially brave, they may try to walk in this seated position, with someone signaling "Right!" "Left!" and so on.

Source: *The New Games Book*, p. 171

LAST DETAILS

—Try this one when the group needs a breather from some of the more raucous activities.

Energy level: Low
Environment: Indoor
Materials: Optional: wearable props, such as glasses, hats, scarves, gloves, buttons.

Directions: Have the group divide into pairs. If you are using props (this can be done successfully without them), let each person select one or two at this time. Each person then faces his or her partner, carefully observing the other's details. When signaled by the leader, players turn their backs to each other, and, within a minute, rearrange six details. Both players face each other again and try to see if they can identify what has been changed.

Source: *More New Games,* p. 29

LEAN-TOO

—A truly cooperative game where balancing the differences makes everyone a winner!

Energy level: Medium
Environment: Open area, soft surface preferable
Materials: None

Directions: Have players stand in a circle and count off alternately by ones and twos and join hands. Keeping backs and legs as straight as possible, have all "ones" lean gently forward toward the center, and all the "twos" lean backward toward the outside. This is a true act of cooperative counterbalance. Once balanced, have the group slowly reverse leaners: "twos" lean in and "ones" lean out. Once a comfortable balance has been attained, have everyone try stepping slowly to the right to move around in a circle.

Source: *The Outrageous Outdoor Games Book,* p. 61

MIME RHYME

—Mime rhyme—perfect anytime

Energy level: Medium
Environment: Indoor
Materials: None

Directions: One person selects a word (say, *rat*) and tells the group a word that rhymes with the word he or she has chosen (such as *mat*).

The group then tries to guess the word by pantomiming words that rhyme. For instance, one at a time, individuals may try to act like a "cat" or a "bat"; or lie down in front of a door to impersonate a "mat"; or do their best beached-whale, just-finished-Thanksgiving-dinner routine to mime "fat!"

Source: *More New Games*, p. 83

MOUSE TRAP

—Who is more cunning, the sneaky mice or the cat who is just pretending to sleep?

Energy level: High
Environment: Open area
Materials: Minimum of 10 players

Directions: To begin, four or five players become The Dreaded Trap by standing in a circle with hands joined and raised in the air to create entrances and exits for the mice. One player is chosen to be the Fearsome Cat. The Cat, who is pretending to sleep, faces away from the trap with eyes closed. Remaining players become the Cunning and Clever Mice who dart quietly in and out of the Trap past the sleepy Cat.

To capture the Mice, the Cat suddenly opens his or her eyes and yells, "Snap!" The players who are the Trap immediately bring their arms down, snaring the rascally rodents. Captured Mice now become part of the Trap. The game continues with the Trap becoming larger and larger until there is only one victorious Mouse.

Source: *The Outrageous Outdoor Games Book*, p. 54

MUTUAL MONSTERS

—Step aside, Dr. Frankenstein; here come the real monster makers!

Energy level: Low
Environment: Tables and chairs
Materials: A sheet of letter-size paper and pencil/crayons/markers for each person

Directions: Distribute paper and pencils and have participants fold their papers in thirds. On the top third, everyone will draw the head of a monster, person, animal, or creature. Have all artists extend the neck a little past the first crease in the paper. When completed, have participants fold back the top third so it is hidden, and pass to a neighbor. Now everyone draws a torso and arms in the middle section of the page, connecting to the neck lines, but without looking at the head. This time, have them extend the waist a little past the second crease. Now fold the paper again and pass to a different neighbor. Everyone now draws legs and feet on the bottom third of the paper, without looking at the other sections. When all players are finished, the papers are unfolded and the creations are shared with the whole group.

Source: *The Incredible Indoor Games Book*, p. 94

NOSE TOES

—This game is sure to keep you on your toes, or is that nose?

Energy level: Medium
Environment: Open space
Materials: None

Directions: To begin, everyone sits in a circle on the floor. The leader begins clapping in rhythm and the group joins in. Once the rhythm is established, the leader turns to a neighbor, points to his or her *toes* and says, "This is my nose." The neighbor repeats, "This is my nose" and points to *toes*, and then adds another silly statement, such as, "This is my knee," while pointing to a *thumb*. The next person in the circle repeats, "This is my knee" and points to a *thumb*, and then adds a new statement and gesture. This continues around the circle. Note: Each person repeats only the statement of the person before him or her—not the statements of all previous players.

Source: *The Incredible Indoor Games Book*, p. 69

PASS THE ORANGE

—This well-known neck-in-neck race is fun as a relay or as just a co-operative challenge once participants get to know each other.

Energy level: Medium
Environment: Open space
Materials: Three to five oranges

Directions: To begin, line players up in two teams. Place an orange under the chin of each team's first player. The object is for the team to pass the orange, neck to neck, chin to chin, all the way down the line to the last player. Players should hold their hands behind their backs to resist the temptation to handle the orange during its tenuous transport.

PASSED OVER

—Much harder to describe than to play, Passed Over is another game that can also be played with water balloons!

Energy level: High
Environment: Field or gym
Materials: A ball

Directions: Two teams (we call them Red and Blue, but you can call them Liver and Onions—whatever) stand face to face in lines, about 4 feet apart. Starting at one end, the ball is passed back and forth, working its way down the row. What makes Passed Over tricky is that, after throwing the ball, players run to become the last person in line on the *opposite* team. For instance (assuming there are 10 players on each team), Red 1 throws the ball to Blue 1 who throws the ball to Red 2 and so on. After Red 1 throws the ball to Blue 1, he or she runs around to stand next to Blue 10. Instead of running behind their own line, however, players run forward, cross, and run behind the other team's line. If this is too easy, try increasing the space between the lines or using more than one ball.

Source: *The Outrageous Outdoor Games Book,* p. 90

PRUI

—Unlike the "Blob," in Blob Tag (see p. 161), which everyone wants to avoid becoming a part of, Prui (pronounced PROO-ee) is a gentle creature that everyone would like to join.

Energy level: High
Environment: Field or gym
Materials: Blindfolds (optional)

Directions: To play, all players stand in a group with their eyes closed. The referee quietly selects someone to be Prui. Prui keeps eyes open, but cannot talk. With eyes closed, everyone else begins milling around. When a player bumps into another player, he or she is to shake hands and ask, "Prui?" If the person replies, "Prui?" then the inquirer has not found the Prui. However, if the player finds someone, shakes hands, and this person does not reply, "Prui," then the player may suspect that the "true" Prui has been found. After checking again to be sure there is no response, the player joins hands with the Prui and opens his or her eyes. Prui, still silent, grows as new players make the discovery and join hands. Participants can only shake the Prui's hand at either end, so if they bump into joined hands, they must make their way to the end of the chain. When the last person joins Prui and opens his or her eyes, Prui breaks the vow of silence and lets out a victorious cheer!

Source: *The New Games Book,* p. 133

PSYCHIC SHAKE

—How can you find your comrades if you can't talk?

Energy level: Medium
Environment: Field or gym
Materials: None

Directions: Have all participants silently select a number—either one, two, or three. Once decided, people quietly circulate, giving each other handshakes of one, two, or three shakes. When players meet someone with the same number, they stick together and search for others of their number. When all is done, for curiosity, see if there are three equal groups.

Source: *More New Games,* p. 177

PUSHPIN SOCCER

—Caution: this game requires goalies to use pushpins!

Energy level: High
Environment: Gym
Materials: Inflated balloons (about two per player); two pushpins; masking tape

Directions: Unlike regular soccer, Pushpin Soccer "goalies" do not defend the goals—they stay in their goal boxes to score points for their team by popping balloons swatted to them by their teammates. To prepare for this activity, use masking tape to create a small soccer court with generous goalie boxes at either end. To begin, have players line up according to height, and, starting with the tallest player, have players count off "red," "blue," "red," "blue," and so on. This will assure two teams of approximately equal heights. Have the teams meet at their goal box and select a goalie. (Of course, everyone will want a turn at being a goalie.)

With each team, review in great detail the importance of safety and the rules that will help assure that the game is played safely: No one is allowed to reach into the goal box. Similarly, the goalie may not reach outside of the goal box for any reason. Adults stationed near each goal can monitor goalies' and players' adherence to safety rules.

Once warned, the goalies are handed their pushpins, and a balloon is brought onto the court. It is tossed into the air, and the game begins. Each team swats the balloon toward its goalie who pops the balloon. Players may swat the balloon with their hands only. For fun, try introducing more than one balloon at a time toward the end of the activity.

Variations: Pushpin soccer also works well in confined spaces (such as hallways). If necessary, goalies can operate from behind a large chair, folding table or other sturdy barricade. If the group has participants of greatly differing heights, consider alternating sets for taller and not-so-tall players.

Source: *More New Games,* p. 69

RED-HANDED

—Keep passing 'cause you wouldn't want to be caught red-handed!

Energy level: Low
Environment: Open area
Materials: One small object, such as a marble

Directions: With his or her eyes closed, one player stands in the middle of a circle of players who continuously circulate a small object such as a key or marble. Whether they have it or not, all players simultaneously pretend to be passing the object. When ready, the center player opens his or her eyes and has three guesses to determine which player has the marble. The player caught "red-handed" (or whoever has the marble after the third unsuccessful guess) becomes the new person in the center.

Source: *The New Games Book,* p. 71

SCRABBLE SCRAMBLE

—Spelling tests should be so much fun!

Energy level: Medium
Environment: Field or gym

Materials: 62 sheets of construction or typing paper, wide black felt-tip marker

Directions: To prepare, make two sets of alphabet cards with an extra A,E,I,O, and U for each set—62 total. Divide the group into two equal teams and have them line up at one end of a gym. Place the two lettered stacks at the opposite end of the gym—about 30 feet away or so. The leader then calls out a category—food, trees, television shows, school subjects, or animals. The teams huddle together, determine a word that will fit the category, and then run to their stack to get the necessary letters. Team members run back with a letter and arrange themselves in proper order. If there are more team members than letters in the word, they can help arrange their team's word. The first team to spell a word is awarded a point for each letter. The team with the most points after a set number of rounds wins.

Source: *The Outrageous Outdoor Games Book*, p. 56

SIGHTLESS SCULPTURE

—Can a person who can no longer hear write music? Of course! Beethoven did. Could a person who can no longer see still make sculptures of friends? Sightless Sculpture, a great low-energy activity, can also be an opportunity to talk about people with disabilities and art.

Energy level: Low
Environment: Inside
Materials: Bandanas

Directions: To begin, groups of three participants decide who will be the Sightless Sculptor, the Blob of Clay, and the Model (a.k.a. the Model Child). The Sculptor (and, if you wish, the Blob of Clay) are blindfolded. The Model then assumes any position he or she can maintain for up to 5 minutes—the wackier the better! The Sculptor then uses his or her hands to determine the Model's position and manipulates the Blob of Clay to create an identical statue. Leaders may need to help the Sculptor locate the Model and the Blob of Clay. (It is best when they are close to the Sculptor.) When the Sculptor feels that the creation is complete, then he or she and the Blob of Clay open their eyes to assess their work. This activity can be done in groups of three, or with three people at a time in front of a group.

Source: *More New Games*, p. 77

STAND-OFF

—Be careful how you throw your weight around in this game. It is easy to lose your balance!

Energy level: Medium
Environment: Open area
Materials: None

Directions: Each player stands with feet together, one arm-length away from his or her partner. To begin, players make palm-to-palm contact and attempt to unbalance their partners by moving their hands and shifting their weight. Points are given when a partner moves a foot, loses balance, or makes contact with any part of the body other than palms. No points are given if you both lose balance.

Source: *The New Games Book*, p. 35

STAND UP

—Included below are variations on this Sibshop classic. Can you and your participants think of others?

Energy level: Medium
Environment: Outdoors or soft surface
Materials: None

Directions: To begin, have pairs of equal height sit back to back, then reach back and lock elbows. On the count of three, everyone yells, "Stand Up!" and players, digging their heels into the ground, push back. If done right, the pair will pop up into a standing position. Can this be done with three or even four people? How about three people facing one another, feet to feet, and holding hands?

Source: *The New Games Book*, p. 65

TAG-O-RAMA

—Also known as Dodge Tag, this is a simple but exciting version of an old standby.

Energy level: High
Environment: Field or gym
Materials: None

Directions: To begin, have the group divide into pairs. Each pair decides who will be It first. Then the group is spread out across the field or gym. At the signal "Go," all players begin their individual games of Tag, dodging other players caught up in their own games.

Source: *The Outrageous Outdoor Games Book*, p. 121

TRIANGLE TAG

—A geometric twist on tag. Also an excellent demonstration of how exhausting running around in circles can be!

Energy level: High
Environment: Field or gym
Materials: Bandanas or wristbands (one per group of four)

Directions: To play, groups of three players hold hands to make a triangle. One wears a wristband or a bandana around the wrist to identify him or her as the "target." A fourth player attempts to tag the target while the triangle maneuvers around to protect the target. There is really only one other rule: The "tagger" cannot reach over the arms of triangle members to reach the target.

Source: *More New Games*, p. 43

TUG OF WAR

—Simple as can be, and great fun for Sibshop participants of all sizes

Energy level: Medium
Environment: Field or gym
Materials: Stout rope

Directions: Tug of War needs little explanation: Divide into two teams, grab a rope, and pull! However, do try some of the variations suggested in *New Games*, including having players wait 10 feet away and, on signal, run to the rope and commence pulling; or stretching the rope over a sprinkler.

Source: *The New Games Book*, p. 153

ULTIMATE NERF

—Somewhat like football—but much more fun

Energy level: High
Environment: Field or gym
Materials: Nerf football or Frisbee

Directions: Ultimate Nerf starts with one team "kicking off" to the other by tossing a Nerf ball, Frisbee, or whatever. Members of the receiving team may run anywhere on the field— except for the person with the ball, who may not move his or her feet until the ball is thrown to a teammate. Members of the opposite team must stand one arm-length away from the person who has the ball. If a passed ball is dropped, thrown out of bounds, or intercepted, the other team immediately takes possession and the direction of the play shifts.

Source: *More New Games*, p. 53

UNDERCOVER LEADER

—Wherein leaders exert a very subtle leadership style

Energy level: Low
Environment: Open space
Materials: None

Directions: To begin, players sit in a circle on the floor. One person is chosen to be It, and leaves the room. Another player in the circle is chosen to be the Undercover Leader. During the game, the Leader starts various body movements, such as head nodding, foot tapping, elbow scratching, or chicken wings, and the rest of the group follows his or her lead. Throughout the game, it is important that players not look directly at the Leader for movement changes, or they might give away the Leader's cover! Once a movement has started, the person who is It is invited back into the room. It watches closely to determine who is the Leader. The Leader, meanwhile, continues to change the movements. When It discovers the Leader's identity, two other players are chosen to become It and the new Undercover Leader, and the play resumes.

Source: *The Incredible Indoor Games Book*, p. 53

VAMPIRE

—Perfect for that late-October Sibshop

Energy level: Medium
Environment: Field or gym
Materials: None

Directions: To begin playing, have all players close their eyes and begin shuffling around. The referee, who must assure that players do not bump into inanimate objects, also secretly appoints one of the players to be the Vampire. The Vampire must also keep his or her eyes closed. When humans bump into humans, nothing happens; but when a player bumps into the Vampire, the ghoul grabs the prey by the arms and lets out a blood-curdling scream. The victim now becomes a Vampire as well, and keeping his or her eyes closed, seeks other humans on which to feast. Lest everyone become vampires too quickly, here's a catch: Any two vampires who try to feast on each other are automatically returned to human status!

Source: *The New Games Book*, p. 123

WATER BRIGADE

—Conjure up images of water-toting brooms and Mickey Mouse by accompanying this game with music from *The Sorcerer's Apprentice.*

Energy level: Medium
Environment: Outside
Materials: Four buckets, a paper cup for each player

Directions: The object here is for each team to transfer water from a full bucket to an empty bucket, by pouring it from cup to cup. To begin, divide the group into two teams and have them stand in parallel lines. Place a full bucket of water at the beginning of each line and an empty bucket at each opposite end. Give each participant a paper cup. At the signal "Go," teams begin transferring the water, one cup at a time. The winning team is the one who finishes first and spills the least amount of water (the fullest end bucket).

Source: *The Outrageous Outdoor Games Book,* p. 58

WIND IN THE WILLOW

—Create a proper mood for this quiet, gentle game by having players make low wind-blowing sounds.

Energy level: Low
Environment: Grassy area or inside
Materials: None

Directions: To begin, have a small circle of players (about eight or so) stand shoulder to shoulder with hands held at shoulder height, palms forward. To maintain balance during this activity, one foot should be behind the other. A volunteer "willow" stands in the middle of the circle with eyes closed, arms crossed at the chest, keeping his or her body as straight as possible. Circle members support the willow as it gently sways back and forth in the "wind."

Source: *More New Games,* p. 67

SAMPLE SIBSHOP FOOD ACTIVITIES

Food activities are among the most rewarding Sibshop activities. When we make and eat food together, we are nourished, we express our creativity, and we derive enjoyment from eating the kid-friendly meal we have prepared together. As we cook and eat, we also laugh, tell bad jokes, learn about our likes and dislikes, and talk about our schools, friends, and families. The sharing and informal support that occurs during the breaking of bread should never be underestimated!

If you have never organized a group cooking activity, here are a few thoughts to keep in mind:

1. *Be prepared.*   Locate and set up your materials before your participants arrive. If you are not familiar with the kitchen, plan on visiting it well before your Sibshop to take an inventory of the tools you need (and prepare a list of tools you will need to bring) and to be sure that necessary equipment, such as ovens, work. Even a simple activity, such as Super Nachos (a good first-time activity), can be difficult if an important ingredient or tool is forgotten.

2. *Keep it simple.*   Especially the first few times. If you cannot remember back that far, kids can be picky eaters. We know that over 50% of Sibshop participants think that tomatoes (much less green peppers, pineapple, or black olives) are just "too weird" to go on nachos. Ditto for mushrooms in pasta sauce. That does not mean that you cannot have some on hand for adults and kids who like them, but do not assume that everyone will want them.

3. *Identify as many jobs as possible.*   We have found that participants would rather be doing something than watching. They frequently display enthusiasm for even the less glamorous chores, like pot scrubbing, which has amazed us and shocked their parents. As you plan your food activity, consider the number of hands you will want to keep busy. If space permits, consider breaking the kitchen into stations, each responsible for a specific chore. When shopping, purchase food that can be readied by your young participants: Buy blocks of cheese for grating rather than pregrated cheese or canned cheese sauce.

4. *Think about how much time you will need for the project.*   Select or adapt projects to accommodate for the time you have available.

To get you started, we have listed some food activities that we and others have enjoyed. Share the foods you love with your young participants, whether it is egg rolls, stir fries, giant chocolate chip cookies, tacos, Belgian waffles, or fruit kabobs!

Super Nachos

The jobs here are grating cheese; chopping tomatoes, green peppers, olives, and maybe onions; spreading tortilla chips; and assembling the dish before running it under the broiler. Good with sour cream, beans, and, of course, salsa. Also a good project when time is limited.

Pizza

For this perennial favorite, try using small pizza rounds and let the young chefs customize their pizzas with a variety of toppings.

Sibshop Subshop

A 6-foot long submarine sandwich roll sold at some bakeries can add an extra dollop of fun to this activity. You can, of course, pile almost anything on a sub, but we think the sprinkling of Italian dressing is what puts it "over the top." Subs can be a good choice when kitchen space and equipment are minimal.

Homemade Pasta

If you have a pasta machine, know how to use it, and your sauce is already made, a group of siblings can turn flour and eggs into home-made linguine or fettucine in less than an hour. It cooks in seconds. Don't forget the candles, the Italian bread, and maybe a Frank Sinatra tape!

Hand-Cranked Ice Cream

A time-honored method of channeling youthful excess energy is to crank an ice cream freezer. If you can find an old-fashioned people-powered ice cream freezer, by all means use it. Making ice cream is as educational as it is rewarding. We are always surprised at the number of children who have never had or made homemade ice cream before. Sometimes we will churn the ice cream early in the program, pack it in ice to harden, and enjoy it at the end of the Sibshop when partici-pants serve it to their parents, their brothers and sisters, and them-selves!

CONCLUSION

Please remember that recreational and food activities are indispensable in creating an appealing, memorable, and sometimes magical Sibshop. As noted at the beginning of this chapter, recreational and food activities provide participants with informal opportunities for support and help keep the program's focus on the participants' many strengths. Select, plan, and present these activities with the same care and attention that you would give to other activities. The energy, joy, and imagination that you and your colleagues bring to these activities will be reflected in faces of the children you are there to serve. Have fun, and they will too!

10

Information Activities, Guest Speakers, and Special Events

As we reviewed in Chapter 4, numerous authors, researchers, and siblings themselves have noted that brothers and sisters have a lifelong need for information on the specifics and implications of their siblings' disability or illness. As with many sibling issues, this need for information is similar to parents' need for information. However, compared to their parents, brothers and sisters usually have far fewer opportunities to acquire this information.

Because of their changing needs as they mature, brothers and sisters will need to have their siblings' conditions and their implications reinterpreted as they grow. This need is best addressed when parents and service providers are aware of sibling concerns and regularly share information with brothers and sisters throughout their lives. (If you have not done so already, read Chapter 3 for implications for parents and service providers.) Activities for parents and service providers, such as workshops and sibling panels (see Chapter 11) can be an important step in creating readily available, natural sources of information for brothers and sisters as they grow up.

WRITTEN SOURCES OF INFORMATION

When available, written information can help brothers and sisters as well. A few agencies, such as the Epilepsy Foundation of America, have prepared materials for children, including some specifically for brothers and sisters. Books such as *Living with a Brother or Sister with Special Needs* (Meyer, Vadasy, & Fewell, 1985) or those listed in Appendix A can provide siblings with information on disabilities, therapies, future concerns, and even emotions they may experience. If children cannot read these books on their own, parents can read them to their children—a practice that can be a wonderful means of keeping the lines of communication open.

SIBSHOPS AS INFORMATION SOURCES

In addition to providing recreation and discussion, Sibshops can also be places to learn. The fourth Sibshop goal is *to provide siblings with an opportunity to learn more about the implications of their brothers' and sisters' special needs.* There are, however, limits to the type and amount of information that can be conveyed at a Sibshop.

Sibshops for brothers and sisters of children with a specific condition—such as hearing impairment or cancer—can be a valuable opportunity to convey information about the nature of a sibling's special needs. These Sibshops are generally held as a part of a state, national, or regional conference. It can be challenging, if not impossible, however, to attract sufficient numbers of siblings of people with a specific condition to make a viable local program. Consequently, most community-based Sibshops are for brothers and sisters of children with various disabilities or illnesses, which can make an in-depth or ongoing discussion about any one disability or illness impractical. Despite these limitations, Sibshops can be a fine place for participants to gain information about topics of common interest, such as those described below.

Services for People with Special Needs

Many participants will have brothers and sisters who receive services from a wide range of professionals, including adapted physical education teachers, audiologists, interpreters, mobility teachers, nurses, occupational and physical therapists, physicians, psychologists, recreational therapists, respite care providers, social workers, and special education teachers. However, many times brothers and sisters have only a vague idea of what these service providers do with their siblings on a daily basis. Consider inviting a therapist or a teacher to your next Sibshop as a guest speaker. Ask the guest to briefly describe what he or she does with kids with special needs and, if at all possible, demonstrate using the "tools of the trade" such as adaptive spoons and therapy balls. Be sure to leave ample time for questions. Listen carefully to the questions asked by participants. They will help you determine participants' knowledge of disabilities, illnesses, and services and can help you plan future informational activities.

Information About Disabilities

Often, siblings are interested in learning more about disabilities, even disabilities other than those that their brothers and sisters have. If your participants seem to have an interest, consider inviting guest speakers who can provide your participants with an overview of a disability and answer their questions. Many disability-related organizations provide community education, often provided by people who have the disability themselves.

Learning about different disabilities can be helpful in at least two ways. First, it provides participants with a fresh, broadened perspective as they listen and compare and contrast their siblings' disabilities with the one presented. Second, as guests speak, common themes (such as self-advocacy or inclusion) frequently emerge, providing siblings with a growing understanding of issues facing all people who have disabilities.

Technology for People with Disabilities

Today's children are fascinated by computers and their many applications. Throughout the United States there are many examples of how computers and other technologies are making life better for people who have disabilities. Two frequent guests to the Seattle area Sibshop are a man who developed a communication-based system that uses head switches and Morse code and a young woman (formerly a special education student and now a university doctoral student) who uses this system. If you are not aware of a local expert on computers for people with special needs, contact your state's Assistive Technology Office (frequently found at University Affiliated Programs) or RESNA, an interdisciplinary association for the advancement of rehabilitation and assistive technology. RESNA's phone number is 703-524-6686. Either should be able to refer you to an appropriate local resource.

Very Special Arts

Most states have Very Special Arts (VSA) organizations. For those unfamiliar with VSA, it is a cultural and educational organization dedicated to providing opportunities in the arts for, by, and with people who have disabilities. In many states, VSA sponsors Artist-in-Residence programs in schools and Very Special Arts Festivals. Like Sibshops, VSA celebrates strengths and diversity. Plan on inviting a representative from your state's VSA organization to be a guest artist at your Sibshop. Also, consider contacting VSA to see how your Sibshop could take part in your state's next Very Special Arts Festival. To locate the VSA organization in your state, call 1-800-933-VSA1.

Kids on the Block

Many communities have Kids on the Block puppet troupes that feature puppets with and without disabilities and chronic health conditions. Sibshop participants are likely to enjoy Kids on the Block's programs, which provide information about a wide range of special needs using accessible, interactive, and frequently humorous short plays. Participants may especially like the program "What It's Like to be the Brother of a Child Who Has a Disability," featuring a puppet without disabilities named Michael Riley. As many siblings have greater knowledge of disabilities than their age peers, these productions allow participants to "show off" what they know about special needs as they interact with the puppets. Most Kids on the Block programs are created for third- through sixth-grade audiences, similar to Sibshop's intended age range. To learn more about Kids on the Block troupes in your state, call 1-800-368-KIDS.

Future Issues

As the research literature suggests, brothers and sisters often have unasked questions about the future. Questions that could be addressed during a Sibshop may include: What will happen to my brother and sister when we grow up? Will my sibling live with me someday? Survey your group to determine which issues are of greatest interest.

To lead an informational discussion on the suggested topics, the facilitator will need to be aware of the range of housing and vocational opportunities available for adults with disabilities, or will need to invite others familiar with the range of services in the community. You may also wish to invite as a guest speaker an adult with a disability who can talk about where he or she lives, works, and plays. If you need help finding appropriate resources or speakers on adult services, a good place to start will be your local Arc. Alternatively, you may wish to sponsor a field trip to supported employment sites and meet adults with disabilities who are working and living in the community.

Parents of Children with Special Needs

Perhaps because of parents' desires to protect their typically developing children, many brothers and sisters have never heard parents candidly discuss the impact of their child's disability, and the unique concerns and rewards parents experience. Brothers and sisters who have an opportunity to hear parents discuss their families can gain insights into the workings of their own parents and families.

When inviting two or three parents to share their families' stories and answer participants' questions, for confidentiality reasons make sure that the parents you invite have more than one child and are not parents of Sibshop participants. It will also help if these presenters have previously spoken to groups about their children and families.

Topics the parents could briefly address are: the family's reaction to the child's diagnosis; the special joys and concerns they have regarding their child and family; and the effect that the child with special needs has had on their family, especially his or her brothers and sisters. We have found that children often find it easier to talk to other children's parents, so leave plenty of time for questions.

Older Siblings

Listening to the experiences of adult brothers and sisters can be instructive and validating for Sibshop participants. Hearing adults talk about growing up as a sibling of a person with special needs will encourage your participants to talk about their lives and will stimulate conversation among the entire group.

To prepare your Sibshop participants, announce the panel at the beginning of the program, and encourage the participants to think of questions for the panel.

To help prepare the panel, you may wish to send them guidelines and questions prior to the Sibshop. A sample letter is shown in Figure 21.

Dear Panelist,

Thanks for agreeing to be on our adult sibling panel at our upcoming Sibshop. As I mentioned on the phone, you and the other panelists will have a chance to informally discuss your experiences growing up with a brother or sister who has special needs with our 8- to 13-year-old Sibshop participants. We'll ask you to share information about:

Yourself. We'll want to know what you do, whether you have a family of your own, where you grew up and went to school, and anything else you wish to share.

Your brother or sister with special needs. We'll want to know what kind of disability your sibling has, how old your sibling is, where he or she went to school, what your sib currently does during the day, where he or she lives, and so on.

Your family. We'll be interested in how many children there are in your family. If you're older than your sib, we'll want to know how old you were when you learned your sib had special needs. If you're younger than your sib, we'll want to know how much younger and if you remember when you realized your older brother or sister had special needs.

What it was like when you were a kid. Did your brother's or sister's special needs cause any problems with your parents, friends, schoolmates, or even strangers? Did you come up with solutions to these problems? Growing up, did you have any questions or secret worries about your sibling's special needs? Were there good things that happened to you or your family as a result of having a brother or sister who has special needs? Does your family have funny, treasured stories about life with your brother or sister?

A desired outcome of the panel will be the discussion with the younger siblings. Frequently, upon hearing the panelists' "testimony," younger siblings will describe similar experiences they have had.

Thanks again for being a part of our program!

Sincerely,

Erica Lewis Erickson

Figure 21.   Sample letter to panel participant. (For the reader's use, this material may be reproduced. From Meyer, D.J., & Vadasy, P.F. [1994]. *Sibshops: Workshops for siblings of children with special needs*. Copyright © 1994 Paul H. Brookes Publishing Co.)

Other Special Guests

When a project seemed to be finished, Walt Disney always encouraged his staff to look at it one more time and "plus it." In other words, how can we make this good experience even better? You will want to "plus" your Sibshop frequently to be sure that it stays fresh and exciting for participants.

Special guests can help keep a Sibshop lively and especially rewarding to attend. As with many Sibshop activities, you are limited only by your imagination when choosing a special guest. Examples of special guests you can invite to help make sure your Sibshops are truly memorable events include: chefs who can show participants how to make a special dish or dessert, clog or tap dancers who are willing to perform and teach a step or two, jugglers who share the basics of their craft, folk singers who can create songs based on participants' suggestions, actors adept at improvisational theater, gymnasts, martial arts instructors, or even a local football hero who would enjoy playing touch football with admiring participants.

11

Workshops for Parents and Service Providers on Sibling Issues

One of the most gratifying aspects of providing training on the Sibshop model has been parents' and professionals' keen interest in sibling issues. Parents, who witness the sibling experience on a daily basis, tell us that they appreciate an opportunity to discuss and learn about sibling relationships in other families. Teachers, administrators, social workers, physicians, and therapists who realize that a child's disability has an impact on all family members tell us that they welcome opportunities to expand their understanding of issues for brothers and sisters. In this chapter we describe how to present three different types of workshops on sibling issues: a panel of siblings, a workshop for parents and service providers, and an informal meeting for parents of Sibshop participants. All three are designed to address the fifth Sibshop goal:

Goal 5: Sibshops will provide parents and other professionals with opportunities to learn more about the concerns and opportunities frequently experienced by brothers and sisters of people with special needs.

Because some parents and professionals prefer to read a book or a newsletter or watch a videotape than attend workshops, we list alternative resources at the end of the chapter.

SIBLING PANELS

Panels of brothers and sisters of people with special needs can be a potent, valuable method of educating parents and professionals about issues facing siblings. Panelists frequently remark that they, too, leave with an expanded understanding of the sibling experience as a result of listening to the other panelists.

Panel Guidelines

Sibling panels are relatively easy to run, considering the value of the information exchanged. Below are guidelines to help assure that a sibling panel is as productive as possible:

1. *Begin early.* As soon as you decide to host a sibling panel, begin to recruit five to seven panelists, using the selection guidelines discussed below. Finding appropriate panelists who are available on the dates you select may take longer than you think. Decide upon location, time (allowing at least 90 minutes), and how you will publicize the event to parents and professionals.
2. *Publicize the event.* As noted above, sibling panels are wonderful learning opportunities. Publicizing the panel will assure that this opportunity is offered to as many parents and professionals as possible. A good turnout will also assure a rich dialogue between panel and audience.
3. *Seek balance.* Ideally, your sibling panel will be balanced with respect to:

Disability or illness type. Unless the purpose of the panel is to discuss the concerns of siblings with a specific disability or illness, attempt to have several disabilities and/or illnesses represented.

Age relative to the sibling with the disability. Attempt to balance the panel by inviting brothers and sisters who are older, younger, and very close in age to their siblings who have special needs. As you can easily imagine, the experiences of a brother who is 10 years older than a sibling with cerebral palsy will be very different from the experiences of a brother who is 1 year younger than a sibling with cerebral palsy.

Gender. Brothers often have different experiences from sisters, especially with regard to caregiving expectations and their involvement with the sibling as an adult. Seek to have equal representation of males and females on the panel.

4. *Invite primarily adult siblings.* Sibling panels benefit from the reflection provided by young adult and older adult brothers and sisters. Although school-age siblings are often more readily available than adult siblings and can comment on issues they currently face, they lack the perspective of older siblings and occasionally suffer from stage fright. If you do include young siblings, invite no more than two panelists between the ages of 8 and 15.
5. *Disinvite parents.* If possible, ask the panelists' parents not to attend the session. This will help assure that panelists feel free to talk about their lives and their families.

Two weeks prior to the sibling panel, send each panelist a sheet (such as the one shown in Figure 22) outlining questions they may be asked during the program. This "advanced organizer" will reduce panelists' anxiety and help them prepare their thoughts on the topic prior to the panel. In the event they forget to bring these sheets along, make additional copies to give panelists before the program begins.

SIBLING PANEL WORKSHOP SHEET

Greetings! Thank you for agreeing to be a member of our sibling panel. During the panel you will have a chance to discuss what life is like for a brother or sister of a person with special needs. You and the other panelists will have a chance to discuss the good parts, the not-so-good parts, and everything in between.

Parents, professionals, and others who attend sibling panels usually say that they left knowing a lot more about sibling issues than they did before. Panelists usually say they learned a lot too.

During the panel, you will be asked to share information on:

Yourself, such as where you live, your work or school status, interests
Your brother or sister with special needs, such as age, work or school status, interests
Your family, such as total number of kids
How you learned about your sibling's illness or disability and how it was explained to you
Whether your sibling's disability or illness ever caused any special problems for you (with friends, at school, at home)
Whether your sibling's disability or illness ever resulted in any unusual opportunities
What comes to mind when you think about your and your sibling's future
Stories or anecdotes about your sibling, your family, or yourself that you would like to share

We'll leave plenty of time for members of the audience to ask questions. This is often the most informative part of the workshop.

At the very end, I may ask:

In retrospect, what do you think your parents did especially well in helping your family accept and adjust to your sibling's special needs?
What things do you wish they had done differently?
What advice would you give to a young brother or sister of a child with special needs? to parents?
What message would you give to service providers who work with families of people with special needs?

Thanks for your thoughts on this important topic!

Figure 22.   The Sibling Panel Workshop Sheet. (For the reader's use, this material may be reproduced. From Meyer, D.J., & Vadasy, P.F. [1994]. *Sibshops: Workshops for siblings of children with special needs.* Copyright © 1994 Paul H. Brookes Publishing Co.)

Hosting the Panel

At the workshop, before the panel members introduce themselves, welcome the panelists and the audience and note the workshop's goal: to provide parents and other professionals with an opportunity to learn about the unique joys, concerns, and issues experienced by brothers and sisters of people with special needs. If time permits, ask audience members to introduce themselves briefly and say what brought them to a sibling panel. Following introductions, let the audience know that they will have an opportunity to ask panel members questions, seek advice from panelists, and share experiences from their families.

As the panel's host, ask the panelists to introduce themselves first, sharing with the audience information suggested in the first question of the workshop sheet. You may then ask them to respond to subsequent questions on the workshop sheet. After asking the panel a few introductory questions, be sure to offer the audience a chance to ask additional questions or make comments. Questions and discussion among parents and panel members will be the most valuable portion of the workshop, so be sure to allow ample time. As parents' concerns surface, you may wish to encourage panel members and other parents to share how their families handled a similar situation. Bring closure to the program by selecting closing questions from the workshop sheet. (What do you think your parents did especially well? What do you wish they had done differently? What advice would you give to a young brother or sister of a child with special needs? to parents? What message would you give to service providers who work with families of people with special needs?)

At the very end, be sure to thank the panel members. The questions posed for the panel members will yield valuable insights. However, questions also will require panelists to examine and comment on a lifetime of experiences with their siblings, families, and friends that were sometimes happy, sometimes sad, and frequently challenging—no easy task.

A WORKSHOP ON SIBLING ISSUES

During this 1½- to 2-hour workshop, parent and service provider participants work together to define and discuss sibling concerns, opportunities, and strategies. Discussions are based on participants' observations and experiences. Rather than using an imported "expert" on sibling issues, this workshop utilizes the group's collective expertise.

At the beginning of the workshop, ask participants to introduce themselves briefly and (if appropriate) their families, and share with the group what brings them to a workshop on sibling issues. Following introductions, acknowledge that for siblings, as for their parents, having a family member with a disability is usually an ambivalent experience. As do their parents, siblings may have unusual concerns (i.e., need for information about the disability, guilt, resentment), but they may also have unusual opportunities (i.e., increased empathy, a special pride, a singular sense of humor).

Suggest to the participants assembled that they, as parents and providers who work with families, are as capable as anyone to define the concerns and opportunities that their typically developing children experience. In short, the collective expertise and wisdom of the group is considerable. Tell them that by sharing and discussing their insights with the rest of the group, everyone in the group can leave with an expanded understanding of the sibling experience.

Prior to a meeting, prepare a four-sided worksheet (two pages, printed front to back, stapled), such as the one shown in Figure 23.

Distribute the sheets to the participants, and provide pens or pencils. Ask each participant to pair off with another participant (and introduce themselves if they have not met) and take 10 minutes to discuss page 1. At the end of this time, ask a representative from each pair to share with the larger group the unusual concerns they have observed or identified. Record the general headings on a chalkboard or, preferably, large sheets of paper.

Next, ask each participant to pair off with a different partner and discuss page 2, strategies to decrease unusual concerns. After 10 minutes, have parents report back to the group. Continue with pages 3 and 4. By the end of the session, participants will have generated a wide range of issues, and have had the opportunity to discuss them individually with four different participants, as well as with the larger group.

Let the participants know that you (or a participant volunteer) will transcribe the concerns, opportunities, and strategies from the sheets or chalkboard and send each participant a copy.

INFORMAL DISCUSSIONS FOR PARENTS OF SIBSHOP PARTICIPANTS

If you hold your Sibshops as a series of meetings, we suggest that you plan one meeting with a concurrent gathering for parents of participants. This meeting for parents, ideally held midway through the series, need not be as long as the Sibshop itself—usually 2 hours will suffice. During the meeting, you may wish to utilize the workshop formats described above, or simply have an open-ended discussion with participants' parents. To begin, ask parents to introduce themselves, describe their families, and share their reasons for enrolling their children in a Sibshop. This will usually be enough to initiate a lively discussion. Your job is to facilitate (i.e., to make easy) conversation and to listen.

This discussion is also an excellent opportunity to seek parents' feedback on the Sibshop. Ask parents what comments their children

SIBLING ISSUE WORKSHEETS

Page 1 (first full page):

BROTHERS AND SISTERS OF CHILDREN WITH SPECIAL NEEDS

The goal of this workshop is to define and discuss the unusual opportunities and concerns experienced by brothers and sisters. By sharing your observations and experiences, you can help all workshop participants gain a broader understanding of the joys, concerns, and challenges that are a part of being a sibling of a child with special needs.

UNUSUAL CONCERNS

With your partner, please take a few minutes to discuss any concerns that you feel brothers and sisters of children with special needs may experience. Please briefly note the concerns you discuss below:

Page 2 (one full page):

STRATEGIES: CONCERNS

Next, please discuss with your partner ways that parents and other professionals can minimize the concerns of siblings of children with special needs. Please briefly list your strategies below:

Page 3 (one full page):

UNUSUAL OPPORTUNITIES

Please discuss benefits or unusual opportunities that brothers and sisters may experience as a result of growing up with a sibling who has special needs. Please briefly note these benefits or opportunities below:

Page 4 (one full page):

STRATEGIES: OPPORTUNITIES

Finally, please discuss how we as parents and service providers can maximize opportunities experienced by brothers and sisters of children with special needs. Please note these strategies below:

Figure 23.   Sibling Issue Worksheet format, prepared as two pages, printed front and back and stapled together. (For the reader's use, this material may be reproduced. From Meyer, D.J., & Vadasy, P.F. [1994]. *Sibshops: Workshops for siblings of children with special needs.* Copyright © 1994 Paul H. Brookes Publishing Co.)

have made about the program, and what suggestions they have to make it better. It is also a good time to discuss the direction of the program and to seek their counsel on how to make Sibshops as responsive and available to families as possible.

This is not, however, a time to share with parents the details of their children's conversations during your Sibshops. Despite some parents' desire to know what their children are saying, the information and opinions shared during Sibshops should be treated as confidential. There is an important exception: If a participant shares information that, in your best judgment, parents *need* to know, it is your responsibility to meet privately with the participant, share your concerns, and discuss strategies for telling his or her parents. Sometimes participants will elect to tell their parents themselves; other times they will appreciate your offer to talk to the parents; and still other times they will want your company as you both discuss your concern with the parents.

OTHER RESOURCES FOR PARENTS AND SERVICE PROVIDERS

Not all parents will be able to (or wish to) attend workshops. Many parents will prefer to learn about sibling issues through written materials or other media. The following are publications you may wish to recommend and have in your library to refer to parents. The videotapes, especially Tom Fish's *The Next Step*, can also be a valuable part of a workshop on sibling issues.

Books

Brothers, Sisters, and Special Needs: Information and Activities for Helping Young Siblings of Children with Chronic Illnesses and Developmental Disabilities. Debra J. Lobato, 1990. Baltimore: Paul H. Brookes Publishing Co.

Brothers & Sisters: A Special Part of Exceptional Families (2nd ed.). Thomas H. Powell and Peggy Ahrenhold Gallagher, 1993. Baltimore: Paul H. Brookes Publishing Co.

Living with a Brother or Sister with Special Needs: A Book for Sibs. Donald Meyer, Patricia Vadasy, and Rebecca Fewell, 1985. Seattle: University of Washington Press.

Profile of the Other Child: A Sibling Guide for Parents. Frances Dwyer McCaffery and Thomas Fish. Publications Office, Nissonger Center UAP, 434 McCampbell Hall, The Ohio State University, 1581 Dodd Drive, Columbus, OH 43210.

Newsletters

The National Association of Sibling Programs (NASP) Newsletter. The Sibling Support Project, CL-09, Children's Hospital and Medical Center, 4800 Sand Point Way, NE, Seattle, WA 98105.

The Sibling Information Network Newsletter. Sibling Information Network, 1776 Ellington Road, South Windsor, CT 06074.

The Bond, the newsletter of the Siblings and Adult Children Network of the National Alliance of the Mentally Ill. NAMI, 2101 Wilson Blvd. Suite 302, Arlington, VA 22201.

Videotapes

Brothers and Sisters: Growing up with a Blind Sibling. (1992). Nancy Chernus-Mansfield and Marilyn Horn, Producers. The Institute for Families of Blind Children, Mailstop 111, P.O. Box 54700, Los Angeles, CA 90054-0700.

Childhood Cancer: Siblings Speak Out. (1983). The Children's Hospital, Producer. The Children's Hospital, Hematology and Oncology Department, Box B115, 1056 E. 19th Avenue, Denver, CO 80218.

The Next Step. (1993). Thomas Fish, Producer. Publications Office, Nissonger Center UAP, 434 McCampbell Hall, The Ohio State University, 1581 Dodd Drive, Columbus, OH 43210.

The Rest of the Family. (1991). Karen Collins, Producer; David Emmerling, Director. The Epilepsy Foundation of America, 4351 Garden City Drive, Landover, MD 20785.

What About Me? (1989). Barbara Turk, Producer. Educational Productions, Inc., 7412 S.W. Beaverton Hillsdale Highway, Suite 210, Portland, OR 97225.

12

Programs for Adult Siblings of People with Disabilities

Increasingly, adults with disabilities of the baby boom and post–baby boom generation are living and working in the community. As their parents age and die, their brothers and sisters who do not have disabilities will be involved in their lives in significant ways. Because of the movement toward community life for people with disabilities and the scarcity of needed resources for adults with disabilities (e.g., residential options and employment opportunities), siblings' roles will likely be greater than in previous generations.

> Carol, who is in her 20s, has a brother Sean, who has cerebral palsy. Carol's mother, who is not nearly as assertive as Carol, depends on Carol to attend IEP meetings to assure that Sean's educational and behavioral needs are being met. She also depends on Carol to keep her up-to-date with information about cerebral palsy. Even though she has other brothers and sisters, it is obvious to Carol who will look after Sean's needs in the years to come.

> Tom is in college. Last year, he and his parents discussed his brother Ron's future with a lawyer. Even though Tom would eventually like to move away from the economically depressed city in which he lives, he feels he cannot, because Ron (who has mental retardation and behavior problems) does not respond well to change. Tom is considering changing his major to adapt to his region's meager job market.

> Michael has one surviving sibling—Jalene, who has autism. Rochelle, their older sister, died last year, as did their dad. Mom will be 82 in May. On his way to work and during odd moments, Michael, who remarried 2 years ago, worries about his future. Rochelle, so it seemed, was planning on caring for Jalene "when the time came." Now Michael feels he must step forward and assume some responsibility for Jalene, but, he thinks, where do you begin? Michael finds it difficult to discuss his sister's future with his mother—she's been

through so much already this year. It's also hard for him to discuss it with his new wife and her children, who still don't know Jalene all that well. Should he plan on having Jalene live with his family someday? Are there places in the community where Jalene could live? Or work? He knows there are services for adults with disabilities, but what are they? Again, where do you begin?

Like Carol, Tom, and Michael, many adult siblings without disabilities will struggle with seemingly incompatible loyalties they feel toward their brothers and sisters and loyalties they have toward their own families.

Adult brothers and sisters are an extraordinarily overlooked population, receiving little attention from agencies serving brothers and sisters of people with special needs. This is despite the fact that siblings generally have the longest-lasting relationship in the family and the fact that there are vast numbers of brothers and sisters: Most of the 43 million people with disabilities in the United States have brothers and sisters. One way to acknowledge the important roles that adult siblings play in the family is to create programs specifically for brothers and sisters that reflect their issues and concerns.

Discussions with adult brothers and sisters of people with special needs reveal that they share many, if not most, of the concerns that parents have about the well-being of the person with the disability. Like groups for parents, groups for adult siblings, while important and useful, will be no panacea. Addressing their concerns, like those of their parents, will require systemic change.

The handful of programs for adult siblings of people with disabilities provide direction for those interested in meeting with groups of adult siblings. Most existing adult sibling programs are, in one way or another, addressing at least three identified needs: information, peer support opportunities, and advocacy skills.

Information. Adult siblings express a desire to learn more about services for their brothers and sisters. Like Michael, they say they need this information to help their siblings make informed choices and plan for the entire family's future. At adult sibling programs, participants have an opportunity to seek and share information on the myriad services for people with disabilities.

Peer support. Like their parents, adult siblings express a desire to talk to a peer who is facing a similar situation. At groups for adult siblings, participants can share—often for the very first time—the unique joys and concerns that are a part of being a sibling of a person with a disability with someone who truly understands.

Advocacy. A third concern that adult siblings have is the desire to advocate for quality services for their brothers and sisters. Like their parents before them, adult siblings know that fundamental change for people with disabilities occurs only when family members effectively advocate on their behalf. Now that many siblings are assuming a more important role in the lives of their brothers and sisters, they express a desire to acquire advocacy skills. Programs for brothers and sisters can provide them with this opportunity.

ADULT SIBLING PROGRAM PROFILES

Below are brief descriptions of five programs for adult brothers and sisters of people with disabilities. As these programs are a relatively recent innovation, some of these programs may be considered "works-in-progress." Nevertheless, they provide their communities with a valuable service and a reminder of the critical roles played by adult brothers and sisters.

Association for the Help of Retarded Children, New York City

The Association for the Help of Retarded Children (AHRC) involves adult siblings in various agency activities, including their Adult Sibling Support Group, which has met monthly on Sunday evenings since 1982. It is sibling-run, using no professional leadership, and is open to any adult sibling wishing to join at any time. According to organizers, a "closed" group model was tried and found not to work. Members are kept in touch via a mailed summary of each meeting. Organizers report that some adult siblings come monthly, some less frequently, some only during times of crisis, and some just for the information. Occasionally guest speakers are invited. In addition to the ongoing support groups, AHRC has hosted meetings for adult siblings on specific topics in various boroughs of New York City. Topics have included: family teamwork and future planning, guardianships, the caregiver experience, entitlements and benefits, and family and professional partnerships.

The Greater Boston Association for Retarded Citizens

The Sibling Support Group of the Greater Boston Association for Retarded Citizens (GBARC) is a 10-session, closed group offered at least once per year for 8–10 adult brothers and sisters. At 4 of the 10 sessions, guest speakers are invited. The sessions follow a predetermined sequence: 1) getting acquainted, 2) advocacy, 3) potluck dinner, 4) residential options, 5) family communications, 6) guardianship and estate planning, 7) vocational training and jobs, 8) friends, 9) genetic counseling, and 10) sibling celebration. According to organizers, the program has a "graduate" group that meets occasionally and refers newly identified brothers and sisters to the 10-session program.

GBARC has a program guide available for purchase ($9.00; Greater Boston Arc, 1249 Boylston Street, Boston, MA, 02215; telephone 617-783-3900).

Siblings for a Significant Change, New York City

As an organization, Siblings for a Significant Change (SSC) has a clear preference for action and advocacy over support activities where participants discuss emotional and family issues. Members meet infrequently as a group. Instead, SSC disseminates information to members and others; provides conferences, workshops, and advocacy training to siblings; and provides direct services such as counseling, crisis intervention, and legal assistance. SSC has been involved with a variety of advocacy issues pertaining to people with disabilities, including the creation of a videotape about siblings (Zatlow, 1987) and appearances on television and radio to discuss sibling and advocacy issues. According to organizers, a certain amount of sharing occurs incidentally, although siblings who have a strong need to discuss such issues are referred to appropriate services. SSC also hosts social events so that members, relatives with disabilities, and providers may meet and informally discuss issues.

Arc Sibling Support Group of Monmouth County, New Jersey

A relatively new effort for adult siblings in New Jersey, the Sibling Support Group (SSG) meets four times per year. According to organizers, turnout at any given meeting is typically low but members are interested. Organizers report many are "apprehensive about what will happen when their parents die" (Meyer & Erickson, 1993, p. 4) and wish to learn about options available for their siblings in a time of diminishing resources. Preferring action and advocacy over discussion of family and emotional issues, SSG meetings have guest speakers and are exploring creative housing opportunities with the local Arc. SSG also occasionally meets at a restaurant for dinners.

Adult Siblings of People with Disabilities of King County, Washington

Adult Siblings of People with Disabilities (ASPD) has served Seattle-area adult siblings since 1991. The group is cosponsored by the Sibling Support Project at Children's Hospital and Medical Center and the Arc of King County. The program began by surveying potential members to determine programmatic interests. The survey revealed that adult siblings had an interest in obtaining information on a wide array of topics, listed here in decreasing order of interest: recreation and leisure opportunities; community living and residential options; sexuality, socialization, and friendships; family communications; employment/day program options; eligibility for services; legal issues; advocacy; and respite care options.

After some experimentation, ASPD adopted a format of informal monthly meetings at members' homes. Every third month, a guest speaker is invited to address a topic chosen by participants. At the remaining meetings, members discuss a wide range of family and disability-related issues and share information about services for their siblings. The group has open membership with about 10 core participants and an equal number coming less frequently. The ASPD program also sponsors picnics for members and their families.

GOALS FOR ADULT SIBLING PROGRAMS

In its fledgling days, ASPD worked to develop goals to focus the group's efforts and meet the needs of its members. The group reviewed the structures and objectives of the adult sibling programs described above and utilized some of the concepts that had shaped their goals. After brainstorming and discussing, prioritizing and drafting, the following are the goals and opportunities that the Seattle ASPD group established to meet their needs (Meyer & Erickson, 1993, pp. 4–6). They are offered as a starting point for new groups for adult siblings.

Support

> To meet other adult siblings of people with disabilities at ASPD-sponsored meetings and social events; and
>
> To share common joys and concerns with other adult brothers and sisters.

Adult brothers and sisters of people with disabilities face issues that are not generally experienced by their peers in the community. ASPD provides opportunities for participants to meet—perhaps for the first time—others who share similar concerns. ASPD offers participants both formal (meetings) and informal (social events, sibling-to-sibling) sources of support.

> To examine the impact of the sibling's disability on the entire family.

At ASPD meetings, participants can discuss the dynamics of the families in which they grew up, their own families, and the families' adaptations to the siblings' disabilities.

> To discuss members' relationships with their brothers and sisters who have disabilities.

At meetings, members can discuss the unique aspects of their relationships with their siblings, including ways to enhance relationships, whether local or long-distance.

> To offer an understanding ear to participants who are experiencing a crisis with their siblings.

Participants will, on occasion, face stressful events concerning their families or siblings. When these events are resolvable, group members may suggest strategies or resources. When unresolvable, participants can turn to the group (or individuals from the group) for support and understanding.

Information

> To learn about programs and services available for their brothers and sisters.

To ensure that their siblings who have disabilities live a full life, it is important for family members, including adult brothers and sisters, to learn about available resources. At ASPD, participants will have opportunities to learn from one another and from guest speakers about resources of interest to group members including, but not limited to: recreational and leisure opportunities; residential options; vocational and day program options; wills, trusts, and guardianships; and medical insurance. Participants who live close to their siblings may be able to provide ideas and suggest resources to a participant who is worried about the well-being of a sibling who lives in another city or state.

> To learn how other participants have resolved issues commonly faced by brothers and sisters.

Adult brothers and sisters face issues not frequently faced by others in the community. At ASPD meetings, participants will have opportunities to seek ideas and information from group members. Learning how others have handled difficult situations can provide participants with a broad array of solutions from which they may choose.

Advocacy

> To acquire necessary skills to become effective advocates for their brothers and sisters.

Advocacy is a skill. At ASPD meetings members will share advocacy strategies and learn, from one another and guest speakers, about legislation affecting people with disabilities and how to advocate effectively for their brothers and sisters.

> To advocate for services for their brothers and sisters with disabilities.

Change for people with disabilities has occurred only when advocates—usually parents—have determinedly demanded it. As many adult siblings are increasingly involved in the lives of their brothers and sisters, members of ASPD may learn ways to advocate effectively for the well-being and advancement of their siblings with disabilities. Furthermore, to assure that their *own* needs are met, participants may learn ways to share their views, *as adult siblings,* with policy makers.

> To explore creation of services to assure that siblings' needs are met.

Assuring a quality lifestyle during times of diminishing resources may require creative action. Members of ASPD may meet for the purposes of creating services, such as housing or respite, to meet the needs of participants' brothers and sisters.

WELCOMING SIBLINGS, ADULT AND OTHERWISE: A CHECKLIST FOR AGENCIES

Many agencies are beginning to realize that siblings are too valuable to ignore, and have begun changing policies and procedures to acknowledge the important roles brothers and sisters play. Here are a few considerations:

Does your agency reach out to adult brothers and sisters? Many agencies and organizations complain that they have difficulty attracting parents of adults with disabilities to meetings, workshops, and other events. Many of these parents have already attended enough meetings to last several lifetimes, and cannot abide one more. Consider targeting the family member who will have increasing involvement in the life of the person with the disability, by making a special effort to invite brothers and sisters to informational, IEP, and transition-planning meetings. Brothers and sisters, after all, are the future.

Does your agency have brothers and sisters on your advisory board? Reserving seats on your board for siblings will provide the board with a unique and important perspective and evidence of your agency's concern for this important family member.

Does your agency educate staff about issues facing young and adult brothers and sisters? Consider utilizing the written materials and

BROTHERS, SISTERS, AND SPECIAL NEEDS:
A MEETING FOR ADULT SIBLINGS OF PEOPLE WITH DISABILITIES

Until recently, young siblings of children with special needs have been a largely over-looked group. Still overlooked are adult brothers and sisters of people with disabili-ties. Tonight, we will focus on issues that are important to you. We feel that service providers and parents have much to learn from your experiences and thoughts.

This evening, we hope you will share your expertise, your concerns, and your experiences, both good and not-so-good. Your thoughts will help us all learn more about what it means to be the adult sibling of a person who has a disability.

To begin, we'll ask participants to introduce themselves briefly to the group. We'll also ask participants to provide some information about their brothers or sis-ters who have disabilities, such as age, school or employment status, and disability type.

Below are some questions you may wish to discuss with the group. Throughout the group, please feel free to ask each other questions and make comments, but pace yourself so everyone gets a turn.

Growing up

What were important issues to you growing up with a sibling who has a disability?

Is the experience of being a sister to a person with a disability different from a brother's experience? If so, how?

Is the experience of being an older sibling to a person with a disability different from a younger sibling's experience? If so, how?

Now

How does your relationship with the sibling who has a disability compare to the relationship your other brothers and sisters have with this sibling?

Has explaining your sibling's current and future special needs been a problem for your children, "significant other," or spouse?

What are your sibling's biggest needs right now?

As an adult, what information (on service, resources, etc.) do you feel is required to assure that your and your sibling's needs are met?

What could agencies (for example, Arcs, UCPs, state developmental disabilities commissions) do to address your concerns as an adult brother or sister of a per-son with a disability?

The future

When you think about your sibling's future, what do you see?

What are your family's plans for your sibling's future? What is your role? Were you involved in this planning? Are you satisfied with these plans?

In retrospect

What advice would you give to a young brother or sister of a child with special needs?

What message would you give to teachers or other professionals who work with families of children with special needs?

In regard to raising a child with special needs: What did your parents do especially well? Is there anything you wish they had done differently?

What is one thing parents should know about brothers and sisters of people with special needs?

Thank you for your thoughts!

Figure 27. Basic Sibshop worksheet for use or adaption. (For the reader's use, this material may be reproduced. From Meyer, D.J., & Vadasy, P.F. [1994]. *Sibshops: Workshops for siblings of children with special needs.* Copyright © 1994 Paul H. Brookes Publishing Co.)

videotapes mentioned in Chapter 11 or hosting a sibling panel, also discussed in Chapter 11.

Does your agency have a program specifically for adult brothers and sisters? You may wish to try a one-time Adult Siblings Only Workshop. A sample workshop sheet may be found in Figure 24. Be sure to publicize the event well in advance. A sample press release may be found in Figure 3.

Does your agency have a policy about the importance of including siblings? For a starting point, read the policy statement in Appendix D, which we adapted from the Illinois Planning Council on Developmental Disabilities.

Does your agency still use limiting terminology? Organizations that use the word *parent* when *family* or *family member* is more appropriate send a message to brothers and sisters, grandparents, and other family members that the program is not for them. With siblings and primary-caregiver grandparents assuming increasingly active roles in the lives of people with disabilities, we cannot afford to exclude anyone.

WORKSHOPS FOR ADULT BROTHERS AND SISTERS

Bringing adult brothers and sisters together to talk can be a powerful learning experience for everyone. For many, these meetings will be the first opportunity they have to talk to another sibling. You may use or adapt the workshop sheet shown in Figure 27 (p. 209). Let us know how it went!

CONCLUSION

If the adult siblings in your community have not had an opportunity to meet as a group, we hope you will consider hosting a one-time meeting, if not an ongoing program. The benefits we have witnessed with our adult sibling group (ASPD) are considerable and farreaching. Members and facilitators gain unique insights on the impact that a person's special needs can have on all family members. Participants frequently have closely held feelings validated, often for the first time. As they learn about services and issues, participants become better advocates for their siblings and others with special needs. And finally, participants go on to represent sibling issues on boards, task forces, and planning councils, and in doing so, help these organizations become truly family focused.

Appendix A
Books About Disabilities
and Illnesses for Young Readers

Erica Lewis Erickson

On the pages that follow are books about disabilities and illnesses for young readers. Some of the books are fiction where a sibling or child with a disability is the central character. Others are nonfiction books that attempt to describe a disability or illness to young readers. Some facilitators use this list to select books to read to younger participants during their Sibshops. You may photocopy this list and share it with participants and parents. The recommended reader ages are given in parentheses at the end of each reference.

AUTISM

Bodenheimer, C. (1979). *Everybody is a person: A book for brothers and sisters of autistic kids.* Syracuse, NY: Jowonio/The Learning Place. (11–14)

Gold, P. (1975). *Please don't say hello.* New York: Human Sciences Press. (8–13)

Parker, R. (1974). *He's your brother.* Nashville, TN: Thomas Nelson. (11–15)

Spence, E. (1977). *The devil hole.* New York: Lothrop, Lee & Shepard. (11–14)

Yashima, T. (1955). *Crow boy.* New York: Viking Press. (4–8)

BLINDNESS AND VISUAL DISABILITIES

Eyerly, J. (1981). *The seeing summer.* Philadelphia: J.B. Lippincott. (8–12)

Hall, L. (1982). *Half the battle.* New York: Charles Scribner's Sons. (11–15)

Kent, D. (1979). *Belonging.* New York: Ace Books. (11–15)

Little, J. (1972). *From Anna.* New York: Harper & Row. (11–16)

Little, J. (1977). *Listen for the singing.* New York: E.P. Dutton. (11–16)

Marcus, R. (1981). *Being blind.* Mamaroneck, NY: Hastings House. (10–15)

McPhee, R. (1981). *Tom and Bear.* New York: Thomas Y. Crowell. (9–15)

Weiss, M.E. (1980). *Blindness.* New York: Franklin Watts. (11–14)

Wolf, B. (1976). *Connie's new eyes.* New York: Harper & Row. (11–15)

CANCER

Amadeo, D.M. (1989). *There's a little bit of me in Jamey.* Morton Grove, IL: Albert Whitman & Co. (8–13)

Murray, G., & Jampolsky, G. (Eds.). (1983). *Straight from the siblings: Another look at the rainbow.* Berkeley, CA: Celestial Arts. (8–18)

Erica Lewis Erickson is Project Assistant at the Sibling Support Project, Children's Hospital and Medical Center, Seattle, Washington.

CEREBRAL PALSY

Emmert, M. (1989). *I'm the big sister now.* Morton Grove, IL: Albert Whitman & Co. (7–11)

Fassler, J. (1975). *Howie helps himself.* Morton Grove, IL: Albert Whitman & Co. (3–7)

Little, J. (1962). *Mine for keeps.* Boston: Little, Brown. (8–12)

Metzger, L. (1992). *Barry's sister.* New York: Atheneum. (9–17)

Nolan, C. (1987). *Under the eye of the clock.* New York: St. Martin's Press. (14 and up)

Perske, R. (1986). *Don't stop the music.* Nashville, TN: Abingdon Press. (11–17)

Rabe, B. (1981). *The balancing girl.* New York: E.P. Dutton. (4–7)

Robinet, H.G. (1980). *Ride the red cycle.* Boston: Houghton Mifflin. (9–14)

Slepian, J. (1980). *The Alfred summer.* New York: Macmillan. (11–17)

Southall, I. (1968). *Let the balloon go.* New York: St. Martin's Press. (9–15)

CYSTIC FIBROSIS

Arnold, K. (1982). *Anna joins in.* Nashville, TN: Abingdon Press. (4–8)

DEAFNESS AND HEARING PROBLEMS

Hlibok, B. (1981). *Silent dancer.* New York: Messner. (3–6)

Hyman, J. (1980). *Deafness.* New York: Franklin Watts. (11–15)

Keller, H. (1982). *Cromwell's glasses.* New York: Greenwillow Books. (3–6)

Peterson, J.W. (1977). *I have a sister, my sister is deaf.* New York: Harper & Row. (11–13)

Walker, L.A. (1985). *Amy: The story of a deaf child.* New York: E.P. Dutton. (7–13)

DIABETES

Kipnis, L., & Adler, S. (1979). *You can't catch diabetes from a friend.* Gainesville, FL: Triad Scientific Publishers. (6–14)

EMOTIONAL AND BEHAVIORAL PROBLEMS/ATTENTION DEFICIT DISORDER

Gehert, J. (1992). *I'm somebody too.* Fairport, NY: Verbal Images Press. (9–17)

Moss, D. (1989). *Shelley, the hyperactive turtle.* Rockville, MD: Woodbine House. (4–8)

EPILEPSY

Epilepsy Foundation of America. (1992). *Brothers and sisters: Just for you!* Landover, MD: Author. (7 through adult)

Hermes, P. (1980). *What if they knew?* New York: Harcourt Brace Jovanovich. (11–14)

Herzig, A., & Mali, J.L. (1982). *A season of secrets.* Boston: Little, Brown. (11–17)

Moss, D. (1989). *Lee, the rabbit with epilepsy.* Rockville, MD: Woodbine House. (4–8)

LEARNING DISABILITIES

Evans, S. (1986). *Don't look at me.* Portland, OR: Multnomah Press. (7–11)

Little, J. (1968). *Take wing.* Boston: Little, Brown. (11–14)

Pevsner, S. (1977). *Keep stompin' till the music stops.* New York: Seabury. (11–15)

Smith, D.B. (1975). *Kelly's creek.* New York: Harper & Row. (11–15)

DEVELOPMENTAL DISABILITIES (INCLUDES DOWN SYNDROME)

Baldwin, A.N. (1978). *A little time.* New York: Viking Press. (9–15)

Bradbury, B. (1970). *Nancy and her Johnny O.* New York: Ives Washburn, Inc. (14 and up)

Byars, B. (1970). *The summer of the swans.* New York: Viking Press. (11–15)

Cairo, S. (1985). *Our brother has Down's syndrome: An introduction for children.* Toronto, Ontario, Canada: Annick Press Ltd. (4–11)

Cleaver, V. (1973). *Me too.* Philadelphia: J.B. Lippincott. (11–15)

Dodds, B. (1993). *My sister Annie.* Honesdale, PA: Caroline House Boyds Mills Press. (11–15)

Edwards, J., & Dawson, D. (1983). *My friend David.* Portland, OR: Ednick Communications. (14 and up)

Friis-Baastad, B. (1967). *Don't take Teddy.* New York: Charles Scribner's Sons. (11–14)

Gillhan, B. (1981). *My brother Barry.* London: Andre Duetsch Ltd. (10–13)

Hansen, M. (1985). *Straight from the heart.* Saskatoon, Saskatchewan, Canada: Saskatchewan Association for the Mentally Retarded. (12–17)

Hesse, K. (1991). *Wish on a unicorn.* New York: Henry Holt & Co. (9–16)

Hirsch, K. (1977). *My sister.* Minneapolis, MN: Carolrhoda Books. (5–8)

Konschuh, S.J. (1991). *My sister.* Calgary, Alberta, Canada: Paperworks Press Ltd. (3–8)

Laird, E. (1989). *Loving Ben.* New York: Delacorte Press. (11–17)

Lasker, J. (1974). *He's my brother.* Morton Grove, IL: Albert Whitman & Co. (3–7)

Litchfield, A. (1984). *Making room for Uncle Joe.* Morton Grove, IL: Albert Whitman & Co. (6–9)

Little, J. (1968). *Take wing.* Boston: Little, Brown. (10–13)

Lynch, M. (1979). *Mary Fran and me.* New York: St. Martin's Press. (14 and up)

Miner, J.C. (1982). *She's my sister: Having a retarded sister.* Mankato, MN: Crestwood House. (11–14)

Nollette, C.D., Lynch, T., Mitby, S., & Seyfried, D. (1985). *Having a brother like David.* Minneapolis, MN: Minneapolis Children's Medical Center. (7–11)

Perske, R. (1984). *Show me no mercy.* Nashville, TN: Abingdon Press. (14 and up)

Reynolds, P. (1968). *A different kind of sister.* New York: Lothrop, Lee & Shepard. (10–14)

Rodowsky, C. (1976). *What about me?* New York: Franklin Watts. (14 and up)

Shyer, M. (1978). *Welcome home, Jellybean.* New York: Scribner. (11–15)

Slepian, J. (1990). *Risk n' roses.* New York: Philomel Books. (9–16)

Smith, L.B. (1977). *A special kind of sister.* New York: Holt, Rinehart and Winston. (5–8)

Sobol, H. (1977). *My brother Steven is retarded.* New York: Macmillan. (5–8)

Thompson, M. (1992). *My brother, Matthew.* Rockville, MD: Woodbine House. (7–11)

Welch, S.K. (1990). *Don't call me Marda.* Wayne, PA: Our Child Press. (8–16)

Wright, B.R. (1981). *My sister is different.* Milwaukee, WI: Raintree Children's Books. (7–12)

PHYSICAL DISABILITIES

Berger, G. (1979). *Physical disabilities.* New York: Franklin Watts. (11–15)

Greenfield, E., & Revis, A. (1981). *Alesia.* New York: Philomel. (11–14)

Muldoon, K.M. (1989). *Princess Pooh.* Morton Grove, IL: Albert Whitman & Co. (7–13)

Rosenberg, M.B. (1983). *My friend Leslie.* New York: Lothrop, Lee & Shepard. (5–8)

Siegel, I.M. (1991). *Everybody's different, nobody's perfect.* Tucson, AZ: Muscular Dystrophy Association. (7–11)

SCHIZOPHRENIA

Knoll, V. (1992). *My sister then and now.* Minneapolis, MN: Carolrhoda Books. (7 and up)

SIBLING LOSS

Hickman, M.W. (1984). *Last week my brother Anthony died.* Nashville, TN: Abingdon Press. (4–8)

LaTour, K. (1983). *For those who live.* Omaha, NE: Centering Corp. (13–18)

SPINA BIFIDA

White, P. (1978). *Janet at school.* New York: Crowell. (3–5)

GENERAL BOOKS ABOUT DISABILITIES

Adams, B. (1979). *Like it is: Facts and feelings about handicaps from kids who know.* New York: Walker & Co. (8–12)

Brown, T. (1982). *Someone special just like you.* New York: Holt, Rinehart and Winston. (3–7)

Kamlen, J. (1979). *What if you couldn't . . . ? A book about special needs.* New York: Charles Scribner's Sons. (11–16)

McConnell, N.P. (1982). *Different and alike.* Colorado Springs, CO: Current Inc. (11–15)

Meyer, D.J., Vadasy, P.F., & Fewell, R.R. (1985). *Living with a brother or sister with special needs: A book for sibs.* Seattle: University of Washington Press. (7–15)

Rosenberg, M.B. (1988). *Finding a way: Living with exceptional brothers and sisters.* New York: Lothrop, Lee & Shepard. (7–14)

Schwier, K.M. (1992). *Keith Edward's different day.* San Luis Obispo, CA: Impact Pubs Cal. (7–11)

Stein, S.B. (1974). *About handicaps.* New York: Walker & Co. (3–8)

Appendix B

Recreation and Discussion Activity Books

The following are books that we consult—some more often than others—as we develop Sibshop activities. Check these out at your library should you wish to be further inspired!

RECREATIONAL ACTIVITIES

Caney, S. (1972). *Steven Caney's toy book*. New York: Workman.

Caney, S. (1975). *Steven Caney's play book*. New York: Workman.

Flugelman, A. (Ed.). (1976). *The new games book*. Garden City, NY: Doubleday.

Flugelman, A. (Ed.). (1981). *More new games!* Garden City, NY: Doubleday.

Gregson, B. (1982). *The incredible indoor games book*. Belmont, CA: Fearon Teacher Aids.

Gregson, B. (1984). *The outrageous outdoor games book*. Belmont, CA: Fearon Teacher Aids.

Le Fevere, D. (1988). *New games for the whole family*. New York: Putnam.

Luvmour, S., & Luvmour, J. (1990). *Everybody wins!* Philadelphia: New Society Publishers.

Orlick, T. (1978). *The cooperative sports & games book*. New York: Pantheon.

Orlick, T. (1982). *The second cooperative sports & games book*. New York: Pantheon.

Sobel, J. (1983). *Everybody wins*. New York: Walker & Co.

DISCUSSION ACTIVITIES

Devencenzi, J., & Pendergast, S. (1988). *Belonging*. San Luis Obispo, CA: Belonging.

Feshbach, N., Feshbach, S., Fauvre, M., & Ballard-Campbell, M. (1983). *Learning to care*. Glenview, IL: Scott, Foresman.

Konczal, D., & Petetski, L. (1983). *We all come in different packages: Activities to increase handicap awareness*. Santa Barbara, CA: The Learning Works.

Landy, L. (1988). *Child support through small group counseling*. Mount Dora, FL: KIDSRIGHTS.

Pincus, D. (1990). *Feeling good about yourself.* Carthage, IL: Good Apple.

Schwartz, L. (1978). *I am special.* Santa Barbara, CA: The Learning Works.

OTHER CURRICULA ON PROGRAMS FOR
SIBLINGS OF CHILDREN WITH SPECIAL NEEDS

Burton, S. (1991). *KIDPOWER: A leader's guide for conducting KIDPOWER groups.* Moscow: Idaho Center on Developmental Disabilities.

Lobato, D.J. (1990). *Brothers, sisters, and special needs: Information and activities for helping young brothers and sisters of children with chronic illnesses and developmental disabilities.* Baltimore: Paul H. Brookes Publishing Co.

Morgan, F. (Ed.). (1992). *The Pittsburgh sibling manual.* Pittsburgh: Easter Seal Society of Allegheny County.

Nollette, C. (1985). *Autism . . . a family affair: A curriculum for use with siblings of special needs children.* Minneapolis: Minneapolis Children's Medical Center.

Appendix C

A Brief Description
of the Sibshop Model

The following pages provide a concise description of the Sibshop model. Use or adapt this description to give to parents, service providers, local media, or funding sources.

The Sibshop model seeks to provide brothers and sisters of children with special needs opportunities for peer support and education through activities designed to accomplish the following goals:

> Goal 1: Sibshops will provide brothers and sisters of children with special needs an opportunity to meet other siblings in a relaxed, recreational setting.

The chance to meet other brothers and sisters in a casual atmosphere and join them in recreational activities has several benefits for participants. First, it can help reduce a sibling's sense of isolation. Participants quickly learn that there are others who experience the special joys and challenges that they do. Second, the casual atmosphere and recreational activities promote informal sharing and friendships among participants. Friendships begun at Sibshops and continued outside of the program offer siblings ongoing sources of support. Third, the recreational setting of the Sibshops helps to ensure that they will be rewarding for the child to attend. If a brother or sister regards any service aimed at siblings as yet another time demand associated with the child with special needs, he or she may find it hard to be receptive to the information presented in the workshop. Furthermore, if a sibling workshop is personally satisfying for the participant, he or she is more likely to attend another one in the future.

> Goal 2: Sibshops will provide brothers and sisters with opportunities to discuss common joys and concerns with other siblings of children with special needs.

> Goal 3: Sibshops will provide brothers and sisters with an opportunity to learn how others handle situations commonly experienced by siblings of children with special needs.

Brothers and sisters of children with special health and developmental needs routinely face problems that are not experienced by other children. Defending a brother or sister from name-calling, responding to questions from friends and strangers, and coping with a lack of attention or exceedingly high expectations from parents are only a few of the problems siblings may experience. At a Sibshop, participants discuss their common concerns, interests, and joys, and thereby decrease the sense that they are alone with their experiences. Furthermore, Sibshop participants have opportunities to learn how others have handled difficult situations. This experience can offer siblings a broad array of solutions from which they may choose.

> Goal 4: Sibshops will provide siblings with an opportunity to learn more about the implications of their brothers' and sisters' special needs.

As noted above, brothers and sisters have a need for information to answer their own questions about their siblings' special needs as well as the questions posed by friends, classmates, and strangers. Sibshops offer participants opportunities to learn about the effect the disability may have on the special child's life, schooling, and future.

> Goal 5: Sibshops will provide parents and other professionals with opportunities to learn more about the concerns and opportunities frequently experienced by brothers and sisters of people with special needs.

Some Sibshop activities attempt to help parents and service providers better understand "life as a sib." One activity allows parents and service providers to meet with a panel of young adult and adult siblings to learn about the joys and challenges of growing up with a special brother or sister. Workshop participants learn about what the panelists believe their parents did especially well to meet their needs growing up. They also learn what panelists wish their parents had done differently.

THE SIBSHOP FORMAT

Although Sibshops have run for as little as 2 hours and as long as a weekend, typical Sibshops are approximately 4 hours long and are presented monthly or bimonthly. Information and discussion activities are scattered throughout a workshop that also includes "New Games" (games designed to be unique, slightly offbeat, and appealing to a wide age and ability range), cooking activities, and special guests who may teach participants mime or how to juggle. A sample schedule of a Sibshop may include the following activities:

Trickle-in activity:	Group juggling
Warm up:	Human Bingo
Discussion #1:	Strengths and Weaknesses
Game:	Sightless Sculpture
Lunch:	Super Nachos
Game:	Pushpin Soccer
Discussion #2:	Dear Aunt Blabby
Guest:	Physical therapist
Closing activity:	Sound-Off

The Sibshop model was originally designed for children 8–13 years of age, but it can be easily adapted for older or younger children. Material throughout this volume may be reproduced for the reader's future use.

Appendix D

Siblings of Persons with Developmental Disabilities Policy Statement

Policy statements acknowledging the roles played by brothers and sisters can be an important first step in changing agencies' behavior toward siblings. Following is a policy statement that we have freely adapted from the Illinois Planning Council on Developmental Disabilities, who adopted their policy on siblings in 1991. Feel free to adapt it further to meet the needs of your agency or planning committee.

Most people with developmental disabilities live with their families, or within the support network of family members, throughout their lifetimes. Sibling relationships are particularly important because they are among the most enduring and meaningful ones individuals may have during their lives. Having a brother or sister with a developmental disability can have a profound impact on one's caregiving responsibilities, social relationships, and well-being. Many siblings view their relationship with their brothers and sisters positively, taking pride in their siblings' abilities and accomplishments and valuing the lessons they have learned about the human condition from their brothers and sisters and parents.

However, even these brothers and sisters may experience unusual concerns throughout their lives. Siblings may experience unequal parental attention, adverse community reactions to their siblings' disabilities, and caregiving demands that begin at an early age and continue to increase throughout their lives. In addition to a traditional sibling role, adult brothers and sisters of people with disabilities may assume other roles as well, such as advocate, housemate, companion, or guardian. As adults, their caregiving responsibilities may range from assisting parents to assuming full responsibility when parents are no longer able.

[This agency/planning council] believes it is important to recognize the role of siblings in efforts to support individuals with developmental disabilities and the family. [The agency/planning council] encourages inviting brothers and sisters to IEP and transition-planning meetings, staffings, and training events, and encouraging involvement in family support initiatives when age-appropriate and when desired by the individual with developmental disabilities.

Any considerations regarding siblings must allow for a range of individual differences in levels and intensity of involvement with the sibling with the disability. These differences will reflect in cultural and familial values and personal resources. Supports and considerations for brothers and sisters should seek to strengthen relationships between siblings, while honoring their individuality.

As parents age, the responsibility for support to the person with developmental disabilities often shifts to the siblings. A brother's or sister's willingness and capacity to assume additional responsibilities must be considered and supported by family members and service providers. When siblings do choose to accept responsibilities, it is critical that they be provided with information and guidance to participate with their brothers and sisters in decision making and long-range planning. Because many brothers and sisters who assume caregiving and guardian roles as adults are unaware of the often confusing array of programs and services available for adults with disabilities, agencies and organizations should reach out to this population in a proactive manner.

[The agency/planning council] recognizes that sibling issues are life-span issues. Like older brothers and sisters, younger siblings will need accurate, up-to-date information about their siblings with disabilities. Like their parents, many siblings—school age and adult—value sharing their common experiences, joys, and concerns with peers. Because their relationship with the person with special needs will most likely be the longest lasting in the family, siblings deserve peer support opportunities throughout their lives.

Adult siblings of people with disabilities continue to be an extraordinarily overlooked population. They are frequently torn between the responsibilities they have for their own families and their allegiance to their sibling with a disability, especially as parents age and pass away.

The roles that siblings play in their brothers' and sisters' health, happiness, and community life are vital. Agencies, including schools, social service agencies, and health care providers, should be encouraged to reach out to siblings of all ages to provide them with the support and information necessary to ensure the well-being of all involved.

Appendix E

Joining the National Association of Sibling Programs

The National Association of Sibling Programs (NASP) is a coalition of family members and professionals who share an interest in the well-being of brothers and sisters of people with special needs. The primary goal of NASP is to act as a network for programs serving brothers and sisters across the United States and Canada. NASP activities offer providers of programs for siblings opportunities to:

Learn more about the rich diversity of programs in the United States, Canada, the United Kingdom, and other countries serving siblings of all ages of people with all manner of special needs
Learn about materials, resources, and activities
Share activities, materials, and information with a larger audience.

NASP publishes the *NASP Newsletter*, which features activities, program descriptions, and other information of interest to providers of programs for siblings. NASP and its sponsoring agency, the Sibling Support Project, maintain the most complete database of existing sibling programs in the United States. If you run a program for brothers and sisters, we would like to include your work in NASP's database.
To join NASP, write:

NASP
The Sibling Support Project
Children's Hospital and Medical Center
P.O. Box C5371, CL-09
Seattle, WA 98105

References

Abramovitch, R., Stanhope, L., Pepler, D., & Corter, C. (1987). The influence of Down's syndrome on sibling interaction. *Journal of Child Psychology and Psychiatry, 28*(6), 865–879.

Antonovsky, A. (1993). The implications of salutogenesis: An outsider's view. In A.P. Turnbull, J.M. Patterson, S.K. Behr, D.L. Murphy, J.G. Marquis, & M.J. Blue-Banning (Eds.), *Cognitive coping, families, & disability* (pp. 111–122). Baltimore, Paul H. Brookes Publishing Co.

1988 award winning summer programs. (1989, March). *Exceptional Parent,* pp. 16–26.

Bank, S.P., & Kahn, M.D. (1982). *The sibling bond.* New York: Basic Books.

Bendor, S.J. (1990). Anxiety and isolation in siblings of pediatric cancer patients: The need for prevention. *Social Work in Health Care, 14,* 17–35.

Binkard, B., Goldberg, M., & Goldberg, P.F. (Eds.). (1987). *Brothers and sisters talk with PACER.* Minneapolis, MN: PACER Center.

Burslem, A. (1991). Never a dull moment! *Mencap News: The Journal of the Society for Mentally Handicapped Children and Adults, 19*(11), 12–13.

Burton, S. (1991). *KIDPOWER: A leader's guide for conducting KIDPOWER groups.* Moscow: Idaho Center on Developmental Disabilities.

Cairns, N., Clark, G., Smith, S., & Lansky, S. (1979). Malignancy. *Journal of Pediatrics, 95*(3), 484–487.

Callahan, C.R. (1990). *Since Owen.* Baltimore: The Johns Hopkins University Press.

Cleveland, D.W., & Miller, N. (1977). Attitudes and life commitments of older siblings of mentally retarded adults: An exploratory study. *Mental Retardation, 15*(3), 38–41.

Cobb, M. (1991). A senior essay. *Outlook, the newsletter of the Down Syndrome Association of Charlotte, NC,* (5)6, 3.

Coleman, S.V. (1990). The sibling of the retarded child: Self-concept, deficit compensation motivation, and perceived parental behavior (Doctoral dissertation, California School of Professional Psychology, San Diego, 1990). *Dissertation Abstracts International, 51*(10-B), 5023. (University Microfilms No. 01147421-AAD91-07868)

Collins, K. (Producer), & Emmerling, D.P. (Director). (1991). *The rest of the family* [Videotape]. Landover, MD: Epilepsy Foundation of America.

Devencenzi, J., & Pendergast, S. (1988). *Belonging.* San Luis Obispo: Belonging Publishing Co.

de Vinck, C. (1985, April 10). Power of the powerless. *The Wall Street Journal,* p. 28.

Dickens, R. (1991). *Notes for siblings/adult children.* (Available from National Alliance for the Mentally Ill, 2101 Wilson Blvd. Suite 302, Arlington, VA 22201)

Doherty, J. (1992). A sibling remembers. *Candlelighters Childhood Cancer Foundation Quarterly Newsletter, 16*(2), 4–6.

Drotar, D., & Crawford, P. (1985). Psychological adaptation of siblings of chronically ill children: Research and practice implications. *Developmental and Behavioral Pediatrics, 6,* 355–362.

Dudish, M.P. (1991). My sister Ellen . . . , my daughter Tara. *Sibling Information Network Newsletter, 7*(3), 1–3.

Duvall, E.M. (1962). *Family development.* Philadelphia: J.B. Lippincott.

Dyson, L., & Fewell, R. (1989). The self-concept of siblings of handicapped children: A comparison. *Journal of Early Intervention, 13*(3), 230–238.

Dyson, L.L. (1989). Adjustment of siblings of handicapped children: A comparison. *Journal of Pediatric Psychology, 14*(2), 215–229.

Ellis, A. (1992). *Siblings: The "forgotten child" in childhood cancer.* Unpublished manuscript.

Emberly, E. (1977). *Ed Emberly's great thumbprint drawing book.* Boston: Little, Brown.

Farber, B. (1960). Family organization and crisis: Maintenance of integration in families with a severely mentally retarded child. *Monographs of the Society for Research in Child Development, 25*(1, Serial No. 75).

Featherstone, H. (1980). *A difference in the family: Life with a disabled child.* New York: Basic Books.

Ferrari, M. (1984). Chronic illness: Psychosocial effects on siblings. 1: Chronically ill boys. *Journal of Child Psychology and Psychiatry, 25,* 459–476.

Feshbach, N., Feshbach, S., Fauvre, M., & Ballard-Campbell, M.(1983). *Learning to care.* Glenview, IL: Scott, Foresman.

Fink, L. (1984, November 6). Looking at the role played by siblings of the retarded. *Newsday,* pp. 6–9.

Fish, T. (Producer). (1993). *The next step* [Videotape]. (Available from Publications Office, Nisonger Center UAP, 434 McCampbell Hall, The Ohio State University, 1581 Dodd Dr., Columbus, OH, 43210)

Fish, T., & Fitzgerald, G.M. (1980, November). *A transdisciplinary approach to working with adolescent siblings of the mentally retarded: A group experience.* Paper presented to Social Work with Groups Symposium, Arlington, TX. (Available from T. Fish, The Nisonger Center, The Ohio State University, 1580 Canon Drive, Columbus, OH, 43210)

Flugelman, A. (Ed.). (1976). *The new games book.* Garden City, NY: Doubleday.

Flugelman, A. (Ed.). (1981). *More new Games!* Garden City, NY: Doubleday.

Fowle, C. (1973). The effect of a severely mentally retarded child on his family. *American Journal of Mental Deficiency, 73,* 468–473.

Gath, A. (1974). Sibling reactions to mental handicap: A comparison of the brothers and sisters of mongol children. *Journal of Child Psychology and Psychiatry, 15,* 187–198.

Gerdel, P. (1986). Who are these researchers and why are they saying such terrible things about me? In M. Hanson & A. Turnbull (Eds.), The family support network series. University of Idaho: *Research in Family Involve-*

ment Practices Monographs, No. 3.

Gregson, B. (1982). *The incredible indoor games book*. Belmont, CA: Fearon Teacher Aids.

Gregson, B. (1984). *The outrageous outdoor games book*. Belmont, CA: Fearon Teacher Aids.

Grossman, F. (1972). *Brothers and sisters of retarded children: An exploratory study*. Syracuse, NY: Syracuse University Press.

Grusza, M.A. (1988). *Family functioning and sibling adjustment in families with a handicapped child*. Unpublished doctoral dissertation. Kingston: University of Rhode Island.

Hanson, M. (1985). *Straight from the heart*. (Available from the Saskatchewan Association for the Mentally Retarded, 331 Louise St., Saskatoon, Saskatchewan, S7J 3L1 Canada)

Harkleroad, D. (1992). Growing up with Raymond. *Parents and Friends Together for People with Deaf-Blindness News*, 1(5), 5.

Harvey, D.H.P., & Greenway, A.P. (1984). The self-concept of physically handicapped children and their nonhandicapped siblings: An empirical investigation. *Journal of Child Psychology and Psychiatry, 25*, 273–284.

Helsel, E., Helsel, B., Helsel, B., & Helsel, M. (1978). The Helsels' story of Robin. In A.P. Turnbull & H.R. Turnbull (Eds.), *Parents speak out: Views from the other side of the two way mirror* (pp. 99–114). Columbus: Charles E. Merrill.

Herndon, L. (1992, November 15). A special brother. *Seattle Times*, p. 2.

Iles, P. (1979). Children with cancer: Healthy siblings' perceptions during the illness experience. *Cancer Nursing, 2*, 371–377.

Itzkowitz, J. (1990). Siblings' perceptions of their needs for programs, services, and support: A national study. *Sibling Information Network Newsletter, 7*(1), 1–4.

"Jennifer." (1990). Mailbag: A column for siblings to speak out. *Sibpage: A Newsletter for and by Brothers and Sisters of Children with Special Needs, 2*(4), 2.

Kazak, A.E., & Clarke, M.W. (1986). Stress in families with myelomeningocele. *Developmental Medicine and Child Neurology, 28*, 220–228.

Koch-Hattem, A. (1986). Siblings' experience of pediatric cancer: Interviews with children. *Health and Social Work, 10*, 107–117.

Konczal, D., & Petetski, L. (1983). *We all come in different packages: Activities to increase handicap awareness*. Santa Barbara: The Learning Works, Inc.

Koocher, G.P., & O'Malley, J.E. (1981). *The Damocles syndrome: Psychological consequences of surviving childhood cancer*. New York: McGraw-Hill.

Landy, L. (1988). *Child support through small group counseling*. Mount Dora, FL: KIDSRIGHTS.

Leder, J. M. (1991). *Brothers and sisters: How they shape our lives*. New York: St. Martin's Press.

Leonard, B. (1992). Siblings of children with chronically ill children: A question of vulnerability versus resilience. *Pediatric Annals, 20*(9), 501–506.

Lobato, D.J. (1990). *Brothers, sisters, and special needs: Information and activities for helping young siblings of children with chronic illnesses and developmental disabilities*. Baltimore: Paul H. Brookes Publishing Co.

Lobato, D., Barbour, L., Hall, L.J., & Miller, C.T. (1987). Psychosocial characteristics of preschool siblings of handicapped and nonhandicapped children. *Journal of Abnormal Child Psychology, 15,* 329–338.

Lynn, M.R. (1989). Siblings' responses in illness situations. *Journal of Pediatric Nursing, 4,* 127–129.

McCullough, M.E. (1981). Parent and sibling definitions of situations regarding transgenerational shift in the care of a handicapped child (Doctoral dissertation, University of Minnesota, 1981). *Dissertation Abstracts International, 42*(1-B), 161. (University Microfilms No. 8115012)

McConachie, H. (1982). Fathers of mentally handicapped children. In N. Beal & J. McGuire (Eds.), *Fathers: Psychological perspectives* (pp. 144–173). London: Junction.

McHale, S., Sloan, J., & Simmeonsson, R.J. (1986). Sibling relationships of children with autistic, mentally retarded, and nonhandicapped brothers and sisters. *Journal of Autism and Developmental Disorders, 16,* 399–413.

McKeever, P. (1983). Siblings of chronically ill children: A literature review with implications for research and practice. *American Journal of Orthopsychiatry, 53*(2), 209–218.

Meyer, D.J. (1986). Fathers of handicapped children. In R. Fewell & P. Vadasy (Eds.), *Families of handicapped children* (pp. 35–73) Austin, TX: PRO-ED

Meyer, D.J., & Erickson, E.L. (1992). [Survey of Seattle-area adult siblings of people with disabilities]. Unpublished raw data.

Meyer, D.J., & Erickson, E.L. (1993, Winter). *The National Association of Sibling Programs Newsletter.*

Meyer, D.J., Vadasy, P.F., & Fewell, R.R. (1985). *Living with a brother or sister with special needs: A book for sibs.* Seattle: University of Washington Press.

Meyer, D.J., Vadasy, P.F., Fewell, R.R., & Schell, G. (1985). *The Fathers Program: How to organize a program for fathers and their handicapped children.* Seattle: University of Washington Press.

Miller, S.G. (1974). An exploratory study of sibling relationships in families with retarded children (Doctoral dissertation, Columbia University, 1974). *Dissertation Abstracts International, 35*(6-B), 2994–2995. (University Microfilms No. 74-26m 606)

Morrow, J. (1992). Terry Cunningham: A brother who sticks up for his siblings. *Parents and Friends Together for People with Deaf-Blindness News, 1*(5), 2.

Moses, K. (1982). Brothers and sisters of special children. *Interactions.* Madison, WI: Harry A. Waisman Center on Mental Retardation, pp. 20–25.

Murphy, A.T. (1979). Members of the family: Sisters and brothers of handicapped children. *Volta Review, 81*(5), 352–362.

Murphy, A.T. (1981). *Special children, special parents.* Englewood Cliffs, NJ: Prentice-Hall.

Murray, G., & Jampolsky, G.G. (Eds.). (1982). *Straight from the siblings: Another look at the rainbow.* Berkeley, CA: Celestial Arts.

Nester, J. (1989, March). Adult sibling panel notes. *Down Syndrome Association of New Jersey, Inc.* [newsletter], p. 4.

Parfit, J. (1975). Siblings of handicapped children. *Special Education: For-*

ward *Trends, 2*(1), 19–21.

Podeanu-Czehotsky, I. (1975). Is it only the child's guilt? Some aspects of family life of cerebral palsied children. *Rehabilitation Literature, 36,* 308–311.

Powell, T.H., & Gallagher, P.A. (1993). *Brothers & sisters: A special part of exceptional families* (2nd ed.). Baltimore: Paul H. Brookes Publishing Co.

Remsberg, B. (1989). *What it means to have a handicapped brother or sister.* Unpublished manuscript.

Rinehart, J. (1992, May). My sister's hand. *Children's Health Issues, 1*(1), 10–11.

Royal, D. (1991). *The other child.* (Unpublished manuscript).

Schild, S. (1976). Counseling with parents of retarded children living at home. In F.J. Turner (Ed.), *Differential diagnosis and treatment in social work* (2nd ed., pp. 476–482). New York: Free Press.

Schorr-Ribera, H. (1992). Caring for siblings during diagnosis and treatment. *Candlelighters Childhood Cancer Foundation Quarterly Newsletter, 16*(2), 1–3.

Seligman, M. (1979). *Strategies for helping parents of exceptional children.* New York: Free Press.

Seligman, M. (1983). Sources of psychological disturbance among siblings of handicapped children. *Personnel and Guidance Journal, 67,* 529–531.

Seligman, M. (1991). Siblings of disabled brothers and sisters. In M. Seligman (Ed.), *The family with a handicapped child* (2nd ed., pp. 181–198). Boston: Allyn & Bacon.

Shanley, S. (1991). My brother Peter. *Sibling Information Network Newsletter, 7*(4), 1–2.

Simeonsson, R., & McHale, S. (1981). Review: Research on handicapped children: Sibling relationships. *Child: Care, Health and Development, 7,* 153–171.

Skrtic, T., Summers, J.A., Brotherson, M.J., & Turnbull, A., (1983). Severely handicapped children and their brothers and sisters. In J. Blacher (Ed.), *Severely handicapped young children and their families: Research in review* (pp. 215–246). New York: Academic Press.

Sourkes, B. (1990). Siblings count too. *Candlelighters Childhood Cancer Foundation Youth Newsletter, 12*(3), 2, 6.

Sourkes, B.M. (1980). Siblings of the pediatric cancer patient. In J. Kellerman (Ed.), *Psychological aspects of childhood cancer* (pp. 47–69). Springfield, IL: Charles C Thomas.

Spinetta, J. (1981). The sibling of the child with cancer. In J. Spinetta & P. Deasy-Spinetta (Eds.), *Living with childhood cancer* (pp. 133–142). St. Louis: C.V. Mosby.

Stoneman, Z., & Brody, G.H. (1993). Sibling relations in the family context. In Z. Stoneman & P.W. Berman (Eds.), *The effects of mental retardation, disability, and illness on sibling relationships* (pp. 3–30). Baltimore: Paul H. Brookes Publishing Co.

Stoneman, Z., Brody, G.H., Davis, C.H., & Crapps, J.M. (1987). Mentally retarded children and their older same-sex siblings: Naturalistic in-home observations. *American Journal on Mental Retardation, 92,* 290–298.

Stoneman, Z., Brody, G.H., Davis, C.H., & Crapps, J.M. (1988). Child care responsibilities, peer relations, and sibling conflict: Older siblings of mentally retarded children. *American Journal on Mental Retardation, 93,* 174–183.

Stoneman, Z., Brody, G.H., Davis, C.H., & Crapps, J.M. (1989). Role relations between mentally retarded children and their older siblings: Observations in three in-home contexts. *Research in Developmental Disabilities, 10,* 61–76.

Stoneman, Z., Brody, G.H., Davis, C.H., Crapps, J.M., & Malone, D.M. (1991). Ascribed role relations between children with mental retardation and their younger siblings. *American Journal on Mental Retardation, 95,* 527–536.

Thibodeau, S.M. (1988). Sibling response to chronic illness: The role of the clinical nurse specialist. *Issues in Comprehensive Pediatric Nursing, 11,* 17–28.

Torrey, E.F. (1992, July). Sibling issues. *Siblings of People with Mental Illness.* Conference sponsored by Washington Alliance for the Mentally Ill, Seattle, WA.

Tritt, S., & Esses, L. (1988). Psychosocial adaptation of siblings of children with chronic medical illnesses. *American Journal of Orthopsychiatry, 58*(2), 211–220.

Turnbull, A.P., & Turnbull, H.R. (1993). Participatory research on cognitive coping: From concepts to research planning. In A.P. Turnbull, J.M. Patterson, S.K. Behr, D.L. Murphy, J.G. Marquis, & M.J. Blue-Banning (Eds.), *Cognitive coping, families, & disability* (pp. 1–14). Baltimore: Paul H. Brookes Publishing Co.

Unruh, S. (1992). Serena. *Parents and Friends Together for People with Deaf-Blindness News, 1*(5), 1.

Usdane, S., & Melmed, R. (1988). *Facilitator's manual, Siblings Exchange Program.* Phoenix, AZ: Phoenix Children's Hospital.

Watson, J. (1991). The Queen. *Down Syndrome News, 15*(8), 108.

Westra, M. (1992). An open letter to my parents. *Sibling Information Network Newsletter, 8*(1), 4.

Wikler, L. (1981). Chronic stresses of families of mentally retarded children. *Family Relations, 30,* 281–288.

Zatlow, G. (1981, Winter). A sister's lament. *Our Home Newsletter and Annual Report, 5,* 1–2.

Zatlow, G. (Producer). (1987). The other children—Brothers and sisters of the developmentally disabled (Videotape). (Available from Special Citizens' Futures Unlimited, Inc., United Charities Building, 105 East 22nd Street, New York, NY 10010)

Zatlow, G. (1992, Fall). Just a sister. *Momentum,* pp. 13–16.

Index

Page numbers followed by *t* or *f* indicate tables or figures, respectively.